CRE**A**TIVE
HOMEOWNER®

# BEST-SELLING
## 1-STORY HOME PLANS

Book content provided by Design America, Inc., St. Louis, MO.

Current Printing (last digit)
10 9 8 7 6 5

Printed in Singapore

*Best-Selling 1-Story Home Plans, Updated 4th Edition*
ISBN: 978-1-58011-795-1

Library of Congress Cataloging-in-Publication Data

Title: Best-selling 1-story home plans.
Other titles: Best-selling one-story home plans
Description: Updated 4th edition. | Mount Joy : Creative Homeowner, 2017. |
   Includes index.
Identifiers: LCCN 2017015313 | ISBN 9781580117951 (pbk.)
Subjects:  LCSH: Single story houses--United States--Designs and plans.
Classification: LCC NA7205 .B4478 2017 | DDC 728/.3730973--dc23
LC record available at https://lccn.loc.gov/2017015313

We are always looking for talented authors. To submit an idea, please send a brief inquiry to acquisitions@foxchapelpublishing.com.

Creative Homeowner®, *www.creativehomeowner.com*, is an imprint of New Design Originals Corporation and distributed exclusively in North America by Fox Chapel Publishing Company, Inc., 800-457-9112, 903 Square Street, Mount Joy, PA 17552, and in the United Kingdom by Grantham Book Services, Trent Road, Grantham, Lincolnshire, NG31 7XQ.

The homes on the cover are: Top, Plan #F04-007D-0055 on page 33; Bottom, left: Plan #F04-013D-0200 on page 45; Top, right: Plan #F04-101D-0045 on page 88; Bottom, right: Plan #101D-0047 on page 162.

# CONTENTS

*Top to bottom: Plan #F04-051D-0670 on page 140; Plan #F04-007D-0060 on page 80; Plan #F04-011D-0526, on page 242; Plan #F04-013D-0022 on page 105; Plan #F04-084D-0052 on page 181; Plan #F04-011D-0007 on page 47.*

# what's the right
# **PLAN** for you?

*Choosing a house design is exciting, but can be a difficult task. Many factors play a role in what home plan is best for you and your family. To help you get started, we have pinpointed some of the major factors to consider when searching for your dream home. Take the time to evaluate your family's needs and you will have an easier time sorting through all of the house designs offered in this book.*

**BUDGET** is the first thing to consider. Many items take part in this budget, from ordering the blueprints to the last doorknob purchased. When you find the perfect house plan, visit houseplansandmore.com and get a cost-to-build estimate to ensure that the finished home will be within your cost range. A cost-to-build report is a detailed summary that gives you the total cost to build a specific home in the zip code where you're wanting to build. It is interactive allowing you to adjust labor and material costs, and it's created on demand when ordered so

all pricing is up-to-date. This valuable tool will help you know how much your dream home will cost before you buy plans (see page 282 for more information).

**FAMILY LIFESTYLE** After your budget is deciphered, you need to assess you and your family's lifestyle needs. Think about the stage of life you are in now, and what stages you will be going through in the future. Ask yourself questions to figure out how much room you need now and if you will need room for expansion. Are you married? Do you have children? How many children do you plan on having? Are you an empty-nester? How long do you plan to live in this home?

Incorporate into your planning any frequent guests you may have, including elderly parents, grandchildren or adult children who may live with you.

Does your family entertain a lot? If so, think about the rooms you will need to do so. Will you need both formal and informal spaces? Do you need a gourmet kitchen? Do you need a game room and/or a wet bar?

**FLOOR PLAN LAYOUTS** When looking through these home plans, imagine yourself walking through the house. Consider the flow from the entry to the living, sleeping and gathering areas. Does the layout ensure privacy for the master bedroom? Does the garage enter near the kitchen for easy unloading? Does the placement of the windows provide enough privacy from any neighboring properties? Do you plan on using furniture you already

have? Will this furniture fit in the appropriate rooms? When you find a plan you want to purchase, be sure to picture yourself actually living in it.

**EXTERIOR SPACES** With many different home styles throughout ranging from Traditional to Contemporary, flip through these pages and find which style appeals to you the most and think about the neighborhood in which you plan to build. Also, think about how the house will fit on your site. Picture the landscaping you want to add to the lot. Using your imagination is key when choosing a home plan.

Choosing a house design can be an intimidating experience. Asking yourself these questions before you get started on the search will help you through the process. With our large selection of sizes and styles, we are certain you will find your dream home in this book.

## *Make a list!*

Experts in the field suggest that the best way to determine your needs is to begin by listing everything you like or dislike about your current home.

# 10 steps to BUILDING your dream home

## 1 talk to a lender

If you plan to obtain a loan in order to build your new home, then it's best to find out first how much you can get approved for before selecting a home design. Knowing the financial information before you start looking for land or a home will keep you from selecting something out of your budget and turning a great experience into a major disappointment. Financing the home you plan to build is somewhat different than financing the purchase of an existing house. You're going to need thousands of dollars for land, labor, and materials. Chances are, you're going to have to borrow most of it. Therefore, you will probably need to obtain a construction loan. This is a short-term loan to pay for building your house. When the house is completed, the loan is paid off in full, usually out of the proceeds from your long-term mortgage loan.

## 2 determine needs

Selecting the right home plan for your needs and lifestyle requires a lot of thought. Your new home is an investment, so you should consider not only your current needs, but also your future requirements. Versatility and the potential for converting certain areas to other uses could be an important factor later on. So, although a home office may seem unnecessary now,

in years to come, the idea may seem ideal. Home plans that include flex spaces or bonus rooms can really adapt to your needs in the future.

## 3 choose a home site

The site for your new home will have a definite impact on the design you select. It's a good idea to select a home that will complement your site. This will save you time and money when building. Or, you can then modify a design to specifically accommodate your site. However, it will most likely make your home construction more costly than selecting a home plan suited for your lot right from the start. For example, if your land slopes, a walk-out basement works perfectly. If it's wooded, or has a lake in the back, an atrium ranch home is a perfect style to take advantage of surrounding backyard views.

### SOME IMPORTANT CRITERIA TO CONSIDER WHEN SELECTING A SITE:

- Improvements will have to be made including utilities, walks and driveways
- Convenience of the lot to work, school, shops, etc.
- Zoning requirements and property tax amounts
- Soil conditions at your future site
- Make sure the person or firm that sells you the land owns it free and clear

## 4 select a home design

We've chosen the "best of the best" of the 1-story home plans found at houseplansandmore.com to be featured in this book. With over 17,000 home plans from the best architects and designers across the country, this book includes the best variety of styles and sizes to suit the needs and tastes of a broad spectrum of homeowners.

## 5 get the cost to build

If you feel you have found "the" home, then before taking the step of purchasing house plans, order an estimated cost-to-build report for the exact zip code where you plan to build. Requesting this custom cost report created specifically for you will help educate you on all costs associated with building your new home. Simply order this report and gain knowledge of the material and labor cost associated with the home you love. Not only does the report allow you to choose the quality of the materials, you can also select options in every aspect of the project from lot condition to contractor fees. This report will allow you to successfully manage your construction budget in all areas, clearly see where the majority of the costs lie, and save you money from start to finish.

A COST-TO-BUILD REPORT WILL DETERMINE THE OVERALL COST OF YOUR NEW HOME INCLUDING THESE 5 MAJOR EXPENSE CATEGORIES:

- Land
- Foundation
- Materials
- General Contractor's fee - Some rules-of-thumb that you may find useful are: (a) the total labor cost will generally run a little higher that your total material cost, but it's not unusual for a builder or general contractor to charge 15-20% of the combined cost for managing the overall project.
- Site improvements - don't forget to add in the cost of your site improvements such as utilities, driveway, sidewalks, landscaping, etc.

## 6 hire a contractor

If you're inexperienced in construction, you'll probably want to hire a general contractor to manage the project. If you do not know a reputable general contractor, begin your search by contacting your local Home Builders Association to get references. Many states require building contractors to be licensed. If this is the case in your state, its licensing board is another referral source. Finding a reputable, quality-minded contractor is a key factor in ensuring that your new home is well constructed and is finished on time and within budget. It can be a smart decision to discuss the plan you like with your builder prior to ordering plans. They can guide you into choosing the right type of plan package option especially if you intend on doing some customizing to the design.

## 7 customizing

Sometimes your general contractor may want to be the one who makes the mod-

ifications you want to the home you've selected. But, sometimes they want to receive the plans ready to build. That is why we offer home plan modification services. Please see page 285 for specific information on the customizing process and how to get a free quote on the changes you want to make to a home before you buy the plans.

## 8 order plans

If you've found the home and are ready to order blueprints, we recommend ordering the PDF file format, which offers the most flexibility. A PDF file format will be emailed to you when you order, and it includes a copyright release from the designer, meaning you have the legal right to make changes to the plan if necessary as well as print out as many copies of the plan as you need for building the home one-time. You will be happy to have your blueprints saved electronically

so they can easily be shared with your contractor, subcontractors, lender and local building officials. We do, however, offer several different types of plan package depending on your needs, so please refer to page 283 for all plan options available and choose the best one for your particular situation.

Another helpful component in the building process that is available for many of the house plans in this book is a material list. A material list includes not only a detailed list of materials, but it also indicates where various cuts of lumber and other building components are to be used. This will save your general contractor significant time and money since they won't have to create this list before building begins. If a material list is available for a home, it is indicated in the plan data box on the specific plan page in this book.

## 9 order materials

You can order materials yourself, or have your contractor do it. Nevertheless, in order to thoroughly enjoy your new home you will want to personally select many of the materials that go into its construction. Today, home improvement stores offer a wide variety of quality building products. Only you can decide what specific types of windows, cabinets, bath fixtures, etc. will make your new home yours. Spend time early on in the construction process looking at the materials and products available.

## 10 move in

With careful planning and organization, your new home will be built on schedule and ready for your move-in date. Be sure to have all of your important documents in place for the closing of your new home and then you'll be ready to move in and start living your dream.

Browse the pages of the Best-Selling 1-Story Home Plans book and discover over 360 designs offered in a huge variety of sizes and styles to suit many tastes. From Craftsman and Country, to Contemporary and Traditional, there is a home design here for everyone with all of the amenities and features homeowners are looking for in a home today. Start your search right now for the perfect 1-Story home!

*Top, left: Plan #F04-055D-0748 on page 8; top, right: Plan #F04-011D-0007 on page 47; bottom, left: Plan #F04-055D-0031 on page 17; bottom, right: Plan #F04-101D-0052, on page 60.*

## Plan #F04-055D-0748

**Dimensions:** 67'2" W x 55'10" D
**Heated Sq. Ft.:** 2,525
**Bedrooms:** 4    **Bathrooms:** 3
**Foundation:** Crawl space or slab, please specify when ordering

| | |
|---|---|
| 5-Sets: | $730 |
| 8-Sets: | $870 |
| PDF File: | $1,340 |
| CAD File: | $2,065 |

*Pricing subject to change*

*Images provided by designer/architect*

## Features

- This expansive one-story design has the split-bedroom floor plan everyone loves
- Stunning columns frame the foyer that leads into the open great room with fireplace, as well as the home theater/living room located right off of the foyer
- The formal dining room, casual breakfast room, and large grilling porch with fireplace provide an abundance of locations for dining opportunities
- Three bedrooms and two baths occupy one side of this home, while the master suite is secluded on the other
- 2-car front entry garage

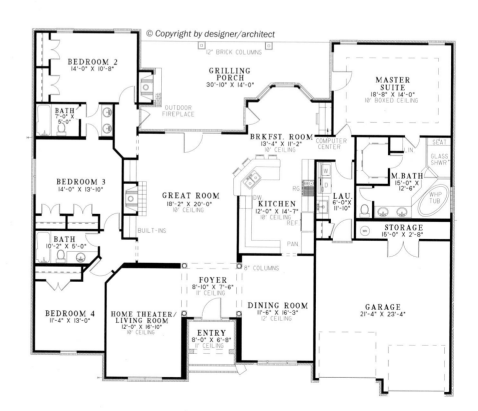

## Plan #F04-033D-0012

| | |
|---|---|
| Dimensions: | 60' W x 43' D |
| Heated Sq. Ft.: | 1,546 |
| Bedrooms: 3 | Bathrooms: 2 |
| Foundation: | Basement |
| PDF File: | $750 |
| 5-Sets: | $800 |
| Reproducible Master: | $800 |
| 8-Sets: | $875 |
| Material List: | $125 |

*Pricing subject to change*

*Images provided by designer/architect*

## Features

- Spacious, open vaulted rooms create a casual atmosphere
- The master bedroom is secluded for privacy and enjoys its own bath and walk-in closet
- The dining room features a large bay window and vaulted ceiling
- The kitchen and dinette combine for added space and include access to the outdoors
- A large laundry room includes a convenient sink with a linen and coat closet nearby
- 2-car front entry garage

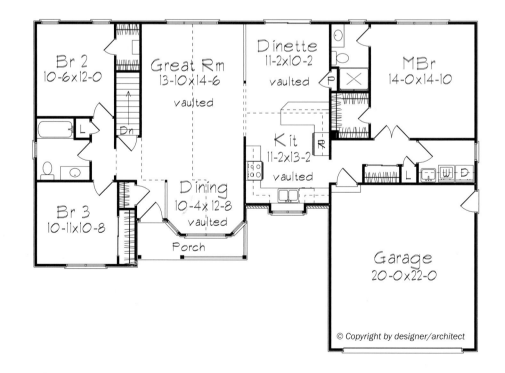

© Copyright by designer/architect

## Plan #F04-077D-0131

| | |
|---|---|
| **Dimensions:** | 69' W x 59'10" D |
| **Heated Sq. Ft.:** | 2,021 |
| **Bedrooms:** 3 | **Bathrooms:** 2½ |

**Foundation:** Basement, slab or crawl space, please specify when ordering

| | |
|---|---|
| **1-Set:** | $990 |
| **5-Sets:** | $1,060 |
| **PDF File:** | $1,200 |
| **CAD File:** | $1,820 |
| **Material List:** | $130 |

*Pricing subject to change*

## Features

- A corner garden tub in the private master bath becomes the ultimate retreat from the stresses of everyday life
- A large eating area extends off the kitchen featuring a center island and access to the covered porch with an outdoor kitchen
- The media/hobby room can be found through double doors in the large great room
- 2-car side entry garage

*Images provided by designer/architect*

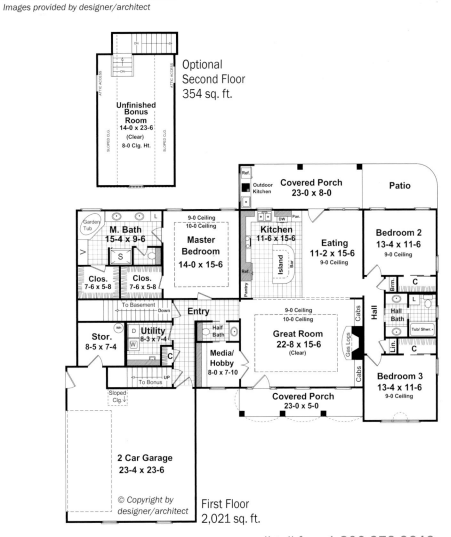

Optional Second Floor 354 sq. ft.

First Floor 2,021 sq. ft.

© Copyright by designer/architect

## Plan #F04-137D-0223

| | |
|---|---|
| Dimensions: | 65'8" W x 56'6" D |
| Heated Sq. Ft.: | 2,185 |
| Bedrooms: 3 | Bathrooms: 2 |
| Foundation: | Slab |
| 5-Sets: | $800 |
| 8-Sets: | $870 |
| PDF File: | $980 |
| Reproducible Master: | $1,030 |

*Pricing subject to change*

*Images provided by designer/architect*

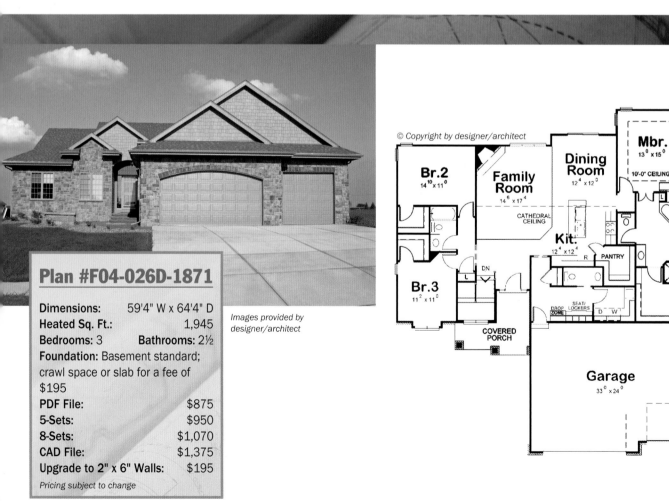

## Plan #F04-026D-1871

| | |
|---|---|
| Dimensions: | 59'4" W x 64'4" D |
| Heated Sq. Ft.: | 1,945 |
| Bedrooms: 3 | Bathrooms: 2½ |

Foundation: Basement standard; crawl space or slab for a fee of $195

| | |
|---|---|
| PDF File: | $875 |
| 5-Sets: | $950 |
| 8-Sets: | $1,070 |
| CAD File: | $1,375 |
| Upgrade to 2" x 6" Walls: | $195 |

*Pricing subject to change*

*Images provided by designer/architect*

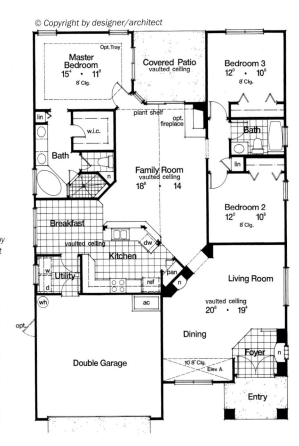

© Copyright by designer/architect

*Images provided by designer/architect*

## Plan #F04-047D-0022

| | |
|---|---|
| Dimensions: | 40' W x 60' D |
| Heated Sq. Ft.: | 1,768 |
| Bedrooms: 3 | Bathrooms: 2 |
| Foundation: | Slab |
| PDF File: | $825 |
| 5-Sets: | $875 |
| Reproducible Master: | $875 |
| CAD File: | $1,725 |

*Pricing subject to change*

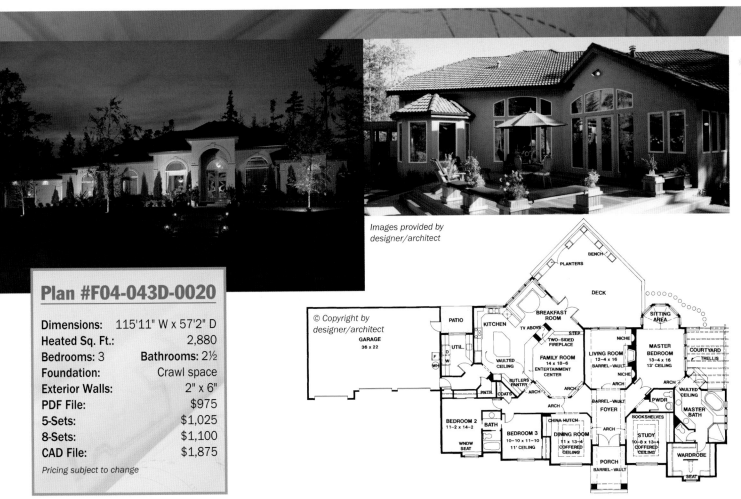

*Images provided by designer/architect*

© Copyright by designer/architect

## Plan #F04-043D-0020

| | |
|---|---|
| Dimensions: | 115'11" W x 57'2" D |
| Heated Sq. Ft.: | 2,880 |
| Bedrooms: 3 | Bathrooms: 2½ |
| Foundation: | Crawl space |
| Exterior Walls: | 2" x 6" |
| PDF File: | $975 |
| 5-Sets: | $1,025 |
| 8-Sets: | $1,100 |
| CAD File: | $1,875 |

*Pricing subject to change*

## Plan #F04-011S-0004

| | |
|---|---|
| **Dimensions:** | 119'6" W x 87'6" D |
| **Heated Sq. Ft.:** | 3,940 |
| **Bedrooms:** | 3 |
| **Bathrooms:** | 2 full, 2 half |
| **Foundation:** Crawl space or post & beam standard; slab for a fee of $350 | |
| **Exterior Walls:** | 2" x 6" |
| **PDF File:** | $1,550 |
| **5-Sets:** | $1,600 |
| **CAD File:** | $3,000 |

*Pricing subject to change*

*Images provided by designer/architect*

## Features

- A pass-through bar connects the spacious great room and kitchen, further expanding the floor space
- The outdoor kitchen and grill is separated from the outdoor living space, allowing for multiple uses of either area
- The bonus room above the garage is available for numerous uses, such as play, media, or game rooms, and offers additional square footage
- The secondary bedrooms have their own vanity and toilet and share an oversized tub
- A home office is tucked away in the rear of the home with a convenient side entrance and half bath nearby
- 3-car side entry garage

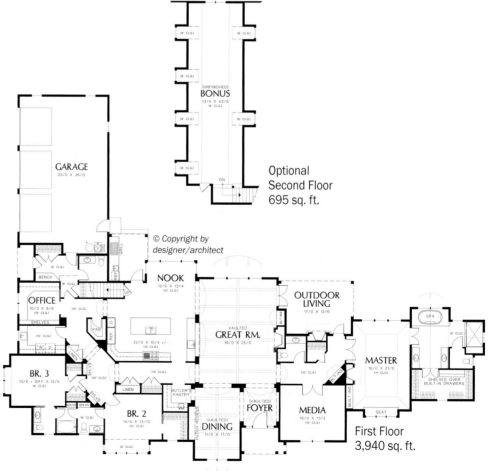

Optional Second Floor 695 sq. ft.

© Copyright by designer/architect

First Floor 3,940 sq. ft.

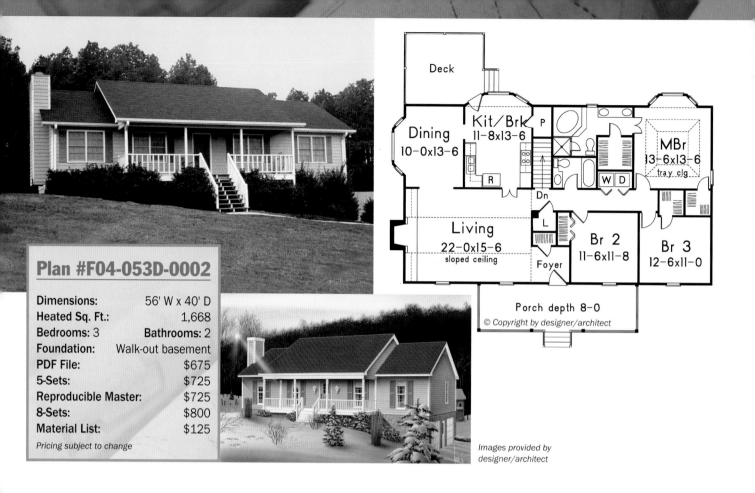

# Plan #F04-053D-0002

| Dimensions: | 56' W x 40' D |
|---|---|
| Heated Sq. Ft.: | 1,668 |
| Bedrooms: 3 | Bathrooms: 2 |
| Foundation: | Walk-out basement |
| PDF File: | $675 |
| 5-Sets: | $725 |
| Reproducible Master: | $725 |
| 8-Sets: | $800 |
| Material List: | $125 |

*Pricing subject to change*

*Images provided by designer/architect*

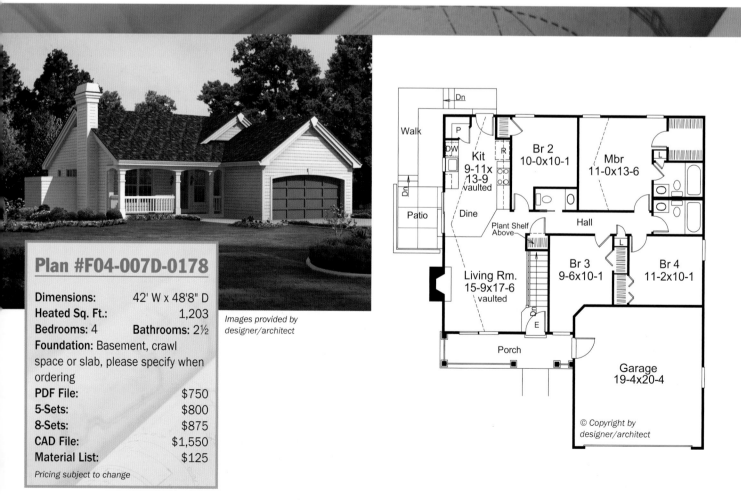

# Plan #F04-007D-0178

| Dimensions: | 42' W x 48'8" D |
|---|---|
| Heated Sq. Ft.: | 1,203 |
| Bedrooms: 4 | Bathrooms: 2½ |

Foundation: Basement, crawl space or slab, please specify when ordering

| PDF File: | $750 |
|---|---|
| 5-Sets: | $800 |
| 8-Sets: | $875 |
| CAD File: | $1,550 |
| Material List: | $125 |

*Pricing subject to change*

*Images provided by designer/architect*

## Plan #F04-055D-0031

| | |
|---|---|
| **Dimensions:** | 58'6" W x 64'6' D |
| **Heated Sq. Ft.:** | 2,133 |
| **Bedrooms:** 3 | **Bathrooms:** 2 |
| **Foundation:** Slab or crawl space standard; basement or walk-out basement for a fee of $250 | |
| **5-Sets:** | $680 |
| **8-Sets:** | $795 |
| **PDF File:** | $1,225 |
| **CAD File:** | $1,885 |
| **Upgrade to 2" x 6" Walls:** | $250 |

*Pricing subject to change*

*Images provided by designer/architect*

© Copyright by designer/architect

First Floor
1,569 sq. ft.

Basement

## Plan #F04-065D-0259

| | |
|---|---|
| **Dimensions:** | 55'6" W x47'6" D |
| **Heated Sq. Ft.:** | 1,569 |
| **Bedrooms:** 3 | **Bathrooms:** 2 |
| **Foundation:** | Basement |
| **5-Sets:** | $695 |
| **8-Sets:** | $799 |
| **PDF File:** | $945 |
| **CAD File:** | $1,320 |
| **Material List:** | $75 |

*Pricing subject to change*

*Images provided by designer/architect*

# Plan #F04-077D-0097

| | |
|---|---|
| **Dimensions:** | 65' W x 56'8" D |
| **Heated Sq. Ft.:** | 1,800 |
| **Bedrooms:** 3 | **Bathrooms:** 2 |

**Foundation:** Slab, basement or crawl space, please specify when ordering

| | |
|---|---|
| **5-Sets:** | $1,015 |
| **PDF File:** | $1,125 |
| **Reproducible Master:** | $1,200 |
| **CAD File:** | $1,680 |
| **Material List:** | $130 |

*Pricing subject to change*

*Images provided by designer/architect*

## Features

- Double doors open into the foyer crowned with a 10' ceiling
- The vaulted great room opens into the kitchen and bayed breakfast area with decorative columns
- Located right off of the foyer is a flex space that can be used for a home office, craft room, exercise room or whatever suits your family's needs
- The master bedroom and bath are tucked away in the rear of this home offering the utmost privacy
- 2-car side entry garage

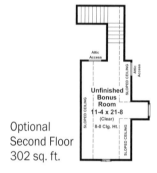

Optional
Second Floor
302 sq. ft.

© Copyright by designer/architect

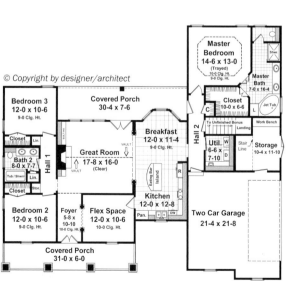

First Floor
1,800 sq. ft.

Images provided by designer/architect

## Plan #F04-007D-0010

| | |
|---|---|
| Dimensions: | 83' W x 42'4" D |
| Heated Sq. Ft.: | 1,845 |
| Bedrooms: 3 | Bathrooms: 2 |

Foundation: Walk-out basement, crawl space or slab, please specify when ordering

| | |
|---|---|
| PDF File: | $900 |
| 5-Sets: | $950 |
| 8-Sets: | $1,025 |
| CAD File: | $1,800 |
| Material List: | $125 |
| Upgrade to 2" x 6" Walls: | $150 |

*Pricing subject to change*

## Features

- The vaulted dining and great rooms are immersed in light from the atrium window wall
- The chef of the family is sure to love this functionally designed kitchen
- 3-car front entry garage

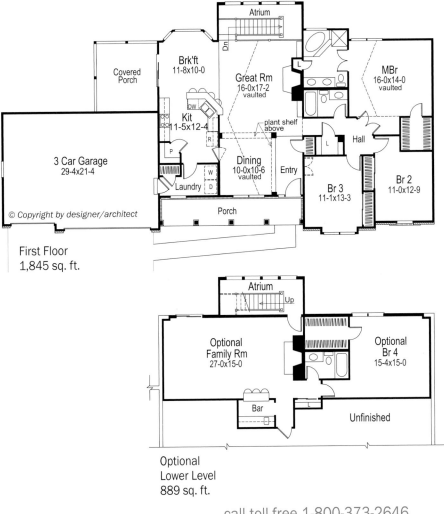

© Copyright by designer/architect

First Floor
1,845 sq. ft.

Optional
Lower Level
889 sq. ft.

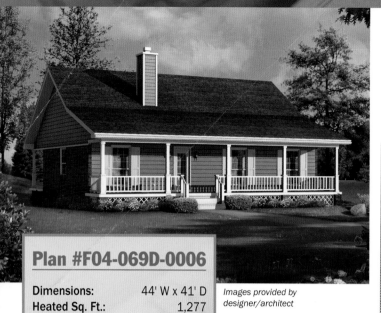

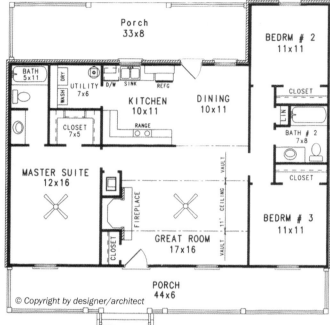

## Plan #F04-069D-0006

| | |
|---|---|
| Dimensions: | 44' W x 41' D |
| Heated Sq. Ft.: | 1,277 |
| Bedrooms: 3 | Bathrooms: 2 |

Foundation: Slab or crawl space, please specify when ordering

| | |
|---|---|
| PDF File: | $675 |
| 5-Sets: | $725 |
| 8-Sets: | $800 |
| CAD File: | $1,475 |
| Material List: | $125 |

*Pricing subject to change*

*Images provided by designer/architect*

Porch 33x8
BATH 5x11
UTILITY 7x6
WASH / DRY
D/W  SINK  REFG
KITCHEN 10x11
DINING 10x11
CLOSET 7x5
RANGE
MASTER SUITE 12x16
FIREPLACE
GREAT ROOM 17x16
11' CEILING VAULT
VAULT
CLOSET
BEDRM # 2 11x11
CLOSET
LIN
BATH # 2 7x8
CLOSET
BEDRM # 3 11x11
PORCH 44x6

© Copyright by designer/architect

---

## Plan #F04-058D-0171

| | |
|---|---|
| Dimensions: | 51' W x 50'4" D |
| Heated Sq. Ft.: | 1,635 |
| Bedrooms: 3 | Bathrooms: 2½ |
| Foundation: | Basement |
| 5-Sets: | $505 |
| 8-Sets: | $575 |
| PDF File: | $575 |
| CAD File: | $675 |
| Material List: | $80 |

*Pricing subject to change*

*Images provided by designer/architect*

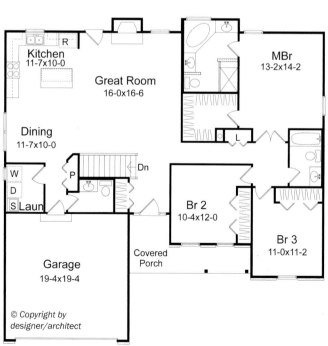

Kitchen 11-7x10-0
Great Room 16-0x16-6
MBr 13-2x14-2
Dining 11-7x10-0
W D S  Laun
P  Dn
L
Br 2 10-4x12-0
Br 3 11-0x11-2
Garage 19-4x19-4
Covered Porch

© Copyright by designer/architect

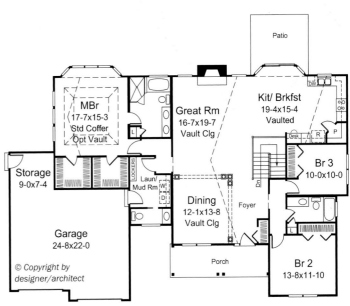

## Plan #F04-121D-0020

| Dimensions: | 70'8" x 47' D |
|---|---|
| Heated Sq. Ft.: | 2,037 |
| Bedrooms: 3 | Bathrooms: 2½ |
| Foundation: | Basement |
| PDF File: | $900 |
| 5-Sets: | $950 |
| 8-Sets: | $1,025 |
| CAD File: | $1,800 |
| Material List: | $125 |
| Upgrade to 2" x 6" Walls: | $150 |

*Pricing subject to change*

*Images provided by designer/architect*

© Copyright by designer/architect

## Plan #F04-155D-0020

| Dimensions: | 73' W x 77'6" D |
|---|---|
| Heated Sq. Ft.: | 2,995 |
| Bedrooms: 3 | Bathrooms: 3 |

Foundation: Crawl space or slab standard; basement, daylight basement or walk-out basement for a fee of $250

| 5-Sets: | $1,100 |
|---|---|
| 8-Sets: | $1,200 |
| PDF File: | $1,850 |
| CAD File: | $2,845 |

*Pricing subject to change*

*Images provided by designer/architect*

Optional Second Floor
1,184 sq. ft.

First Floor
2,995 sq. ft.

## Plan #F04-024D-0055

| | |
|---|---|
| Dimensions: | 72' W x 85'6" D |
| Heated Sq. Ft.: | 2,968 |
| Bedrooms: 4 | Bathrooms: 3½ |
| Foundation: | Slab |
| Exterior Walls: | 2" x 6" |
| 3-Sets: | $940 |
| 5-Sets: | $1,010 |
| 8-Sets: | $1,120 |
| PDF File: | $1,375 |

*Pricing subject to change*

*Images provided by designer/architect*

## Features

- Decorative columns accent the entrance and define the formal dining room
- A full wall of windows brightens the living room that also enjoys an inviting fireplace
- The spacious kitchen is designed for efficiency and opens to the splendid breakfast room
- Relax and retreat to a luxurious master bedroom complete with a corner fireplace and private bath with separate tub and shower, and a double bowl vanity
- 2-car side entry garage

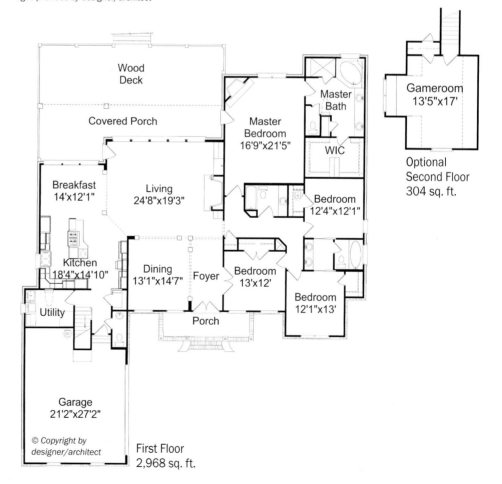

First Floor
2,968 sq. ft.

Optional Second Floor
304 sq. ft.

## Plan #F04-001D-0024

Dimensions: 68' W x 38' D
Heated Sq. Ft.: 1,360
Bedrooms: 3    Bathrooms: 2
Foundation: Basement, slab or crawl space, please specify when ordering

| | |
|---|---:|
| PDF File: | $825 |
| 5-Sets: | $875 |
| 8-Sets: | $950 |
| CAD File: | $1,725 |
| Material List: | $125 |

*Pricing subject to change*

*Images provided by designer/architect*

### Features

- The kitchen/dining room features an island workspace and plenty of dining area
- The master bedroom has a large walk-in closet and a private bath
- The laundry room is adjacent to the kitchen for easy access
- There is a convenient workshop located in the garage
- The large closets in the secondary bedrooms maintain organization
- 2-car side entry garage with workshop space

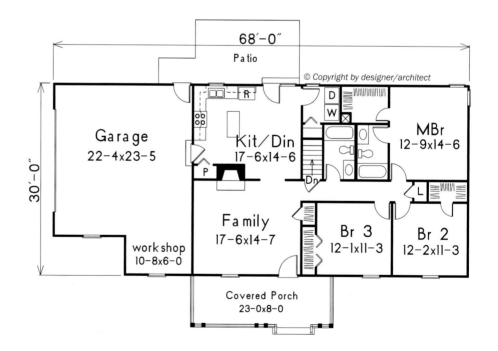

© Copyright by designer/architect

68'-0"

30'-0"

Patio

Garage
22-4x23-5

Kit/Din
17-6x14-6

MBr
12-9x14-6

workshop
10-8x6-0

Family
17-6x14-7

Br 3
12-1x11-3

Br 2
12-2x11-3

Covered Porch
23-0x8-0

## Plan #F04-013D-0134

| | |
|---|---|
| **Dimensions:** | 55' W x 58' D |
| **Heated Sq. Ft.:** | 1,496 |
| **Bedrooms:** 3 | **Bathrooms:** 2 |

**Foundation:** Slab standard; basement for a fee of $250

| | |
|---|---|
| **PDF File:** | $845 |
| **5-Sets:** | $895 |
| **8-Sets:** | $945 |
| **CAD File:** | $1,195 |
| **Material List:** | $125 |

*Pricing subject to change*

*Images provided by designer/architect*

## Features

- This country cottage features spacious open rooms and an easy flow from the welcoming front porch stone walkway to the breezy screened porch off of the family room and master bedroom

- The family room features a cozy corner fireplace

- Isolated from the secondary bedrooms, the master bedroom is an owner's retreat with a sitting area, a large walk-in closet, and a private bath with a separate tub and a shower

- The bonus room above the garage has an additional 301 square feet of living area

- 2-car front entry garage

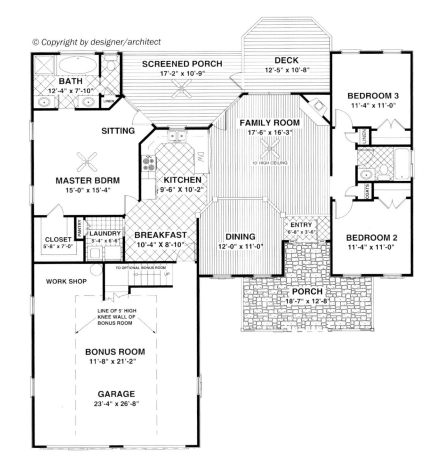

© Copyright by designer/architect

## Plan #F04-048D-0008

| | |
|---|---|
| Dimensions: | 61'8" W x 50'4" D |
| Heated Sq. Ft.: | 2,089 |
| Bedrooms: 4 | Bathrooms: 3 |
| Foundation: | Slab |
| PDF File: | $825 |
| 5-Sets: | $875 |
| Reproducible Master: | $875 |
| CAD File: | $1,725 |
| Material List: | $125 |

*Pricing subject to change*

*Images provided by designer/architect*

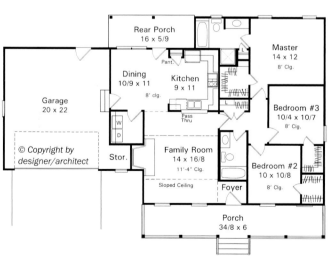

© Copyright by designer/architect

## Plan #F04-039D-0001

| | |
|---|---|
| Dimensions: | 61'3" W x 40'6" D |
| Heated Sq. Ft.: | 1,253 |
| Bedrooms: 3 | Bathrooms: 2 |
| Foundation: | Crawl space or slab, please specify when ordering |
| 5-Sets: | $750 |
| 8-Sets: | $800 |
| PDF File: | $675 |
| CAD File: | $1,475 |

*Pricing subject to change*

*Images provided by designer/architect*

© Copyright by designer/architect

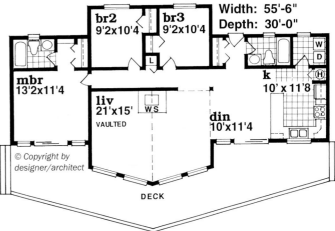

**Width: 55'-6"**
**Depth: 30'-0"**

br2 9'2x10'4
br3 9'2x10'4
mbr 13'2x11'4
liv 21'x15' VAULTED
din 10'x11'4
k 10' x 11'8

© Copyright by designer/architect

DECK

## Plan #F04-062D-0047

| | |
|---|---|
| Dimensions: | 55'6" W x 30' D |
| Heated Sq. Ft.: | 1,230 |
| Bedrooms: 3 | Bathrooms: 2 |
| Foundation: Crawl space or basement, please specify when ordering | |
| Exterior Walls: | 2" x 6" |
| PDF File: | $750 |
| 5-Sets: | $800 |
| 8-Sets: | $875 |
| CAD File: | $1,550 |
| Material List: | $125 |

*Pricing subject to change*

*Images provided by designer/architect*

## Plan #F04-121D-0046

| | |
|---|---|
| Dimensions: | 60' W x 61' D |
| Heated Sq. Ft.: | 1,983 |
| Bedrooms: 3 | Bathrooms: 2½ |
| Foundation: | Basement |
| PDF File: | $750 |
| 5-Sets: | $800 |
| 8-Sets: | $875 |
| CAD File: | $1,550 |

*Pricing subject to change*

*Images provided by designer/architect*

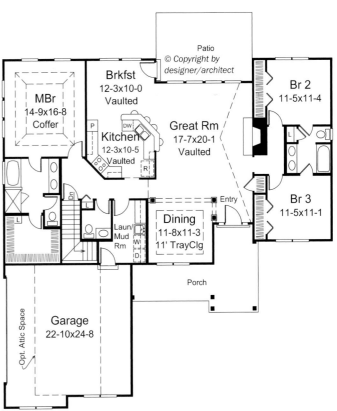

Patio

© Copyright by designer/architect

MBr 14-9x16-8 Coffer

Brkfst 12-3x10-0 Vaulted

Kitchen 12-3x10-5 Vaulted

Great Rm 17-7x20-1 Vaulted

Br 2 11-5x11-4

Entry

Laun/ Mud Rm

Dining 11-8x11-3 11' TrayClg

Br 3 11-5x11-1

Porch

Opt. Attic Space

Garage 22-10x24-8

## Plan #F04-007D-0140

| | |
|---|---|
| Dimensions: | 62' W x 45' D |
| Heated Sq. Ft.: | 1,591 |
| Bedrooms: 3 | Bathrooms: 2 |
| Foundation: | Basement |
| PDF File: | $900 |
| 5-Sets: | $950 |
| 8-Sets: | $1,025 |
| CAD File: | $1,800 |
| Material List: | $125 |
| Upgrade to 2" x 6" Walls: | $150 |

*Pricing subject to change*

*Images provided by designer/architect*

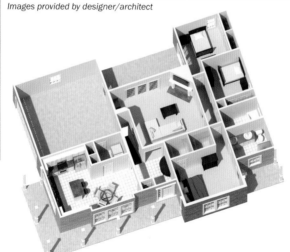

### Features

- The large entry leads to a cheerful kitchen and breakfast area that welcomes the sun through a wide array of windows

- The great room features a vaulted ceiling, a corner fireplace, a wet bar, and access to the rear patio

- Two walk-in closets, a private porch, and a luxury bath, are highlights of the vaulted master bedroom suite

- 2-car side entry garage

© Copyright by designer/architect

Garage 21-4x19-8

Patio

Bar

Br 3 11-4x10-0

Br 2 10-0x10-9

Hall

Great Rm 17-3x16-4 vaulted

Kitchen 11-5x15-8

Laun.

Brk fst 13-6x11-0

Entry

MBr 15-4x12-0 vaulted

Covered Porch

Porch

## Plan #F04-007D-0137

| | |
|---|---|
| Dimensions: | 72'8" W x 44'4" D |
| Heated Sq. Ft.: | 1,568 |
| Bedrooms: 2 | Bathrooms: 2 |
| Foundation: | Crawl space |
| PDF File: | $825 |
| 5-Sets: | $875 |
| Reproducible Master: | $875 |
| 8-Sets: | $950 |
| Material List: | $125 |

*Pricing subject to change*

*Images provided by designer/architect*

## Features

- Multiple entrances from porches help to bring the outdoors inside
- The lodge-like great room features a vaulted ceiling, a stone fireplace, a step-up entrance foyer, and it opens to a huge vaulted screened porch
- 3-car side entry garage

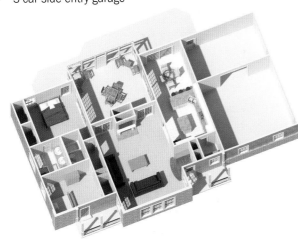

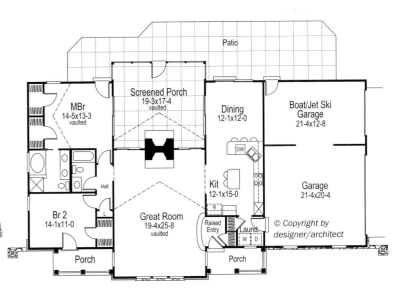

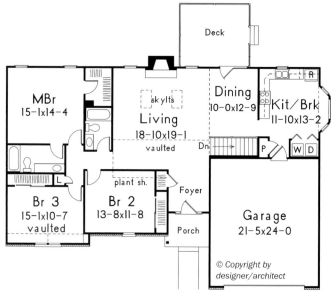

Deck

MBr
15-1x14-4

skylts
Living
18-10x19-1
vaulted

Dining
10-0x12-9

Kit/Brk
11-10x13-2

Dn

plant sh.

Br 3
15-1x10-7
vaulted

Br 2
13-8x11-8

Foyer

Porch

Garage
21-5x24-0

© Copyright by
designer/architect

## Plan #F04-003D-0002

*Images provided by
designer/architect*

| | |
|---|---|
| Dimensions: | 64' W x 44' D |
| Heated Sq. Ft.: | 1,676 |
| Bedrooms: 3 | Bathrooms: 2 |

Foundation: Basement, crawl
space or slab, please specify when
ordering

| | |
|---|---|
| PDF File: | $825 |
| 5-Sets: | $875 |
| Reproducible Master: | $875 |
| 8-Sets: | $950 |
| Material List: | $125 |

*Pricing subject to change*

PORCH NO. 2
10'-0" DEEP

LAUNDRY/HOBBY ROOM
10'2" X 18'-0"

POSSIBLE FUTURE CABINET LOCATION

FREEZER

STORAGE 1
10'-0" X 10'2"

STORAGE 2
14'-2" X 10'-2"

BEDROOM NO. 3
14'-0" X 12'-0"

KITCHEN/DINING
22'-0" X 14'-0"

SNACK BAR

REF.

PANTRY

MASTER
BATH
7'-10" X 15'-10"

© Copyright by
designer/architect

TWO CAR GARAGE
24'-2" X 24'-0"

LINEN

BATH NO. 2

CLOSET
10'-0" wide

BEDROOM NO. 2
14'-0" X 14'-0"

GREAT ROOM
22'-0" X 20'-0"

MASTER BEDROOM
18'-0" X 14'-0"

PORCH NO. 1
8'-0" DEEP

## Plan #F04-028D-0047

| | |
|---|---|
| Dimensions: | 80'4" W x 52' D |
| Heated Sq. Ft.: | 2,091 |
| Bedrooms: 3 | Bathrooms: 2 |

Foundation: Crawl space or slab,
please specify when ordering

| | |
|---|---|
| 5-Sets: | $860 |
| 8-Sets: | $960 |
| PDF File: | $1,010 |

*Pricing subject to change*

*Images provided by
designer/architect*

## Plan #F04-139D-0043

| | |
|---|---|
| Dimensions: | 39'5" W x 39'1" D |
| Heated Sq. Ft.: | 1,225 |
| Bedrooms: 2 | Bathrooms: 2 |
| Foundation: Crawl space standard; basement for a fee of $450 | |
| Exterior Walls: | 2" x 6" |
| 5-Sets: | $1,245 |
| PDF File: | $1,320 |
| CAD File: | $2,995 |

*Pricing subject to change*

*Images provided by designer/architect*

© Copyright by designer/architect

DECK
11'-10" x 10'-0"

KITCHEN
11'-2" x 20'-4"

BEDROOM #1
10'-0" x 10'-0"

WIC

WIC

LIN

LIN

BEDROOM #2
10'-0" x 10'-0"

UTILITY

COAT

PAN

DINING
11'-0" x 12'-3"

HALF-WALL

BOOK SHELVES

FAMILY
16'-7" x 17'-4"

SCREENED PORCH
10'-5" x 10'-6"

PORCH
7'-6" x 5'-2"

DN

---

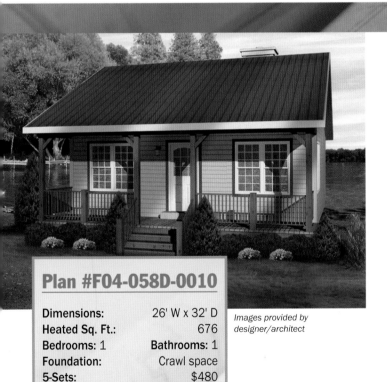

## Plan #F04-058D-0010

| | |
|---|---|
| Dimensions: | 26' W x 32' D |
| Heated Sq. Ft.: | 676 |
| Bedrooms: 1 | Bathrooms: 1 |
| Foundation: | Crawl space |
| 5-Sets: | $480 |
| PDF File: | $500 |
| 8-Sets: | $550 |
| CAD File: | $625 |
| Material List: | $70 |
| Upgrade to 2" x 6" Walls: | $75 |

*Pricing subject to change*

*Images provided by designer/architect*

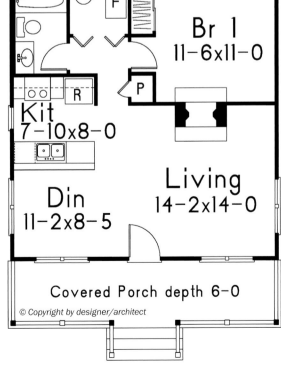

F

Br 1
11-6x11-0

P

Kit
7-10x8-0

R

Living
14-2x14-0

Din
11-2x8-5

Covered Porch depth 6-0

© Copyright by designer/architect

## Plan #F04-077D-0043

| | |
|---|---|
| **Dimensions:** | 64' W x 45'10" D |
| **Heated Sq. Ft.:** | 1,752 |
| **Bedrooms: 3** | **Bathrooms: 2** |

**Foundation:** Slab, basement or crawl space, please specify when ordering

| | |
|---|---|
| **5-Sets:** | $1,015 |
| **PDF File:** | $1,125 |
| **Reproducible Master:** | $1,200 |
| **CAD File:** | $1,680 |
| **Material List:** | $130 |

*Pricing subject to change*

*Images provided by designer/architect*

## Features

- The gas fireplace is framed by elegant built-in cabinets
- The media/hobby room is a great workspace with its large work counter
- The large island in the kitchen provides extra counterspace as well as a snack bar for casual meals
- The vaulted master bedroom features two walk-in closets, a private bath with a double-bowl vanity, a separate shower, a garden tub and a toilet closet
- 2-car side entry garage

## Plan #F04-007D-0055

| Dimensions: | 67' W x 51'4" D |
|---|---|
| Heated Sq. Ft.: | 2,029 |
| Bedrooms: 3 | Bathrooms: 2 |

**Foundation:** Slab, basement or crawl space, please specify when ordering

| | |
|---|---|
| PDF File: | $975 |
| 5-Sets: | $1,025 |
| 8-Sets: | $1,100 |
| CAD File: | $1,875 |
| Material List: | $125 |
| Upgrade to 2" x 6" Walls: | $ 150 |

*Pricing subject to change*

*Images provided by designer/architect*

## Features

- Stonework, gables, a roof dormer and double porches create a country flavor
- The kitchen/dining area enjoys an island snack bar, a built-in pantry, multiple tall windows, extravagant cabinetry, and extended counterspace
- An angled staircase descends from the large entry with wood columns and is open to a vaulted great room with a corner fireplace
- The master bedroom boasts two walk-in closets, a private bath with a double-door entry, and a secluded porch
- 2-car side entry garage

© Copyright by designer/architect

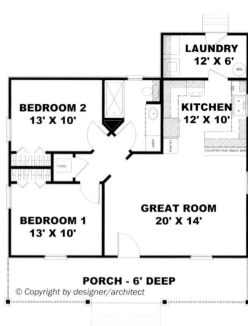

## Plan #F04-028D-0001

| | |
|---|---|
| Dimensions: | 33' W x 36' D |
| Heated Sq. Ft.: | 864 |
| Bedrooms: 2 | Bathrooms: 1 |
| Foundation: Crawl space or slab, please specify when ordering | |
| 5-Sets: | $700 |
| 8-Sets: | $800 |
| PDF File: | $850 |
| Material List: | $80 |

*Pricing subject to change*

*Images provided by designer/architect*

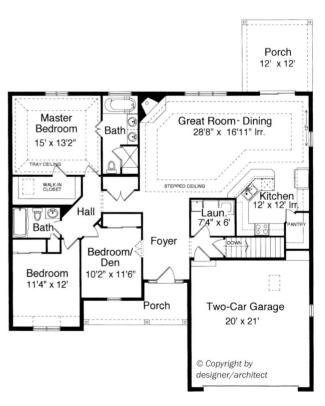

## Plan #F04-065D-0074

| | |
|---|---|
| Dimensions: | 51'8" W x 61'8" D |
| Heated Sq. Ft.: | 1,698 |
| Bedrooms: 3 | Bathrooms: 2 |
| Foundation: | Basement |
| 5-Sets: | $695 |
| 8-Sets: | $799 |
| PDF File: | $945 |
| Reproducible Master: | $945 |
| Material List: | $75 |

*Pricing subject to change*

*Images provided by designer/architect*

## Plan #F04-055D-0030

**Dimensions:** 62'8" W x 62'1" D
**Heated Sq. Ft.:** 2,107
**Bedrooms:** 4      **Bathrooms:** 2½
**Foundation:** Slab or crawl space standard; basement or walk-out basement for a fee of $250

| | |
|---|---|
| 5-Sets: | $730 |
| 8-Sets: | $870 |
| PDF File: | $1,340 |
| CAD File: | $2,065 |

*Pricing subject to change*

*Images provided by designer/architect*

© Copyright by designer/architect

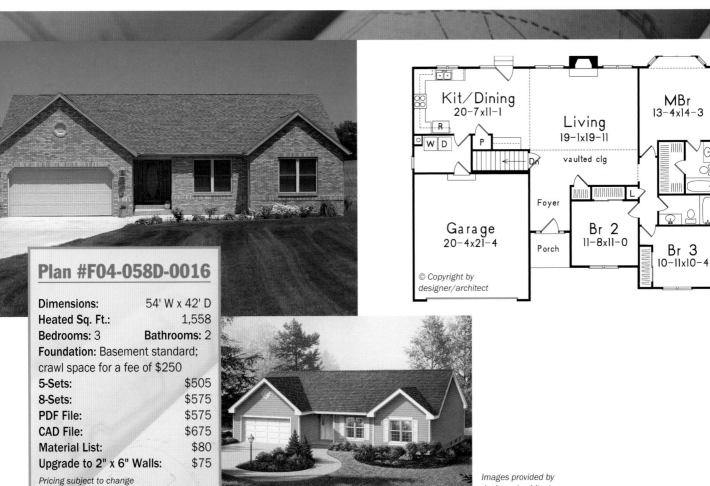

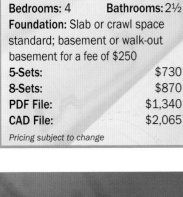

## Plan #F04-058D-0016

**Dimensions:** 54' W x 42' D
**Heated Sq. Ft.:** 1,558
**Bedrooms:** 3      **Bathrooms:** 2
**Foundation:** Basement standard; crawl space for a fee of $250

| | |
|---|---|
| 5-Sets: | $505 |
| 8-Sets: | $575 |
| PDF File: | $575 |
| CAD File: | $675 |
| Material List: | $80 |
| Upgrade to 2" x 6" Walls: | $75 |

*Pricing subject to change*

© Copyright by designer/architect

*Images provided by designer/architect*

## Plan #F04-011S-0001

| | |
|---|---|
| **Dimensions:** | 130'3" W x 79'3" D |
| **Heated Sq. Ft.:** | 4,732 |
| **Bedrooms:** 4 **Bathrooms:** | 3 full |
| | 2 half |

**Foundation:** Trusjoist floor system or walk-out basement, please specify when ordering

| | |
|---|---|
| **Exterior Walls:** | 2" x 6" |
| **PDF File:** | $1,750 |
| **5-Sets:** | $1,825 |
| **CAD File:** | $3,400 |

*Pricing subject to change*

*Images provided by designer/architect*

© Copyright by designer/architect

First Floor
2,902 sq. ft.

Lower Level
1,830 sq. ft.

## Features

- A gourmet kitchen, a nook, and the great room offer ample entertainment space, especially when utilized with the fully equipped outdoor kitchen

- An adjoining theater room and wet bar with separate wine cellar complements three lower level bedrooms perfectly

- The luxurious master bedroom has abundant his and hers closet space with built-in dressers

- 4-car garage

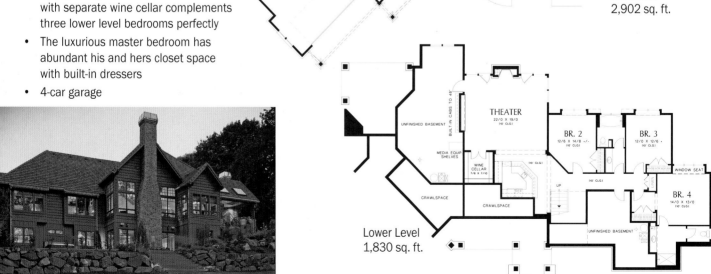

First Floor
2,016 sq. ft.

© Copyright by
designer/architect

BONUS ROOM

Optional
Second Floor
453 sq. ft.

## Plan #F04-051D-0696

| | |
|---|---|
| Dimensions: | 84'8" W x 50' D |
| Heated Sq. Ft.: | 2,016 |
| Bedrooms: 3 | Bathrooms: 2 |
| Foundation: | Basement |
| Exterior Walls: | 2" x 6" |
| 5-Sets: | $883 |
| 8-Sets: | $924 |
| PDF File: | $1,107 |
| CAD File: | $1,755 |

*Pricing subject to change*

*Images provided by
designer/architect*

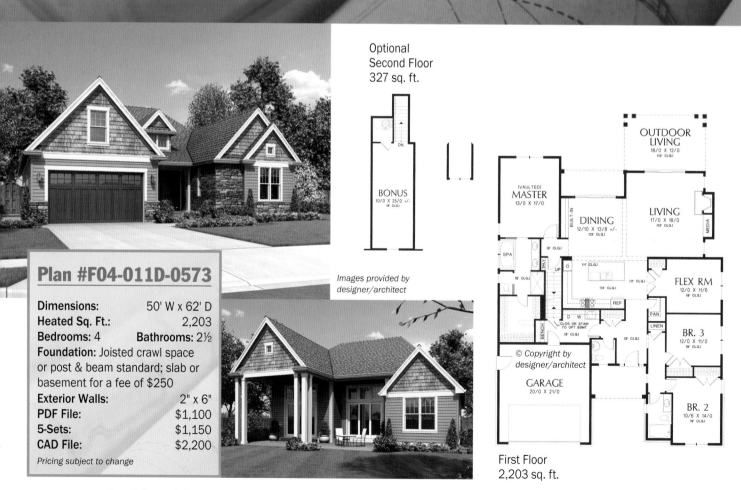

Optional
Second Floor
327 sq. ft.

BONUS

*Images provided by
designer/architect*

OUTDOOR LIVING

MASTER

DINING

LIVING

FLEX RM

BR. 3

BR. 2

GARAGE

© Copyright by
designer/architect

First Floor
2,203 sq. ft.

## Plan #F04-011D-0573

| | |
|---|---|
| Dimensions: | 50' W x 62' D |
| Heated Sq. Ft.: | 2,203 |
| Bedrooms: 4 | Bathrooms: 2½ |
| Foundation: | Joisted crawl space or post & beam standard; slab or basement for a fee of $250 |
| Exterior Walls: | 2" x 6" |
| PDF File: | $1,100 |
| 5-Sets: | $1,150 |
| CAD File: | $2,200 |

*Pricing subject to change*

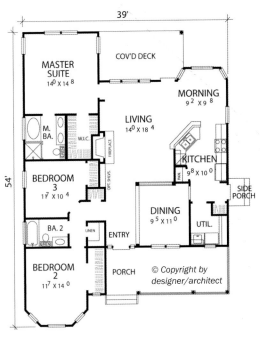

Images provided by designer/architect

© Copyright by designer/architect

## Plan #F04-111D-0038

| | |
|---|---|
| Dimensions: | 39' W x 54' D |
| Heated Sq. Ft.: | 2,041 |
| Bedrooms: 4 | Bathrooms: 2 |
| Foundation: | Slab |
| 5-Sets: | $800 |
| PDF File: | $980 |
| Reproducible Master: | $1,030 |
| CAD File: | $1,660 |

*Pricing subject to change*

## Plan #F04-121D-0030

| | |
|---|---|
| Dimensions: | 76'4" W x 52' D |
| Heated Sq. Ft.: | 2,156 |
| Bedrooms: 3 | Bathrooms: 2 |
| Foundation: | Basement |
| PDF File: | $825 |
| 5-Sets: | $875 |
| 8-Sets: | $950 |
| CAD File: | $1,725 |

*Pricing subject to change*

*Images provided by designer/architect*

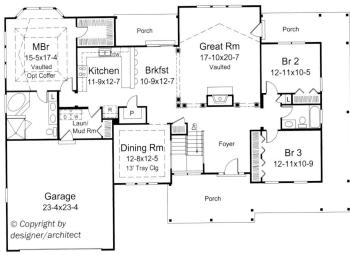

© Copyright by designer/architect

## Plan #F04-005D-0001

| | |
|---|---|
| Dimensions: | 72' W x 34'4" D |
| Heated Sq. Ft.: | 1,400 |
| Bedrooms: 3 | Bathrooms: 2 |
| Foundation: Basement or crawl space, please specify when ordering | |
| PDF File: | $825 |
| 5-Sets: | $875 |
| 8-Sets: | $950 |
| CAD File: | $1,725 |
| Material List: | $125 |

*Pricing subject to change*

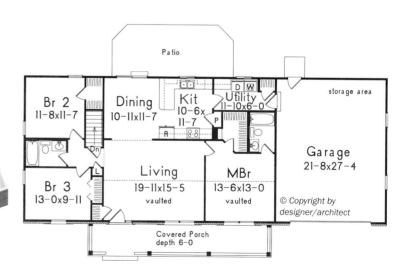

*Images provided by designer/architect*

## Features

- The large utility room has additional cabinet space
- The covered front porch provides an outdoor seating area
- Roof dormers add curb appeal to the front facade
- The living room and master bedroom feature vaulted ceilings
- 2-car garage with storage area

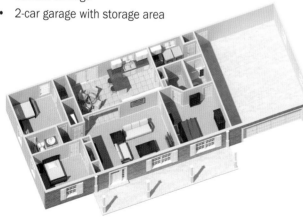

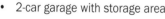

## Plan #F04-001D-0031

| | |
|---|---|
| Dimensions: | 48' W x 66' D |
| Heated Sq. Ft.: | 1,501 |
| Bedrooms: 3 | Bathrooms: 2 |

Foundation: Basement, crawl space or slab, please specify when ordering

| | |
|---|---|
| PDF File: | $825 |
| 5-Sets: | $875 |
| 8-Sets: | $950 |
| CAD File: | $1,725 |
| Material List: | $125 |

*Pricing subject to change*

*Images provided by designer/architect*

## Features

- The spacious kitchen/dining area is open to the covered porch
- A convenient utility room with large coat closet is adjacent to the garage
- The master bedroom has a private bath, a dressing area, and access to the large rear covered porch
- The large family room with fireplace creates openness
- 2-car side entry garage

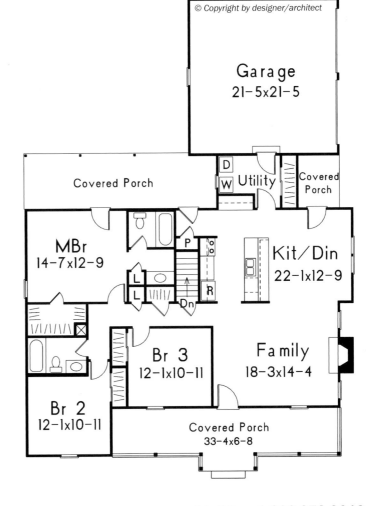

© Copyright by designer/architect

Garage
21-5x21-5

Covered Porch

D
W  Utility

Covered Porch

MBr
14-7x12-9

P

Kit/Din
22-1x12-9

L
L
R
Dn

Br 3
12-1x10-11

Family
18-3x14-4

Br 2
12-1x10-11

Covered Porch
33-4x6-8

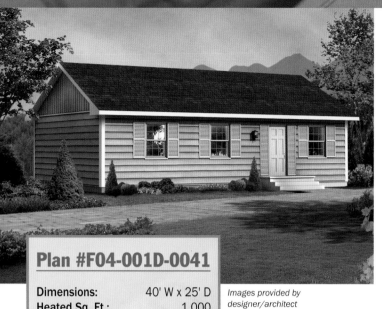

## Plan #F04-001D-0041

| | |
|---|---|
| Dimensions: | 40' W x 25' D |
| Heated Sq. Ft.: | 1,000 |
| Bedrooms: 3 | Bathrooms: 1 |

Foundation: Crawl space, slab or basement, please specify when ordering

| | |
|---|---|
| PDF File: | $750 |
| 5-Sets: | $800 |
| Reproducible Master: | $800 |
| 8-Sets: | $875 |
| Material List: | $125 |

*Pricing subject to change*

*Images provided by designer/architect*

© Copyright by designer/architect

MBr
11-8x11-8

Kit/Dining
16-7x11-8

W
D

Furn    R

L

L

Br 2
11-8x9-0

Br 3
10-4x9-0

Great Rm
14-5x12-5

Porch

---

## Plan #F04-077D-0128

| | |
|---|---|
| Dimensions: | 69' W x 59'10" D |
| Heated Sq. Ft.: | 2,000 |
| Bedrooms: 3 | Bathrooms: 2½ |

Foundation: Slab or crawl space, please specify when ordering

| | |
|---|---|
| 5-Sets: | $1,060 |
| PDF File: | $1,200 |
| Reproducible Master: | $1,270 |
| CAD File: | $1,820 |
| Material List: | $130 |

*Pricing subject to change*

*Images provided by designer/architect*

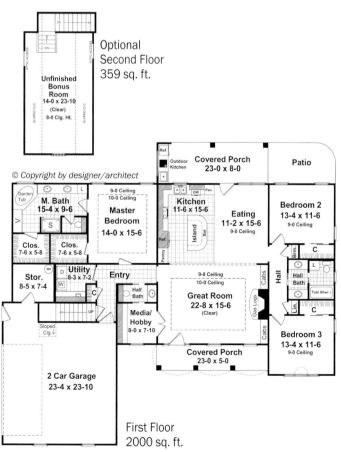

Optional Second Floor 359 sq. ft.

Unfinished Bonus Room
14-0 x 23-10
(Clear)
8-0 Clg. Ht.

© Copyright by designer/architect

Covered Porch
23-0 x 8-0

Patio

Outdoor Kitchen

Garden Tub

M. Bath
15-4 x 9-6

9-0 Ceiling
10-0 Ceiling

Master Bedroom
14-0 x 15-6

Kitchen
11-6 x 15-6

Island

Eating
11-2 x 15-6
9-0 Ceiling

Bedroom 2
13-4 x 11-6
9-0 Ceiling

Clos.
7-6 x 5-8

Clos.
7-6 x 5-8

Utility
8-3 x 7-2

Entry

Hall Bath

Stor.
8-5 x 7-4

Half Bath

9-0 Ceiling
10-0 Ceiling

Great Room
22-8 x 15-6
(Clear)

Gas Logs

Media/ Hobby
8-0 x 7-10

Sloped Clg.

2 Car Garage
23-4 x 23-10

Covered Porch
23-0 x 5-0

Bedroom 3
13-4 x 11-6
9-0 Ceiling

First Floor 2000 sq. ft.

Patio

Brkfst/ Dining
12-8x14-11

Great Rm
16-9x21-11
12' Clg

MBr
12-8x14-6
Coffer Clg

Kitchen
12-8x12-9

Dn

Garage
22-8x24-0

Foyer

Br 2
12-8x11-0

Porch

© Copyright by
designer/architect

## Plan #F04-121D-0048

*Images provided by designer/architect*

| | |
|---|---|
| Dimensions: | 44' W x 53'4" D |
| Heated Sq. Ft.: | 1,615 |
| Bedrooms: 2 | Bathrooms: 2 |
| Foundation: | Basement |
| PDF File: | $750 |
| 5-Sets: | $800 |
| 8-Sets: | $875 |
| CAD File: | $1,550 |
| Material List: | $125 |
| Upgrade to 2" x 6" Walls: | $150 |

*Pricing subject to change*

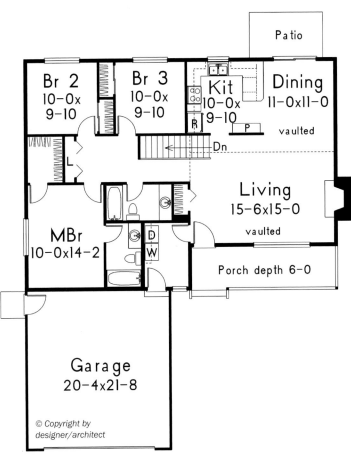

Patio

Br 2
10-0x
9-10

Br 3
10-0x
9-10

Kit
10-0x
9-10

Dining
11-0x11-0
vaulted

Dn

Living
15-6x15-0
vaulted

MBr
10-0x14-2

Porch depth 6-0

Garage
20-4x21-8

© Copyright by
designer/architect

## Plan #F04-014D-0005

*Images provided by designer/architect*

| | |
|---|---|
| Dimensions: | 47' W x 54' D |
| Heated Sq. Ft.: | 1,314 |
| Bedrooms: 3 | Bathrooms: 2 |
| Foundation: | Basement |
| Exterior Walls: | 2" x 6" |
| PDF File: | $675 |
| 5-Sets: | $725 |
| 8-Sets: | $800 |
| CAD File: | $1,475 |
| Material List: | $125 |

*Pricing subject to change*

## Plan #F04-013D-0019

| | |
|---|---|
| **Dimensions:** | 63' W x 57'2" D |
| **Heated Sq. Ft.:** | 1,992 |
| **Bedrooms:** 3 | **Bathrooms:** 2½ |

**Foundation:** Slab, crawl space or basement, please specify when ordering

| | |
|---|---|
| **PDF File:** | $895 |
| **5-Sets:** | $945 |
| **8-Sets:** | $995 |
| **CAD File:** | $1,395 |
| **Material List:** | $125 |
| **Upgrade to 2" x 6" Walls:** | $250 |

*Pricing subject to change*

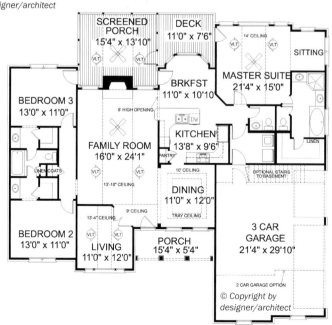

*Images provided by designer/architect*

## Features

- The bayed breakfast room overlooks the outdoor deck and connects to the screened porch
- The private formal living room in the front of the home could easily be converted to a home office or study
- An efficient kitchen is situated between the breakfast and dining rooms
- 3-car side entry garage

## Plan #F04-013D-0200

| | |
|---|---|
| **Dimensions:** | 71'2" W x 64'6" D |
| **Heated Sq. Ft.:** | 2,156 |
| **Bedrooms:** 3 | **Bathrooms:** 3 |

**Foundation:** Basement standard; crawl space or slab for a fee of $250

| | |
|---|---|
| **Exterior Walls:** | 2" x 6" |
| **PDF File:** | $995 |
| **5-Sets:** | $1,045 |
| **8-Sets:** | $1,095 |
| **CAD File:** | $1,495 |

*Pricing subject to change*

## Features

- The spacious country kitchen is open to the vaulted family room and has views of the deck
- The private master suite is topped with a tray ceiling and features two walk-in closets, a sitting area, deck access and a luxury outfitted bath
- Double doors directly off the foyer lead to a formal living room which could be perfect as a home office
- The large family room with fireplace creates openness
- 3-car side entry garage

*Images provided by designer/architect*

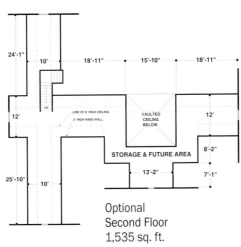

Optional
Second Floor
1,535 sq. ft.

© Copyright by
designer/architect

Optional
Lower Level
2,352 sq. ft.

First Floor
2,021 sq. ft.

## Plan #F04-001D-0013

| | |
|---|---|
| Dimensions: | 60'10" W x 51'2" D |
| Heated Sq. Ft.: | 1,882 |
| Bedrooms: 3 | Bathrooms: 2 |
| Foundation: | Basement |
| PDF File: | $825 |
| 5-Sets: | $875 |
| 8-Sets: | $950 |
| CAD File: | $1,725 |
| Material List: | $125 |
| Upgrade to 2" x 6" Walls: | $150 |

*Pricing subject to change*

## Plan #F04-137D-0065

| | |
|---|---|
| Dimensions: | 62' W x 67'10" D |
| Heated Sq. Ft.: | 2,361 |
| Bedrooms: 3 | Bathrooms: 3 |
| Foundation: | Slab |
| PDF File: | $825 |
| 5-Sets: | $875 |
| Reproducible Master: | $875 |
| 8-Sets: | $950 |

*Pricing subject to change*

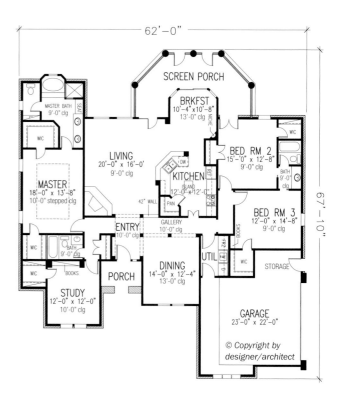

## Plan #F04-011D-0007

| | |
|---|---|
| **Dimensions:** | 50' W x 48' D |
| **Heated Sq. Ft.:** | 1,580 |
| **Bedrooms:** 3 | **Bathrooms:** 2½ |
| **Foundation:** Crawl space, Trusjoist floor system or post & beam standard; slab or basement for a fee of $225 | |
| **PDF File:** | $900 |
| **5-Sets:** | $950 |
| **CAD File:** | $1,800 |

*Pricing subject to change*

*Images provided by designer/architect*

PORCH

DINING
11/2 X 12/8
(9' CLG.)

VAULTED
MASTER
12/8 X 15/2

VAULTED
GREAT RM.
16/8 X 17/0

11/4 X 12/10

© Copyright by designer/architect

GARAGE
20/6 X 21/0

MEDIA

FOYER
(10' CLG.)

BR. 3/
DEN
10/6 X 11/4
(9' CLG.)

BR. 2
11/0 X 10/0
(9' CLG.)

PORCH

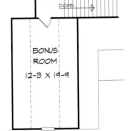

## Plan #F04-076D-0259

| | |
|---|---|
| **Dimensions:** | 46' W x 57'2" D |
| **Heated Sq. Ft.:** | 1,730 |
| **Bedrooms:** 3 | **Bathrooms:** 2 |
| **Foundation:** | Slab |
| **5-Sets:** | $625 |
| **8-Sets:** | $775 |
| **Reproducible:** | $950 |
| **CAD File:** | $1,200 |

*Pricing subject to change*

*Images provided by designer/architect*

Optional
Second Floor
312 sq. ft.

BONUS ROOM
12-3 X 19-9

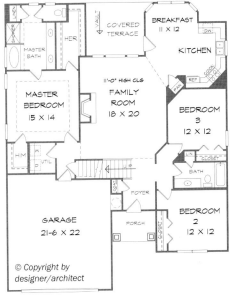

BREAKFAST
11 X 12

KITCHEN

MASTER BATH

HER

COVERED TERRACE

MASTER BEDROOM
15 X 14

11'-0" HIGH CLG
FAMILY ROOM
18 X 20

BEDROOM 3
12 X 12

HIM

UTIL

FOYER

PORCH

BEDROOM 2
12 X 12

GARAGE
21-6 X 22

© Copyright by designer/architect

First Floor
1,730 sq. ft.

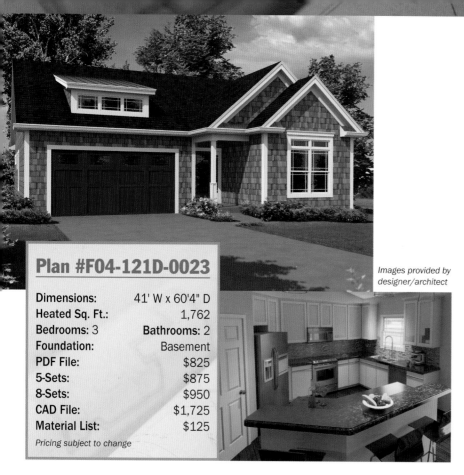

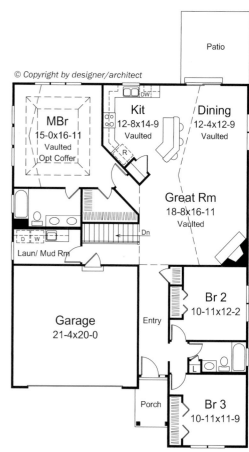

**Kit**
12-8x14-9
Vaulted

**Dining**
12-4x12-9
Vaulted

**MBr**
15-0x16-11
Vaulted
Opt Coffer

**Great Rm**
18-8x16-11
Vaulted

**Laun/ Mud Rm**

**Garage**
21-4x20-0

**Entry**

**Br 2**
10-11x12-2

**Br 3**
10-11x11-9

**Porch**

Patio

*Images provided by designer/architect*

## Plan #F04-121D-0023

| | |
|---|---|
| Dimensions: | 41' W x 60'4" D |
| Heated Sq. Ft.: | 1,762 |
| Bedrooms: 3 | Bathrooms: 2 |
| Foundation: | Basement |
| PDF File: | $825 |
| 5-Sets: | $875 |
| 8-Sets: | $950 |
| CAD File: | $1,725 |
| Material List: | $125 |

*Pricing subject to change*

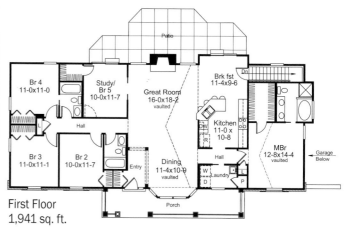

**Br 4**
11-0x11-0

**Study/
Br 5**
10-0x11-7

**Great Room**
16-0x18-2
vaulted

**Brk fst**
11-4x9-6

**Br 3**
11-0x11-1

**Br 2**
10-0x11-7

**Kitchen**
11-0 x
10-8

**Dining**
11-4x10-9
vaulted

**MBr**
12-8x14-4
vaulted

**Entry**

**Hall**

**Hall**

**Laundry**

**Garage Below**

**Porch**

**First Floor**
1,941 sq. ft.

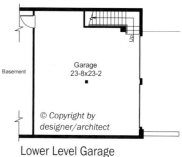

**Basement**

**Garage**
23-8x23-2

**Lower Level Garage**

*Images provided by designer/architect*

## Plan #F04-007D-0151

| | |
|---|---|
| Dimensions: | 70'4" W x 35'8" D |
| Heated Sq. Ft.: | 1,941 |
| Bedrooms: 5 | Bathrooms: 3 |
| Foundation: | Walk-out basement |
| PDF File: | $825 |
| 5-Sets: | $875 |
| 8-Sets: | $950 |
| CAD File: | $1,725 |
| Material List: | $125 |

*Pricing subject to change*

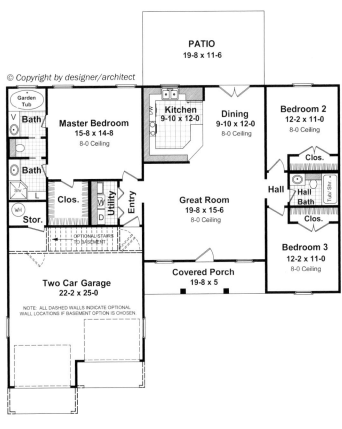

**PATIO**
19-8 x 11-6

**Master Bedroom**
15-8 x 14-8
8-0 Ceiling

Garden Tub

Bath

Bath

Clos.

Stor.

WH

**Kitchen**
9-10 x 12-0

**Dining**
9-10 x 12-0
8-0 Ceiling

Clos.

Utility

W D

Entry

**Great Room**
19-8 x 15-6
8-0 Ceiling

**Bedroom 2**
12-2 x 11-0
8-0 Ceiling

Clos.

Hall

Hall Bath

Tub/Shr.

Clos.

**Bedroom 3**
12-2 x 11-0
8-0 Ceiling

OPTIONAL STAIRS TO BASEMENT

**Two Car Garage**
22-2 x 25-0

**Covered Porch**
19-8 x 5

NOTE: ALL DASHED WALLS INDICATE OPTIONAL WALL LOCATIONS IF BASEMENT OPTION IS CHOSEN.

## Plan #F04-77D-0019

| | |
|---|---|
| Dimensions: | 54' W x 47' D |
| Heated Sq. Ft.: | 1,400 |
| Bedrooms: 3 | Bathrooms: 2 |

Foundation: Slab, basement or crawl space, please specify when ordering

| | |
|---|---|
| 5-Sets: | $915 |
| PDF File: | $1,050 |
| Reproducible Master: | $1,130 |
| CAD File: | $1,615 |
| Material List: | $130 |

*Pricing subject to change*

*Images provided by designer/architect*

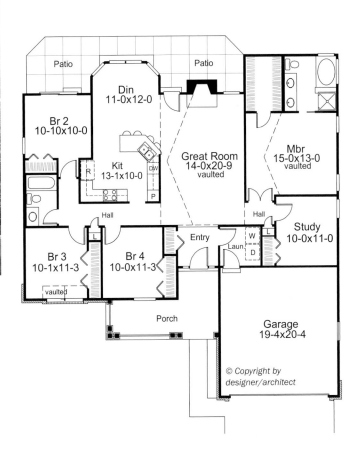

Patio

Patio

**Din**
11-0x12-0

**Br 2**
10-10x10-0

**Kit**
13-1x10-0

R

DW

P

**Great Room**
14-0x20-9
vaulted

**Mbr**
15-0x13-0
vaulted

Hall

Hall

**Br 3**
10-1x11-3

**Br 4**
10-0x11-3

Entry

Laun

W D

L

**Study**
10-0x11-0

vaulted

Porch

**Garage**
19-4x20-4

## Plan #F04-007D-0164

| | |
|---|---|
| Dimensions: | 53' W x 55' D |
| Heated Sq. Ft.: | 1,741 |
| Bedrooms: 4 | Bathrooms: 2 |

Foundation: Crawl space, basement or slab, please specify when ordering

| | |
|---|---|
| PDF File: | $825 |
| 5-Sets: | $875 |
| Reproducible Master: | $875 |
| 8-Sets: | $950 |
| Material List: | $125 |

*Pricing subject to change*

*Images provided by designer/architect*

## Plan #F04-047D-0056

| | |
|---|---|
| Dimensions: | 82'4" W x 83'8" D |
| Heated Sq. Ft.: | 3,424 |
| Bedrooms: 5 | Bathrooms: 4 |
| Foundation: | Slab |
| PDF File: | $1,050 |
| 5-Sets: | $1,100 |
| Reproducible Master: | $1,100 |
| CAD File: | $1,950 |
| Material List: | $125 |

*Pricing subject to change*

*Images provided by designer/architect*

## Features

- The enormous master bath features double walk-in closets and a huge whirlpool tub under a bay window
- Angled walls throughout this home add interest in every room
- The family room with its unique center fireplace flanked by angled walls add a dramatic view from any angle
- An open and airy kitchen looks into a cozy breakfast nook as well as the casual family room
- Framing - only concrete block available
- 3-car side entry garage

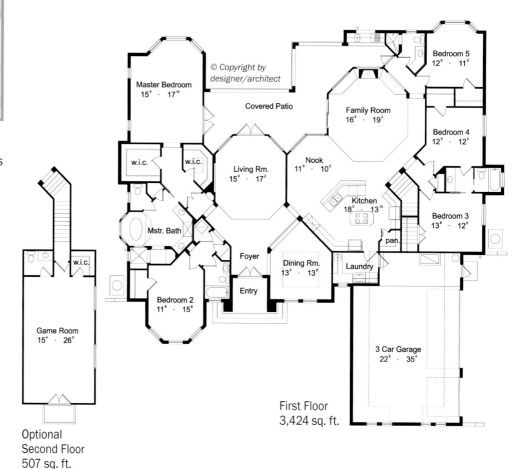

Optional
Second Floor
507 sq. ft.

First Floor
3,424 sq. ft.

# a place of *Refuge* is the wave of the future

There's a lot of irony in today's home building trends. Today's homeowners are constantly searching for the next "big thing" especially when it comes to smart home technology. At the same time, they're wanting to feel secure and back to nature with a sharp focus on ways to live more simply and purposeful. Is it safe to say homeowners want it all? Is today's ideal home one with The Jetsons-like technology, but also with that inviting feel like Grandma's house? In many ways, the answer is yes!

Trends in all areas of life are born from the unique combination of the current environment, economy and demographics. So, no place or time in history is ever exactly the same, and although it may seem as though trends resurface all of the time, they are never exactly the same as they once were. Today's trends in home design are a result of several lifestyle factors that include our intense need to feel connected, while also wanting to be able to detach from the world. So, no doubt home designers have their work cut out for them! Homeowners are sensible and are no longer interested in being wasteful. And, because information on every topic imaginable is available at their fingertips anytime of day, they are smarter than ever before. And, because of their ability to research anything at anytime they feel as though anything they see can be attainable.

From Baby Boomers to Millennials, homeowners are taking today's technology and mixing it with yesterday's vintage furnishings, retro design elements, and reclaimed natural materials that once had another purpose entirely. Homeowners have become resourceful, imaginative, and driven to live in a home that offers them refuge from their busy lives, while spotlighting their personality and interests. The current home design trends speak volumes on how today's homeowners want to live.

Today's these home design trends offer solutions for homeowners, while also providing comfort and security.

## LONELY NO MORE

Although social media allows us to feel connected, people are yearning for ways to feel more connected face-to-face. Because of this need for community, many generations of family are choosing to live together. Whether it's for convenience or community, homes are being universally designed so they are comfortable and accessible for all ages. Having adult children at home, or a parent or in-law requires a thoughtful floor plan that combines openness and privacy for everyone. Split bedroom floor plans have become the most popular option meaning the master suite is separated from the other bedrooms for privacy. Gone are the days of all of the bedrooms doors being side-by-side down one small hallway. Now, master suites are hidden in one side of the house and the other bedrooms are scattered in other areas or placed near each other on the opposite side of the house.

*Page 52 top: Plan #F04-101D-0056 on page 270, Warren Diggles Photography; bottom: Plan #F04-055D-0748 on page 8; Page 53 top: Plan #F04-011S-0001 on page 36; left, Plan #F04-101D-0056 on page 270, Warren Diggles Photography.*

Other popular design options include one-level living with a finished lower level featuring an in-law suite. Keep in mind however, that as the older individual continues to age accessibility to another level of the home will get even more difficult. So, it's very important to plan for the future when choosing a layout. A few other options are being designed to offer even more privacy. Home designers are developing home layouts with apartments connected, or inside of the home. Apartment garages and tiny homes are also hot and offer alternative ways in creating privacy, while adding additional living space to your home's living conditions or property.

## NOT AGAINST THE GRAIN

With sustainability continuing to be popular, it comes as no surprise that texture and wood grain are trending in home design. The use of sustainable materials such as cork and bamboo also are included in the mix. With both cork and bamboo being highly renewable resources, they are great options for those wanting to make less of an impact on the environment when building or remodeling a home. These natural and textured materials are being used in a variety of creative ways from exposed ceiling beams, flooring, wall covering ("think ship lap"), and one-of-a-kind hearths. Even vintage wood furniture pieces are becoming unique bathroom vanities, kitchen islands, or desks in home offices.

With all of these natural elements filling our homes again, taupe is the new gray. It appears people are craving warmth once again and so beige and other warmer tone colors are making a comeback. Although white never goes out of style, even today's hottest kitchen designs are featuring lots of white with rough sewn timber shelving, or a wood butcher-block countertops adding that warmer element to the starkness of the white. With homeowners searching for a cozy, natural and warm living environment it only makes sense beige would be the color of choice.

*Page 54 top: Plan #F04-101D-0052 on page 60, Damon Searles, photographer; left: Plan #F04-101D-0045 on page 88, Warren Diggles Photography; Page 55, top right clockwise: Plan #026D-0252, houseplansandmore.com; Plan #065D-0041 on page 218; Plan #F04-101D-0047 on page 162, Warren Diggles Photography; Plan #071S-0001, houseplansandmore.com; Backyard putting green, Sport Court St. Louis; Plan #F04-101D-0045 on page 88, Warren Diggles Photography.*

## ALL WORK AND NO PLAY?

We're spending more time than ever working. Even with all of the technology that should be simplifying life for us, we still spend more time away from home than ever before. With people working longer and harder, including many delaying retirement, or starting a second career, homes are becoming more playful and offering ways to decompress. How do you like to spend your free time? With little free time in most people's lives, being able to do the things you love under your own roof is very important. Areas that encourage people to relax and unwind are topping new homeowner's wish lists. From exercise or meditation rooms, to libraries or reading rooms designed purposely without technology, new homeowners are making a statement that technology is important, but not in all aspects of their lives and homes. In order to truly decompress and unplug, many want to have a refuge that frees them from all of the never-ending noise technology creates. Other playful additions being added to homes today include sports rooms, indoor pools and putting greens, and for those who enjoy cooking to unwind, even pizza ovens. Outdoor living spaces are also deemed as a must-have for homeowners. Offering a refuge in nature, these outdoor rooms are extensions of the interior providing space for dining and relaxing and often including fireplaces, kitchens and other functions.

## HONEST SPACES

Homes may be getting smarter, but there's a reason, they have to! Today's new homes are getting smaller; so space is in high demand and that means great function is a necessity. With people choosing to live with less space, the space they do have must be able to handle all of a person's or family's needs. Architects and residential designers are catering specifically to a person's wants and needs rather than creating floor plans without their personality in mind. With every square foot so important, no corner can be wasted. If a home is designed to cater to a larger audience, then it's being designed with flexible spaces that can be adapted to many different scenarios from dining rooms to home offices. The birth of the open floor plan also solves smaller home issues by offering one large, open space that integrates gathering, working, cooking and dining. Why separate these spaces with walls when all of these tasks can be freely done in one place? This promotes not only spaciousness in a home design, but once again a feeling of community with family members. Incorporating open wood beams, vaulted ceilings, and larger windows combines several of today's best trends into the perfect living space everyone will find comfortable and inviting.

*Page 56, top: Plan #F04-032D-0887 on page 276; bottom, Plan #F04-101D-0052 on page 60, Damon Searles; Page 57 top: Plan #091S-0001, houseplansandmore.com; bottom, left: Technology drawer, ClosetMaid®; bottom, right: Kitchen office desk planning center, ClosetMaid®.*

## GREEN FEELS CLEAN

Green building is remaining an important factor in new home design, but many home buyers and designers are initially choosing less costly surface upgrades using efficient green materials rather than overhauling all of the appliances and the HVAC system for more efficient models. But, people are more mindful than ever of toxic indoor chemicals and materials we're exposed to everyday that are affecting our home's air and water quality. From water purifiers to low VOC paint brands, all of these subtle choices result in a healthier home for all who dwell there. This trend continues to expand with essential oils allowing indoor environments to be filled with scents that can calm, or energize. There are even new light fixtures that will mimic natural circadian sleep patterns promoting better quality sleep. Home buyers are leaving no stone unturned when it comes to their health, so even fireplaces have become ventless, or being more commonly built for outdoor use on covered patios or porches.

## WORK-LIFE BALANCE ACHIEVED

As we maintain our position on how important a playful home refuge is, it is also very important there is a place within today's homes for work. More people work from home than ever before and there must be a place that promotes effective and productive work free from noise and distraction, while encouraging a healthier work-life balance. However, thanks to the literally shrinking size of our technology, we need less space than ever for work tasks. So, don't picture a huge study or home office any longer, a small computer niche off the mud room or kitchen can easily suffice. In fact, many homes are now including a technology center where additional outlets, charging stations, and storage spaces for safely housing smart phones, hand held devices, and other popular electronic necessities we all seem to believe we can't live without can be kept. Typically, this technology center is designed near the laundry room, mud room, or a rear foyer, so these items can easily be grabbed on your way out the door.

*Make* furniture multi-functional, sometimes it's a home office, sometimes it's just a place to sort mail, and pay bills.

Today's home design trends are so much more than features within a house. The features homeowners desire provide therapy from our non-stop lives outside our home; they shelter us from dangerous chemicals in the environment; and they promote a feeling of contentment and togetherness we're all craving now more than ever. Today's home designs provide sanity and peace and a life better lived.

## TAKE-AWAYS: 5 HOME DECORATING TRENDS

### EVERYTHING OLD IS NEW AGAIN

Vintage, retro and reclaimed is the thing. Re-purposed and refurbished home furnishings and materials are continuing to see new life again. Styles from the 50s, 60s, and 70s including velvet, tapered legs, geometric accents, and curved back seating are becoming popular once again. So, stray away from overly matching décor and opt for a playful furniture addition from the 50s, 60s, or 70s. Not only is vintage in, but it's also a great way to use older furniture pieces in a whole new light. Even appliances are having fun with this hot trend and refrigerators and kitchen appliances have gone retro and can be found in styles reminiscent of the 50s in bold candy-colored colors sure to add personality to kitchens of any size.

### GO FOR THE BOLD

When it comes to color, think bold. Not only will turquoise and green colors remain popular, so will jewel tones in plum and red. Also, with all of the use of wood, like previously mentioned beige is back. And don't be surprised to see close to neon colors being used for outdoor furniture. Bold patterned wallpaper especially in tropical prints is being seen in rooms creating little need for adding expensive artwork.

### THINGS ARE LOOKING UP

Embellished ceilings are a popular focal point in decorating. Don't be surprised to see ceilings painted in bold colors, architecturally enhanced ceiling designs with beams, and other natural textures and materials using herringbone patterns. Quirky and fun statement lighting fixtures are everywhere and add a unique look. Hang a fun light fixture in an unexpected place such as a bedroom, bathroom or even a closet.

## KEEP IT SIMPLE

As home sizes decrease, the need for keeping things organized and in their place increases. It is essential to have an organized home when it's smaller, so anything that can be functional while helping you organize is popular right now. Kitchen islands, banquettes and integrated office spaces keep everything organized and functional. Kitchen storage walls also do just that and require little space. Smart home features like smart phone charging technology built into furniture and pop-up outlets including USB ports promote less clutter, too.

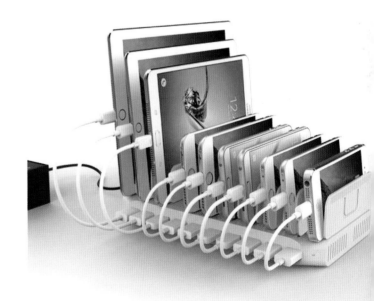

## EASY BEING GREEN

While "living green" may not exactly be a new trend, it is one that is here to stay. Now that people are more educated on how even the little things can greatly and positively impact the environment, homeowners continue to be drawn to recycled or reused products for their homes. Homeowners have learned that LED lighting, eco-friendly light bulbs and other simple swaps are worth every penny in the end.

*Page 58 top, left: Plan #F04-101D-0056 on page 270, Warren Diggles Photography; bottom, left: Plan #128D-0006, houseplansandmore.com; top, right: Smeg 50's Retro Style Aesthetic Refrigerator Item# FAB28URDR1, smegusa. com; bottom, right: Kohler Karbon style faucet, kohler.com; Page 59 top, left: Plan #F04-101-0052 on page 60; top, right: Selje Nightstand with wireless charging, Item#: 690.949.54, ikea.com; middle: Mockett Pop-Up Kitchen Power™, Item #PCS77-23G, mockett.com; bottom, right: UNITEK 96W/2.4A 10-Port USB Charging Station with Quick Charge 3.0, amazon.com.*

## Plan #F04-101D-0052

**Dimensions:** 129'8" W x 70'8" D
**Heated Sq. Ft.:** 2,611
**Bedrooms:** 2 **Bathrooms:** 2½
**Foundation:** Daylight basement or basement, please specify when ordering
**Exterior Walls:** 2" x 6"
**5-Sets:** $950
**PDF File:** $1,250
**CAD File:** $1,800

*Pricing subject to change*

### Features

- Open living at its finest in this Craftsman style home with barrier free living spaces
- An angled den off the foyer creates a private home office
- Highlighting the U-shaped kitchen is the large center island
- Convenient mud room and laundry as you enter from the garage
- 3-car garage

*Images provided by designer/architect*

© Copyright by designer/architect

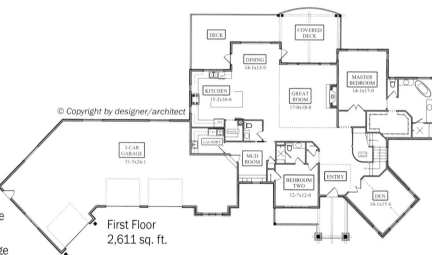

First Floor
2,611 sq. ft.

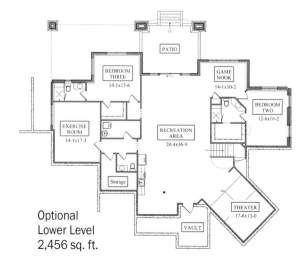

Optional
Lower Level
2,456 sq. ft.

## Plan #F04-076D-0223

| Dimensions: | 91'9" W x 81'6" D |
|---|---|
| Heated Sq. Ft.: | 2,818 |
| Bedrooms: 3 | Bathrooms: 2½ |

Foundation: Basement, slab or crawl space, please specify when ordering

| 5-Sets: | $875 |
|---|---|
| 8-Sets: | $1,125 |
| PDF File: | $1,325 |
| CAD File: | $1,650 |

*Pricing subject to change*

*Images provided by designer/architect*

## Features

- The vaulted foyer creates a grand entrance into this amazing home
- The kitchen in this home is a chef's dream with plenty of open space and an oversized walk-in pantry
- The rear covered terrace is great for enjoying the outdoors in comfort
- The master suite features an amazing vaulted master bath
- 2-car side entry garage

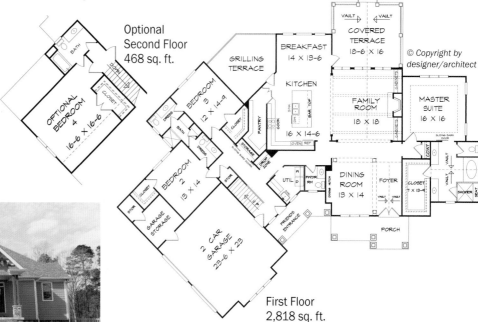

Optional Second Floor 468 sq. ft.

© Copyright by designer/architect

First Floor 2,818 sq. ft.

## Plan #F04-026D-1890

| | |
|---|---|
| Dimensions: | 69' W x 68' D |
| Heated Sq. Ft.: | 2,449 |
| Bedrooms: 3 | Bathrooms: 2½ |
| Foundation: | Slab |
| PDF File: | $925 |
| 5-Sets: | $1,000 |
| 8-Sets: | $1,120 |
| CAD File: | $1,425 |
| Upgrade to 2" x 6" Walls: | $195 |

*Pricing subject to change*

*Images provided by designer/architect*

## Features

- The bedrooms are placed for maximum privacy in a wing to themselves
- Both the entry foyer and great room feature 11' ceilings that add volume and grandeur to this home
- Combining the kitchen, dining and great room is family living at its finest
- Located as you enter through the garage is a drop zone, lockers, shelves and a closet that work together to keep clutter out of the kitchen and add organization to a homeowner's busy schedule
- 2-car side entry garage, with optional additional 1-car front entry garage

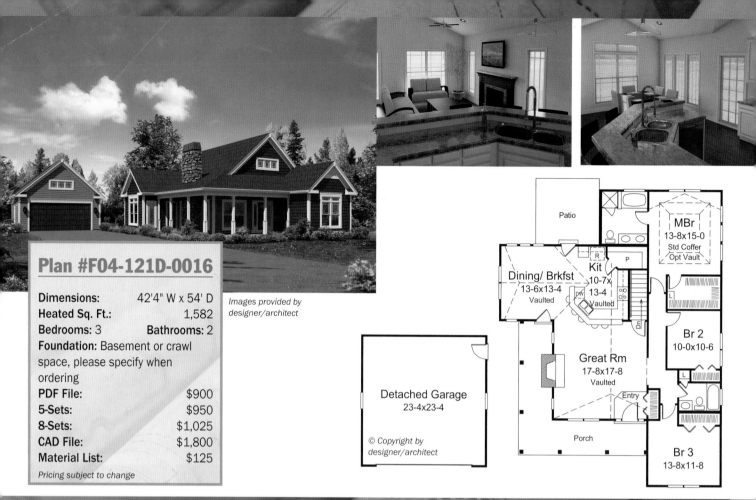

## Plan #F04-121D-0016

| | |
|---|---|
| Dimensions: | 42'4" W x 54' D |
| Heated Sq. Ft.: | 1,582 |
| Bedrooms: 3 | Bathrooms: 2 |
| Foundation: Basement or crawl space, please specify when ordering | |
| PDF File: | $900 |
| 5-Sets: | $950 |
| 8-Sets: | $1,025 |
| CAD File: | $1,800 |
| Material List: | $125 |

*Pricing subject to change*

*Images provided by designer/architect*

© Copyright by designer/architect

Detached Garage
23-4x23-4

Patio

MBr
13-8x15-0
Std Coffer
Opt Vault

Dining/ Brkfst
13-6x13-4
Vaulted

Kit
10-7x 13-4
Vaulted

Br 2
10-0x10-6

Great Rm
17-8x17-8
Vaulted

Entry

Porch

Br 3
13-8x11-8

## Plan #F04-007D-0105

| | |
|---|---|
| Dimensions: | 35' W x 40'8" D |
| Heated Sq. Ft.: | 1,084 |
| Bedrooms: 2 | Bathrooms: 2 |
| Foundation: | Basement |
| PDF File: | $750 |
| 5-Sets: | $800 |
| Reproducible Master: | $800 |
| 8-Sets: | $875 |
| Material List: | $125 |

*Pricing subject to change*

*Images provided by designer/architect*

© Copyright by designer/architect

Br 2
10-0x13-0

MBr
11-7x15-6

Hall

Brk'ft
12-0x9-0

Dining

Patio

Kit
10-9x9-0

Living Rm.
14-0x18-9
vaulted

Porch

Entry

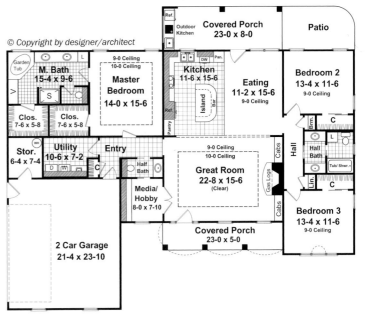

© Copyright by designer/architect

*Images provided by designer/architect*

## Plan #F04-077D-0098

| | |
|---|---|
| Dimensions: | 67' W x 56' D |
| Heated Sq. Ft.: | 2,000 |
| Bedrooms: 3 | Bathrooms: 2½ |

Foundation: Basement, slab or crawl space, please specify when ordering

| | |
|---|---|
| 5-Sets: | $1,060 |
| PDF File: | $1,200 |
| Reproducible Master: | $1,270 |
| CAD File: | $1,820 |
| Material List: | $130 |

*Pricing subject to change*

© Copyright by designer/architect

*Images provided by designer/architect*

## Plan #F04-051D-0675

| | |
|---|---|
| Dimensions: | 54' W x 54' D |
| Heated Sq. Ft.: | 1,569 |
| Bedrooms: 2 | Bathrooms: 2 |
| Foundation: | Basement |
| Exterior Walls: | 2" x 6" |
| 5-Sets: | $823 |
| 8-Sets: | $865 |
| PDF File: | $1,032 |
| CAD File: | $1,630 |

*Pricing subject to change*

## Plan #F04-055D-0456

**Dimensions:** 34'10" W x 83' D
**Heated Sq. Ft.:** 1,811
**Bedrooms:** 3    **Bathrooms:** 2
**Foundation:** Crawl space or slab, please specify when ordering

| | |
|---|---|
| 5-Sets: | $630 |
| 8-Sets: | $720 |
| PDF File: | $1,105 |
| CAD File: | $1,700 |

*Pricing subject to change*

*Images provided by designer/architect*

## Plan #F04-137D-0087

**Dimensions:** 43'8" W x 74'8" D
**Heated Sq. Ft.:** 1,496
**Bedrooms:** 3    **Bathrooms:** 2
**Foundation:** Slab

| | |
|---|---|
| PDF File: | $675 |
| 5-Sets: | $725 |
| Reproducible Master: | $725 |
| 8-Sets: | $800 |

*Pricing subject to change*

*Images provided by designer/architect*

call toll-free 1-800-373-2646   houseplansandmore.com

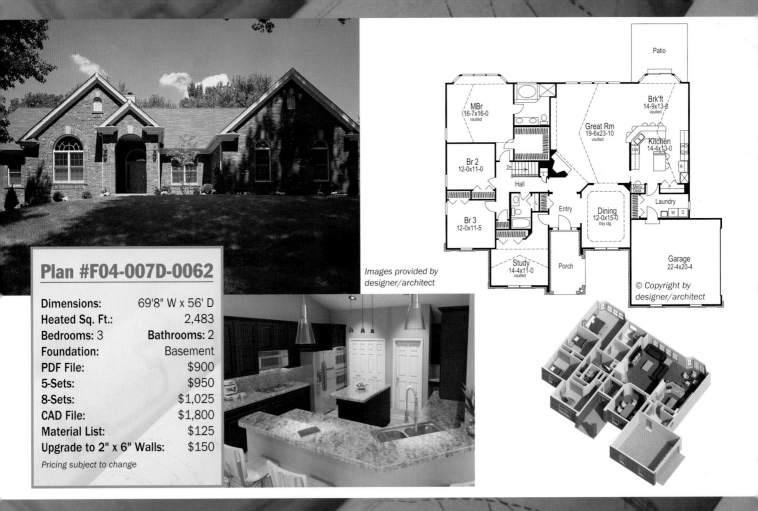

## Plan #F04-007D-0062

| | |
|---|---|
| Dimensions: | 69'8" W x 56' D |
| Heated Sq. Ft.: | 2,483 |
| Bedrooms: 3 | Bathrooms: 2 |
| Foundation: | Basement |
| PDF File: | $900 |
| 5-Sets: | $950 |
| 8-Sets: | $1,025 |
| CAD File: | $1,800 |
| Material List: | $125 |
| Upgrade to 2" x 6" Walls: | $150 |

*Pricing subject to change*

Images provided by
designer/architect

© Copyright by
designer/architect

## Plan #F04-016D-0053

| | |
|---|---|
| Dimensions: | 60' W x 39' D |
| Heated Sq. Ft.: | 1,466 |
| Bedrooms: 3 | Bathrooms: 2 |
| Foundation: | Slab or crawl space standard; basement for a fee of $175 |
| PDF File: | $795 |
| 5-Sets: | $795 |
| 8-Sets: | $875 |
| CAD File: | $1,595 |
| Material List: | $95 |

*Pricing subject to change*

Images provided by
designer/architect

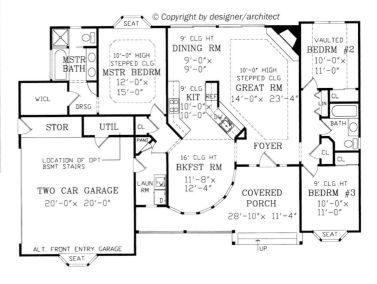

© Copyright by designer/architect

© Copyright by designer/architect

First Floor
2,780 sq. ft.

Optional
Second Floor
432 sq. ft.

## Plan #F04-076D-0237

| | |
|---|---|
| Dimensions: | 91'5" W x 79' D |
| Heated Sq. Ft.: | 2,780 |
| Bedrooms: 4 | Bathrooms: 2½ |

Foundation: Crawl space or slab, please specify when ordering

| | |
|---|---|
| 5-Sets: | $850 |
| 8-Sets: | $1,100 |
| Reproducible Master: | $1,300 |
| CAD File: | $1,600 |

*Pricing subject to change*

*Images provided by designer/architect*

© Copyright by designer/architect

## Plan #F04-051D-0800

| | |
|---|---|
| Dimensions: | 66'8" W x 55' D |
| Heated Sq. Ft.: | 1,709 |
| Bedrooms: 2 | Bathrooms: 2 |
| Foundation: | Basement |
| Exterior Walls: | 2" x 6" |
| 5-Sets: | $823 |
| 8-Sets: | $865 |
| PDF File: | $1,032 |
| CAD File: | $1,630 |

*Pricing subject to change*

*Images provided by designer/architect*

## Plan #F04-007D-0163

**Dimensions:** 50'8" W x 50'4" D
**Heated Sq. Ft.:** 1,580
**Bedrooms:** 3    **Bathrooms:** 2
**Foundation:** Basement, slab or crawl space, please specify when ordering

| | |
|---|---|
| PDF File: | $825 |
| 5-Sets: | $875 |
| Reproducible Master: | $875 |
| 8-Sets: | $950 |
| Material List: | $125 |

*Pricing subject to change*

*Images provided by designer/architect*

© Copyright by designer/architect

© Copyright by designer/architect

## Plan #F04-051D-0807

**Dimensions:** 66'4" W x 55'8" D
**Heated Sq. Ft.:** 2,154
**Bedrooms:** 3    **Bathrooms:** 2
**Foundation:** Basement
**Exterior Walls:** 2" x 6"

| | |
|---|---|
| 5-Sets: | $883 |
| 8-Sets: | $924 |
| PDF File: | $1,107 |
| CAD File: | $1,755 |

*Pricing subject to change*

*Images provided by designer/architect*

© Copyright by designer/architect

## Plan #F04-139D-0001

**Dimensions:** 39'7" W x 51'9" D
**Heated Sq. Ft.:** 1,068
**Bedrooms:** 2    **Bathrooms:** 1
**Foundation:** Crawl space standard;
slab or basement for a fee of $450
**Exterior Walls:** 2" x 6"
**5-Sets:** $1,245
**PDF File:** $1,320
**CAD File:** $2,995
*Pricing subject to change*

*Images provided by designer/architect*

## Plan #F04-135D-0005

**Dimensions:** 13'6" W x 44'10" D
**Heated Sq. Ft.:** 559
**Bedrooms:** 1    **Bathrooms:** 1
**Foundation:** Crawl space
**Exterior Walls:** 2" x 6"
**PDF File:** $525
**5-Sets:** $575
**Reproducible Master:** $575
**8-Sets:** $650
*Pricing subject to change*

*Images provided by designer/architect*

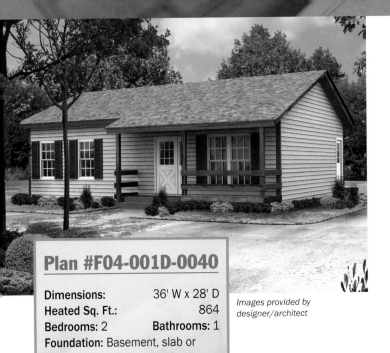

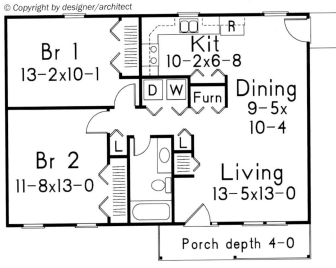

© Copyright by designer/architect

## Plan #F04-001D-0040

| | |
|---|---|
| Dimensions: | 36' W x 28' D |
| Heated Sq. Ft.: | 864 |
| Bedrooms: 2 | Bathrooms: 1 |
| Foundation: Basement, slab or crawl space, please specify when ordering | |
| PDF File: | $675 |
| 5-Sets: | $725 |
| Reproducible Master: | $725 |
| 8-Sets: | $800 |
| Material List: | $125 |
| *Pricing subject to change* | |

*Images provided by designer/architect*

Br 1
13-2x10-1

Kit
10-2x6-8

D W Furn

Dining
9-5x 10-4

Br 2
11-8x13-0

Living
13-5x13-0

Porch depth 4-0

## Plan #F04-007D-0252

| | |
|---|---|
| Dimensions: | 67' W x 51' D |
| Heated Sq. Ft.: | 1,979 |
| Bedrooms: 3 | Bathrooms: 3 |
| Foundation: | Basement |
| PDF File: | $975 |
| 5-Sets: | $1,025 |
| Reproducible Master: | $1,025 |
| 8-Sets: | $1,100 |
| Material List: | $125 |
| *Pricing subject to change* | |

*Images provided by designer/architect*

Garage
34-4x23-4

Optional Second Floor
614 sq. ft.

First Floor
1,979 sq. ft.

Std Loft Area
32-2x18-0

Opt Br 4
13-10x10-7

Opt Office
15-7x18-0

Sloped Clg

Balcony to Great Rm Below

Open to Great Rm Below

Brkfst/ Hearth
12-0x16-8

Patio

Patio

Laundry

Grilling Porch

MBr
15-5x16-8
Std Vault Clg
Opt Coffer Clg

Kitchen
12-0x9-7

Great Rm
19-10x24-8
Vault Clg

Br 2
11-2x12-0

Br 3
10-1x12-0

Foyer

© Copyright by designer/architect   Porch

## Plan #F04-077D-0052

| | |
|---|---|
| Dimensions: | 65' W x 50'10 D |
| Heated Sq. Ft.: | 1,802 |
| Bedrooms: 3 | Bathrooms: 2 |

Foundation: Slab, crawl space or basement, please specify when ordering

| | |
|---|---|
| 5-Sets: | $1,015 |
| PDF File: | $1,125 |
| Reproducible Master: | $1,200 |
| CAD File: | $1,680 |
| Material List: | $130 |

*Pricing subject to change*

*Images provided by designer/architect*

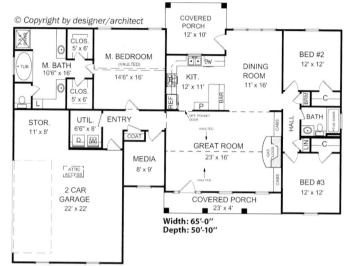

© Copyright by designer/architect

**Width: 65'-0"**
**Depth: 50'-10"**

## Plan #F04-007D-0134

| | |
|---|---|
| Dimensions: | 73'8" W x 32' D |
| Heated Sq. Ft.: | 1,310 |
| Bedrooms: 3 | Bathrooms: 2 |

Foundation: Basement, slab or crawl space, please specify when ordering

| | |
|---|---|
| PDF File: | $750 |
| 5-Sets: | $800 |
| 8-Sets: | $875 |
| CAD File: | $1,550 |
| Material List: | $125 |
| Upgrade to 2" x 6" Walls: | $150 |

*Pricing subject to change*

*Images provided by designer/architect*

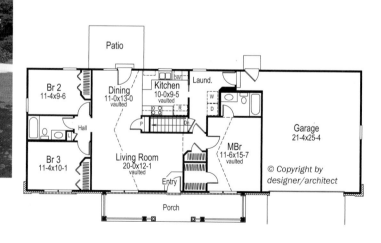

© Copyright by designer/architect

## Plan #F04-011D-0590

| | |
|---|---|
| Dimensions: | 75'6" W x 85'6" D |
| Heated Sq. Ft.: | 3,044 |
| Bedrooms: 3 | Bathrooms: 2½ |
| Foundation: | Post & Beam |
| Exterior Walls: | 2" x 6" |
| PDF File: | $1,250 |
| 5-Sets: | $1,300 |
| CAD File: | $2,400 |

*Pricing subject to change*

*Images provided by designer/architect*

© Copyright by designer/architect

## Plan #F04-055D-0205

| | |
|---|---|
| Dimensions: | 64'2" W x 49' D |
| Heated Sq. Ft.: | 1,989 |
| Bedrooms: 4 | Bathrooms: 3 |

Foundation: Slab or crawl space standard; basement or walk-out basement for a fee of $250

| | |
|---|---|
| 5-Sets: | $730 |
| 8-Sets: | $870 |
| PDF File: | $1,340 |
| CAD File: | $2,065 |
| Upgrade to 2" x 6" Walls: | $250 |

*Pricing subject to change*

*Images provided by designer/architect*

© Copyright by designer/architect

## Plan #F04-055D-1049

| | |
|---|---|
| **Dimensions:** | 85'6" W x 61'3" D |
| **Heated Sq. Ft.:** | 2,470 |
| **Bedrooms:** 4 | **Bathrooms:** 3½ |

**Foundation:** Slab or crawl space standard; walk-out basement or basement a for a fee of $250

| | |
|---|---|
| **5-Sets:** | $880 |
| **8-Sets:** | $1,095 |
| **PDF File:** | $1,685 |
| **CAD File:** | $2,595 |
| **Upgrade to 2" x 6" Walls:** | $250 |

*Pricing subject to change*

### Features

- This home's open floor plan creates a wonderfully inviting feel to the gathering spaces since they seem larger than their true size
- The private master suite enjoys its own private bath, direct access to the outdoor living and covered grilling porch, and a sizable walk-in closet
- All other bedrooms include roomy walk-in closets for maintaining organization
- The bonus room above the garage has an additional 602 square feet of living area
- 2-car side entry garage and a 1-car front entry garage

*Images provided by designer/architect*

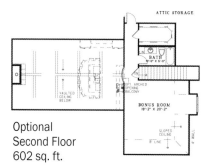
Optional Second Floor
602 sq. ft.

© Copyright by designer/architect

First Floor
2,470 sq. ft.

call toll-free 1-800-373-2646   © Copyright by designer/architect   houseplansandmore.com

## Plan #F04-013D-0015

| | |
|---|---|
| **Dimensions:** | 55'8" W x 56'6" D |
| **Heated Sq. Ft.:** | 1,787 |
| **Bedrooms:** 3 | **Bathrooms:** 2 |
| **Foundation:** Walk-out basement, slab or crawl space, please specify when ordering | |
| **PDF File:** | $895 |
| **5-Sets:** | $945 |
| **8-Sets:** | $995 |
| **CAD File:** | $1,395 |
| **Material List:** | $125 |
| **Upgrade to 2" x 6" Walls:** | $250 |

*Pricing subject to change*

*Images provided by designer/architect*

## Features

- Skylights brighten the screen porch that connects to the family room, master bedroom, and the deck outdoors
- The master bedroom features a comfortable sitting area, a large private bath, and a huge walk-in closet
- The kitchen has a serving bar that extends dining into the family room
- The bonus room above the garage has an additional 263 square feet of living area
- 2-car side entry garage

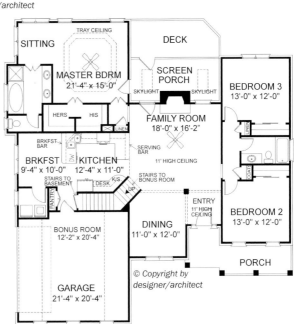

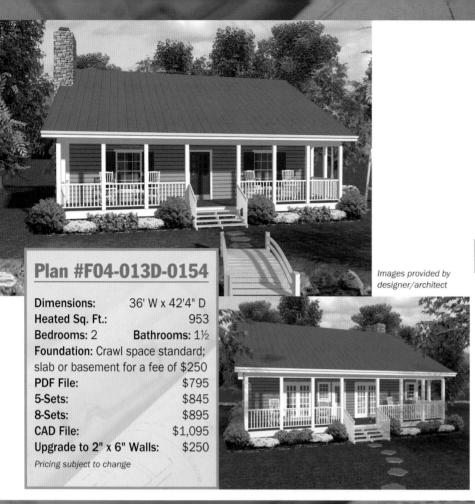

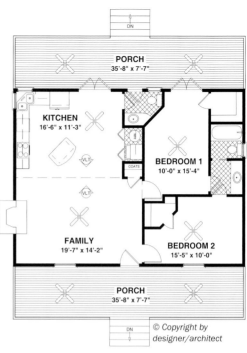

*Images provided by designer/architect*

© Copyright by designer/architect

## Plan #F04-013D-0154

| | |
|---|---|
| Dimensions: | 36' W x 42'4" D |
| Heated Sq. Ft.: | 953 |
| Bedrooms: 2 | Bathrooms: 1½ |

Foundation: Crawl space standard; slab or basement for a fee of $250

| | |
|---|---|
| PDF File: | $795 |
| 5-Sets: | $845 |
| 8-Sets: | $895 |
| CAD File: | $1,095 |
| Upgrade to 2" x 6" Walls: | $250 |

*Pricing subject to change*

---

## Plan #F04-013D-0198

| | |
|---|---|
| Dimensions: | 61'9" W x 37'3" D |
| Heated Sq. Ft.: | 1,399 |
| Bedrooms: 3 | Bathrooms: 2 |

Foundation: Slab standard; crawl space or basement for a fee of $250

| | |
|---|---|
| PDF File: | $845 |
| 5-Sets: | $895 |
| 8-Sets: | $945 |
| CAD File: | $1,195 |
| Upgrade to 2" x 6" Walls: | $250 |

*Pricing subject to change*

*Images provided by designer/architect*

© Copyright by designer/architect

## Plan #F04-130D-0368

| | |
|---|---|
| Dimensions: | 31' W x 53' D |
| Heated Sq. Ft.: | 1,277 |
| Bedrooms: 3 | Bathrooms: 2 |
| Foundation: Slab standard; crawl space or basement for a fee of $150 | |
| PDF File: | $845 |
| 5-Sets: | $970 |
| 8-Sets: | $1,045 |
| CAD File: | $1,095 |
| Upgrade to 2" x 6" Walls: | $150 |

*Pricing subject to change*

*Images provided by designer/architect*

© Copyright by designer/architect

31'-0"

53'-0"

**Storage**

**BED #1**
12 x 15-4
*9' Ceiling*

**Hers**

**His**

**BED #2**
12 x 10
*9' Ceiling*

**DINING ROOM**
12-4 x 11
*9' Ceiling*

12-4 x 10-3

**Pantry**

**Island**

**Ref.**

**KIT**

DW   Sink

Eating Bar

**BED #3**
12 x 10
*9' Ceiling*

Opt. Basement Stairs

Slope 9' to 11'

**LIVING ROOM**
16 x 18
*11' Ceiling*

Slope 9' to 11'

**PORCH**
23 x 8
*9' Ceiling*

---

## Plan #F04-011S-0106

| | |
|---|---|
| Dimensions: | 60' W x 59'6" D |
| Heated Sq. Ft.: | 3,602 |
| Bedrooms: 4 | Bathrooms: 3½ |
| Foundation: | Walk-out basement |
| PDF File: | $1,400 |
| 5-Sets: | $1,450 |
| CAD File: | $2,700 |

*Pricing subject to change*

*Images provided by designer/architect*

© Copyright by designer/architect

**DECK**

**VAULTED MASTER**
13/6 X 17/10

SPA

TILE SHWR

BENCH

**VAULTED DINING**
12/6 X 18/0

**VAULTED GREAT RM.**
19/0 X 19/0
(10' CLG.)

12/6 X 16/0 +/-
(10' CLG.)

**GARAGE**
20/0 X 22/6
(10'-6" CLG. +/-)

**GARAGE**
11/0 X 19/6
(9' CLG. +/-)

**FOYER**
(12' CLG.)

PAN

REF

DN.

**VAULTED OFFICE**
14/0 X 10/6 + BAY

**First Floor**
2,065 sq. ft.

**BR. 2**
12/10 X 14/4
(9' CLG.)

**BR. 3**
12/6 X 11/4
(9' CLG.)

CRAWL SPACE

**GAMES RM.**
20/6 X 18/4
(9' CLG.)

**UNFINISHED MECH.**
13/4 X 5/4

**BR. 4**
12/6 X 11/4
(9' CLG.)

**WINE**
7/4 X 5/3
(9' CLG.)

STORAGE

UP

**UNFINISHED STORAGE**
13/8 X 10/2

**Lower Level**
1,537 sq. ft.

## Plan #F04-011D-0347

Dimensions: 113'4" W x 62'8" D
Heated Sq. Ft.: 2,910
Bedrooms: 3    Bathrooms: 3
Foundation: Post & beam or joisted continuous footings standard; slab or basement for a fee of $275
Exterior Walls: 2" x 6"
PDF File: $1,100
5-Sets: $1,150
CAD File: $2,200

*Pricing subject to change*

*Images provided by designer/architect*

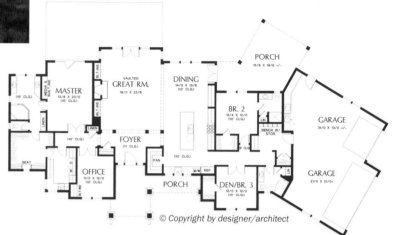

© Copyright by designer/architect

## Plan #F04-007D-0162

Dimensions: 47'8" W x 47'4" D
Heated Sq. Ft.: 1,519
Bedrooms: 4    Bathrooms: 2
Foundation: Basement, slab or crawl space, please specify when ordering
PDF File: $825
5-Sets: $875
8-Sets: $950
CAD File: $1,725
Material List: $125

*Pricing subject to change*

*Images provided by designer/architect*

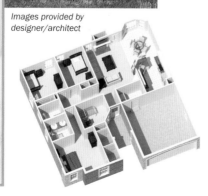

© Copyright by designer/architect

## Plan #F04-008D-0148

| | |
|---|---|
| Dimensions: | 28' W x 28' D |
| Heated Sq. Ft.: | 784 |
| Bedrooms: 3 | Bathrooms: 1 |
| Foundation: | Pier |
| PDF File: | $675 |
| 5-Sets: | $725 |
| 8-Sets: | $800 |
| CAD File: | $1,475 |
| Material List: | $125 |

*Pricing subject to change*

*Images provided by designer/architect*

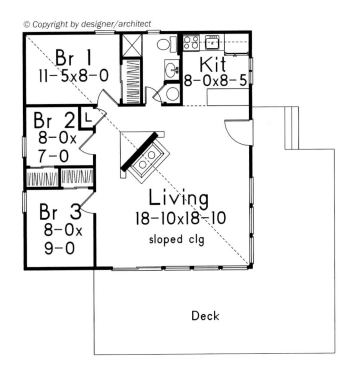

© Copyright by designer/architect

Br 1
11-5x8-0

Kit
8-0x8-5

Br 2
8-0x
7-0

Br 3
8-0x
9-0

Living
18-10x18-10
sloped clg

Deck

## Plan #F04-036D-0216

| | |
|---|---|
| Dimensions: | 50' W x 45' D |
| Heated Sq. Ft.: | 1,603 |
| Bedrooms: 3 | Bathrooms: 2 |
| Foundation: | Slab |
| 5-Sets: | $895 |
| 8-Sets: | $1,035 |
| PDF File: | $1,185 |
| Reproducible Master: | $1,185 |

*Pricing subject to change*

*Images provided by designer/architect*

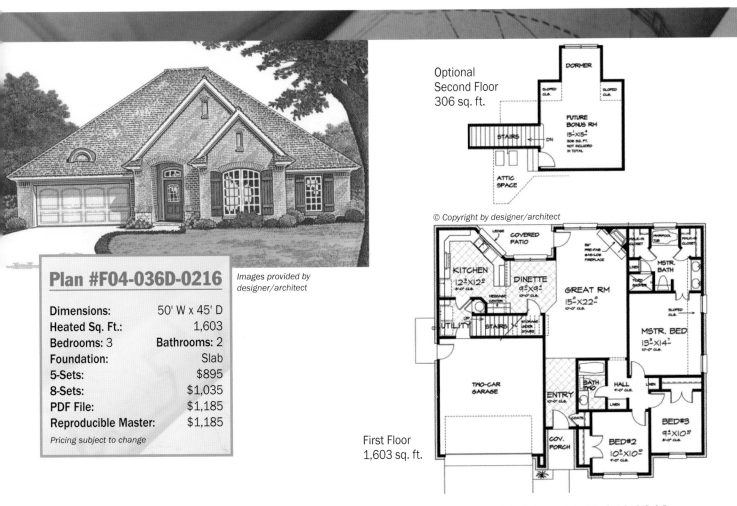

Optional
Second Floor
306 sq. ft.

DORMER

SLOPED CLG.

SLOPED CLG.

FUTURE BONUS RM
15'-X15'-4
306 SQ. FT.
NOT INCLUDED IN TOTAL

STAIRS        DN

ATTIC SPACE

© Copyright by designer/architect

COVERED PATIO

KITCHEN
12'³X12'²

DINETTE
9'⁵X9'²

GREAT RM
15'-X22'-³

MSTR. BATH

MSTR. BED
13'⁵X14'²

UTILITY

STAIRS

TWO-CAR GARAGE

ENTRY

BATH

HALL

BED#2
10'³X10'⁴

BED#3
9'⁴X10'²

COV. PORCH

First Floor
1,603 sq. ft.

## Plan #F04-007D-0060

**Dimensions:** 38'8" W x 48'4" D
**Heated Sq. Ft.:** 1,268
**Bedrooms:** 3    **Bathrooms:** 2
**Foundation:** Basement, slab or crawl space, please specify when ordering

| | |
|---|---|
| **5-Sets:** | $800 |
| **8-Sets:** | $870 |
| **PDF File:** | $980 |
| **CAD File:** | $1,660 |
| **Material List:** | $125 |
| **Upgrade to 2" x 6" Walls:** | $150 |

*Pricing subject to change*

*Images provided by designer/architect*

### Features

- Multiple gables, a large porch, and arched windows create a classy exterior with tons of curb appeal
- This innovative design provides openness in the great room, the kitchen, and the breakfast area
- The secondary bedrooms have a private hall with a bath
- The cheerful bayed breakfast area leads to the backyard patio, perfect for a grill
- 2-car front entry garage

© Copyright by designer/architect

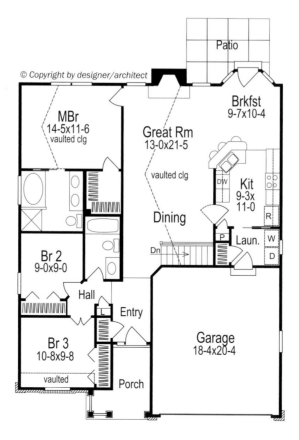

## Plan #F04-016D-0062

| | |
|---|---|
| Dimensions: | 48' W x 43'4" D |
| Heated Sq. Ft.: | 1,380 |
| Bedrooms: 3 | Bathrooms: 2 |

**Foundation:** Slab or crawl space standard; walk-out basement for a fee of $175

| | |
|---|---|
| PDF File: | $795 |
| 5-Sets: | $795 |
| 8-Sets: | $875 |
| CAD File: | $1,595 |
| Material List: | $95 |

*Pricing subject to change*

*Images provided by designer/architect*

### Features

- Built-in bookshelves complement the fireplace in the great room
- An abundance of storage space is found near the laundry room and the kitchen in the utility closet
- The rear covered porch has a view of the deck and backyard
- The bonus area has an additional 385 square feet of living area
- Optional 2-car side entry garage

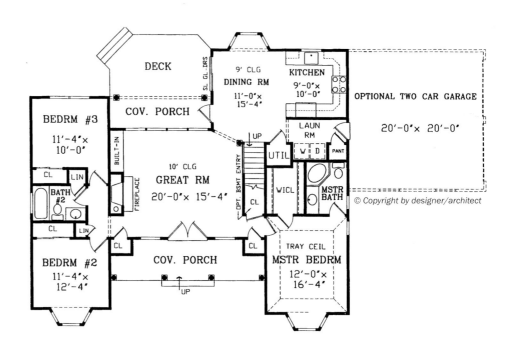

© Copyright by designer/architect

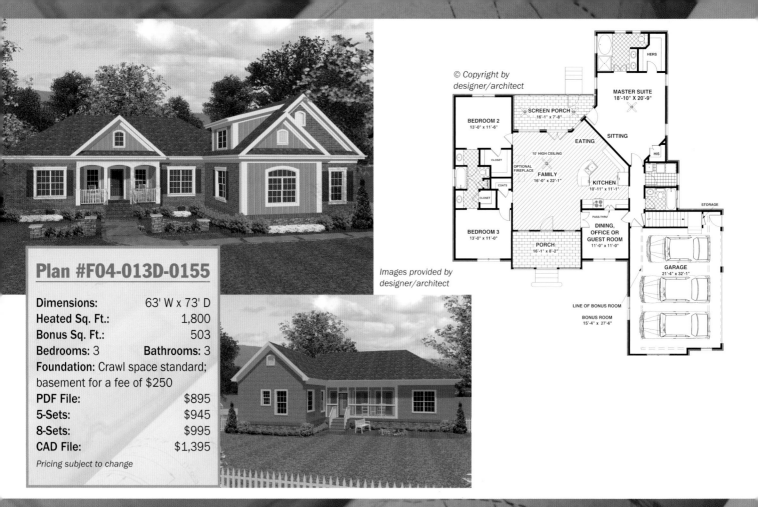

© Copyright by designer/architect

Images provided by designer/architect

## Plan #F04-013D-0155

| | |
|---|---|
| Dimensions: | 63' W x 73' D |
| Heated Sq. Ft.: | 1,800 |
| Bonus Sq. Ft.: | 503 |
| Bedrooms: 3 | Bathrooms: 3 |

Foundation: Crawl space standard; basement for a fee of $250

| | |
|---|---|
| PDF File: | $895 |
| 5-Sets: | $945 |
| 8-Sets: | $995 |
| CAD File: | $1,395 |

*Pricing subject to change*

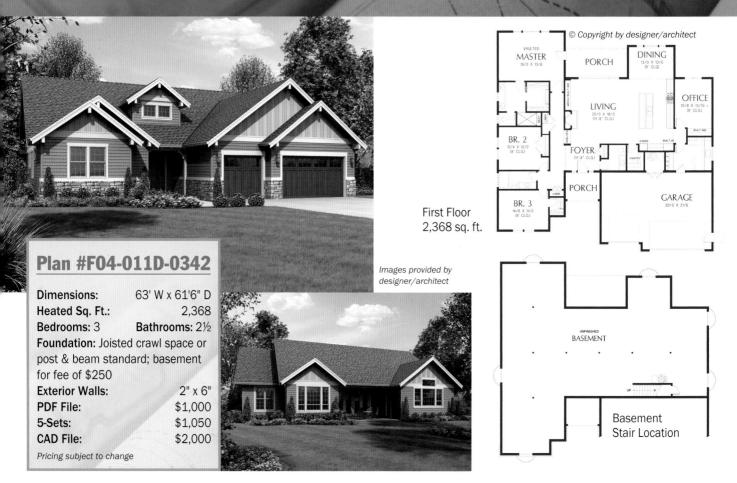

© Copyright by designer/architect

First Floor
2,368 sq. ft.

Images provided by designer/architect

Basement
Stair Location

## Plan #F04-011D-0342

| | |
|---|---|
| Dimensions: | 63' W x 61'6" D |
| Heated Sq. Ft.: | 2,368 |
| Bedrooms: 3 | Bathrooms: 2½ |

Foundation: Joisted crawl space or post & beam standard; basement for fee of $250

| | |
|---|---|
| Exterior Walls: | 2" x 6" |
| PDF File: | $1,000 |
| 5-Sets: | $1,050 |
| CAD File: | $2,000 |

*Pricing subject to change*

© Copyright by designer/architect

## Plan #F04-055D-0192

| | |
|---|---|
| Dimensions: | 69'2" W x 74'10" D |
| Heated Sq. Ft.: | 2,096 |
| Bedrooms: 3 | Bathrooms: 2½ |

Foundation: Crawl space or slab standard; basement or walk-out basement for a fee of $250

| | |
|---|---|
| 5-Sets: | $780 |
| 8-Sets: | $945 |
| PDF File: | $1,450 |
| CAD File: | $2,235 |
| Upgrade to 2" x 6" Walls: | $250 |

*Pricing subject to change*

*Images provided by designer/architect*

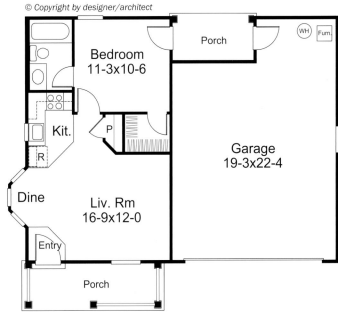

© Copyright by designer/architect

## Plan #F04-007D-0199

| | |
|---|---|
| Dimensions: | 39' W x 33' D |
| Heated Sq. Ft.: | 496 |
| Bedrooms: 1 | Bathrooms: 1 |
| Foundation: | Slab |
| PDF File: | $600 |
| 5-Sets: | $650 |
| 8-Sets: | $725 |
| CAD File: | $1,110 |
| Material List: | $125 |

*Pricing subject to change*

*Images provided by designer/architect*

## Plan #F04-007D-0136

| | |
|---|---|
| Dimensions: | 71'8" W x 38' D |
| Heated Sq. Ft.: | 1,532 |
| Bedrooms: 3 | Bathrooms: 2 |
| Foundation: | Walk-out basement |
| PDF File: | $900 |
| 5-Sets: | $950 |
| 8-Sets: | $1,025 |
| CAD File: | $1,800 |
| Material List: | $125 |
| Upgrade to 2" x 6" Walls: | $150 |

*Pricing subject to change*

### Features

- Multiple gables and stonework deliver a warm and inviting exterior
- The vaulted great room has a fireplace and spectacular views accomplished with a two-story atrium window wall
- A covered rear deck is easily accessed from the breakfast room or garage
- 2-car front entry garage

*Images provided by designer/architect*

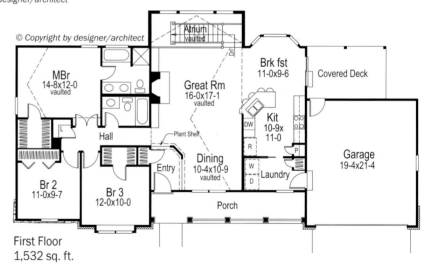

First Floor
1,532 sq. ft.

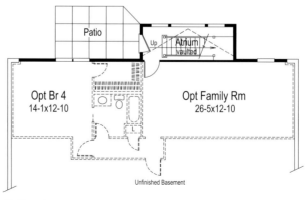

Optional
Lower Level
740 sq. ft.

Rear View

## Plan #F04-013D-0201

| | |
|---|---|
| **Dimensions:** | 71'2" W x 64'6" D |
| **Heated Sq. Ft.:** | 2,294 |
| **Bedrooms:** 3 | **Bathrooms:** 3½ |

**Foundation:** Crawl space standard; basement or slab for a fee of $250

| | |
|---|---|
| **PDF File:** | $995 |
| **5-Sets:** | $1,045 |
| **8-Sets:** | $1,095 |
| **CAD File:** | $1,495 |
| **Upgrade to 2" x 6" Walls:** | $250 |

*Pricing subject to change*

### Features

- This country style home has the perfect split bedroom floor plan ensuring everyone has his or her privacy
- Flanking the entry foyer is the formal dining room and a library also great as a home office
- Every bedroom in this home has its own walk-in closet and private bath
- 2-car side entry garage

*Images provided by designer/architect*

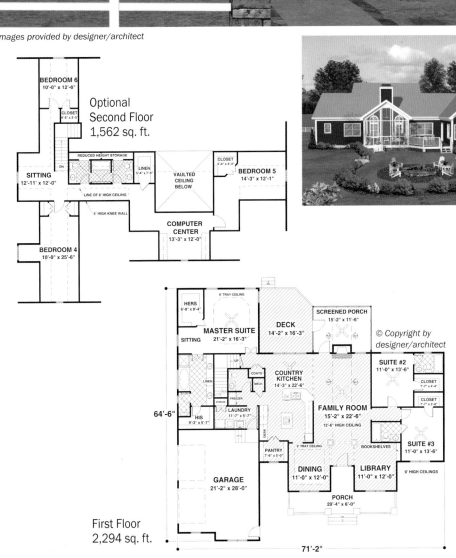

Optional Second Floor 1,562 sq. ft.

First Floor 2,294 sq. ft.

© Copyright by designer/architect

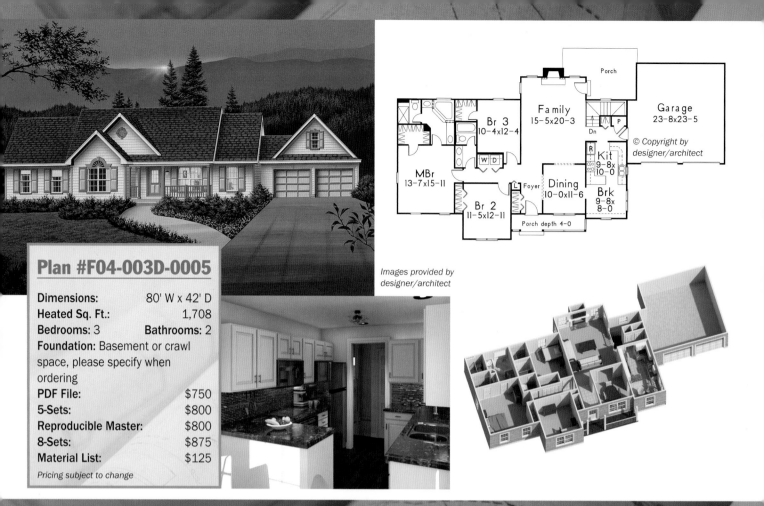

## Plan #F04-003D-0005

| | |
|---|---|
| Dimensions: | 80' W x 42' D |
| Heated Sq. Ft.: | 1,708 |
| Bedrooms: 3 | Bathrooms: 2 |
| Foundation: Basement or crawl space, please specify when ordering | |
| PDF File: | $750 |
| 5-Sets: | $800 |
| Reproducible Master: | $800 |
| 8-Sets: | $875 |
| Material List: | $125 |

*Pricing subject to change*

Images provided by designer/architect

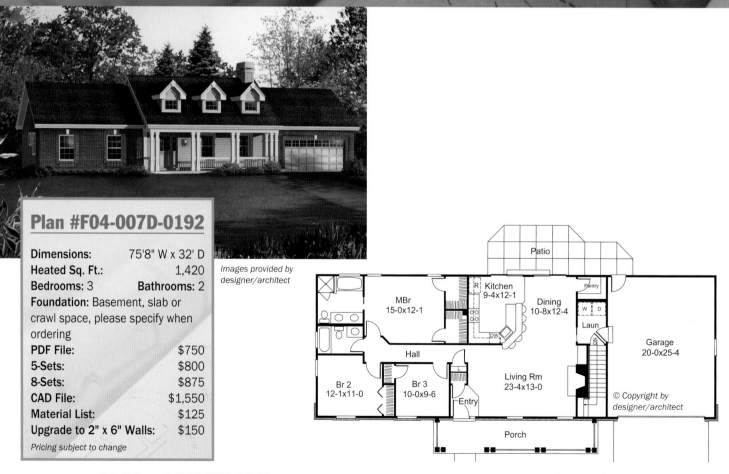

## Plan #F04-007D-0192

| | |
|---|---|
| Dimensions: | 75'8" W x 32' D |
| Heated Sq. Ft.: | 1,420 |
| Bedrooms: 3 | Bathrooms: 2 |
| Foundation: Basement, slab or crawl space, please specify when ordering | |
| PDF File: | $750 |
| 5-Sets: | $800 |
| 8-Sets: | $875 |
| CAD File: | $1,550 |
| Material List: | $125 |
| Upgrade to 2" x 6" Walls: | $150 |

*Pricing subject to change*

Images provided by designer/architect

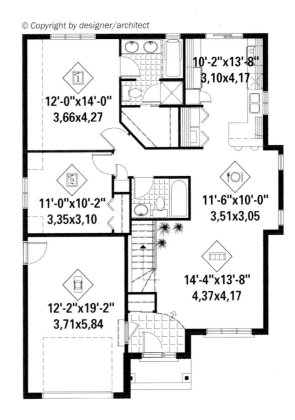

© Copyright by designer/architect

12'-0"x14'-0"
3,66x4,27

10'-2"x13'-8"
3,10x4,17

11'-0"x10'-2"
3,35x3,10

11'-6"x10'-0"
3,51x3,05

12'-2"x19'-2"
3,71x5,84

14'-4"x13'-8"
4,37x4,17

*Images provided by designer/architect*

## Plan #F04-126D-0449

| | |
|---|---|
| Dimensions: | 34' W x 46' D |
| Heated Sq. Ft.: | 1,100 |
| Bedrooms: 2 | Bathrooms: 2 |
| Foundation: | Basement |
| Exterior Walls: | 2" x 6" |
| 5-Sets: | $675 |
| 8-Sets: | $720 |
| PDF File: | $825 |
| CAD File: | $1,380 |
| Material List: | $105 |

*Pricing subject to change*

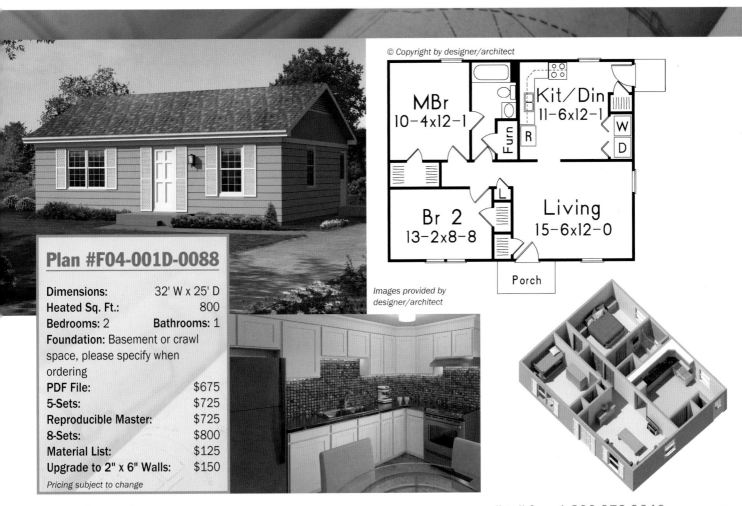

© Copyright by designer/architect

MBr
10-4x12-1

Kit/Din
11-6x12-1

Furn

Br 2
13-2x8-8

Living
15-6x12-0

Porch

*Images provided by designer/architect*

## Plan #F04-001D-0088

| | |
|---|---|
| Dimensions: | 32' W x 25' D |
| Heated Sq. Ft.: | 800 |
| Bedrooms: 2 | Bathrooms: 1 |
| Foundation: | Basement or crawl space, please specify when ordering |
| PDF File: | $675 |
| 5-Sets: | $725 |
| Reproducible Master: | $725 |
| 8-Sets: | $800 |
| Material List: | $125 |
| Upgrade to 2" x 6" Walls: | $150 |

*Pricing subject to change*

## Plan #F04-101D-0045

| | |
|---|---|
| Dimensions: | 69' W x 68'3" D |
| Heated Sq. Ft.: | 1,885 |
| Bedrooms: 2 | Bathrooms: 2½ |
| Foundation: | Basement |
| Exterior Walls: | 2" x 6" |
| 5-Sets: | $850 |
| PDF File: | $1,150 |
| CAD File: | $1,650 |

*Pricing subject to change*

### Features

- The open floor plan maximizes space creating a flowing open layout
- A dual fireplace warms the family room as well as the outdoor covered patio
- The spacious and private master suite has includes its own bath and walk-in closet
- Guests will never want to leave the guest bedroom with its own bath and large walk-in closet
- 3-car front entry garage

*Images provided by designer/architect*

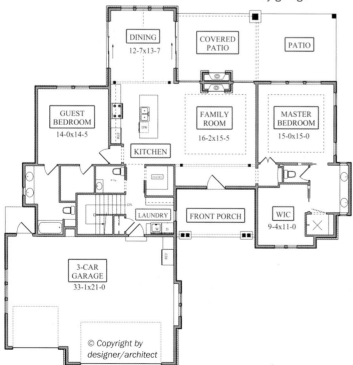

© Copyright by designer/architect

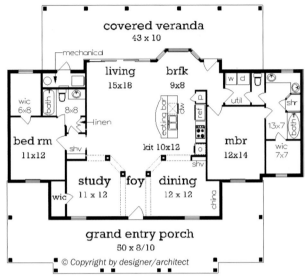

## Plan #F04-020D-0358

| | |
|---|---|
| Dimensions: | 58' W x 50' D |
| Heated Sq. Ft.: | 1,516 |
| Bedrooms: 2 | Bathrooms: 2 |
| Foundation: | Crawl space |
| Exterior Walls: | 2" x 6" |
| PDF File: | $850 |
| 5-Sets: | $875 |
| 8-Sets: | $920 |
| CAD File: | $1,638 |
| Optional Garage Plan: | $100 |

*Pricing subject to change*

*Images provided by designer/architect*

**covered veranda**
43 x 10

mechanical

wic
6x8

bath
8x8

living
15x18

brfk
9x8

eating bar

dw

w d

util

13x7

bath

shr

bed rm
11x12

shv

linen

kit 10x12

ref

shv

mbr
12x14

wic
7x7

wic

study
11 x 12

foy

dining
12 x 12

china

**grand entry porch**
50 x 8/10

© Copyright by designer/architect

## Plan #F04-013D-0130

| | |
|---|---|
| Dimensions: | 54' W x 56'2" D |
| Heated Sq. Ft.: | 1,798 |
| Bonus Sq. Ft.: | 328 |
| Bedrooms: 3 | Bathrooms: 2½ |
| Foundation: | Slab standard; crawl space or basement for a fee of $250 |
| PDF File: | $895 |
| 5-Sets: | $945 |
| 8-Sets: | $995 |
| CAD File: | $1,395 |

*Pricing subject to change*

*Images provided by designer/architect*

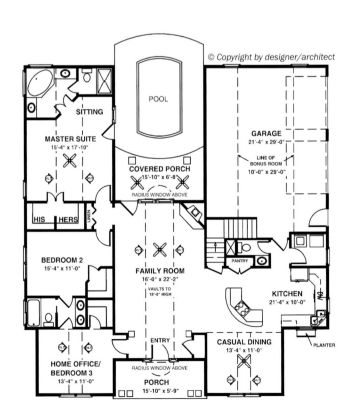

© Copyright by designer/architect

POOL

SITTING

MASTER SUITE
15'-4" x 17'-10"

GARAGE
21'-4" x 29'-0"

LINE OF
BONUS ROOM
10'-0" x 29'-0"

COVERED PORCH
15'-10" x 6'-8"

RADIUS WINDOW ABOVE

HIS
HERS
LINEN

BEDROOM 2
15'-4" x 11'-0"

FAMILY ROOM
16'-0" x 22'-2"

VAULTS TO
18'-8" HIGH

PANTRY

KITCHEN
21'-4" x 10'-0"

ENTRY

CASUAL DINING
13'-4" x 11'-0"

PLANTER

HOME OFFICE/
BEDROOM 3
13'-4" x 11'-0"

PORCH
15'-10" x 5'-9"

RADIUS WINDOW ABOVE

## Plan #F04-001D-0072

| | |
|---|---|
| Dimensions: | 46' W x 32' D |
| Heated Sq. Ft.: | 1,288 |
| Bedrooms: 3 | Bathrooms: 2 |

**Foundation:** Basement, slab or crawl space, please specify when ordering

| | |
|---|---|
| PDF File: | $750 |
| 5-Sets: | $800 |
| Reproducible Master: | $800 |
| 8-Sets: | $875 |
| Material List: | $125 |

*Pricing subject to change*

*Images provided by designer/architect*

© Copyright by designer/architect

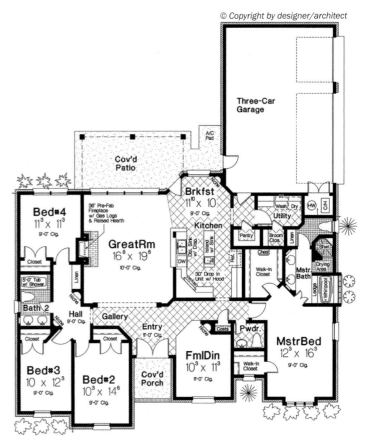

## Plan #F04-036D-0212

| | |
|---|---|
| Dimensions: | 60' W x 72'7" D |
| Heated Sq. Ft.: | 2,291 |
| Bedrooms: 4 | Bathrooms: 2½ |
| Foundation: | Slab |
| 5-Sets: | $1,045 |
| 8-Sets: | $1,185 |
| PDF File: | $1,335 |
| Reproducible Master: | $1,335 |

*Pricing subject to change*

*Images provided by designer/architect*

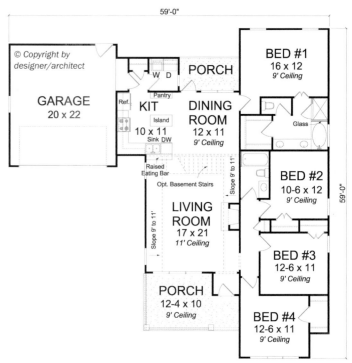

59'-0"

© Copyright by designer/architect

GARAGE
20 x 22

W D

PORCH

Ref.

KIT
10 x 11
Island
Sink DW

Pantry

DINING
ROOM
12 x 11
9' Ceiling

BED #1
16 x 12
9' Ceiling

Glass

Raised
Eating Bar

Opt. Basement Stairs

Slope 9' to 11'

BED #2
10-6 x 12
9' Ceiling

Slope 9' to 11'

LIVING
ROOM
17 x 21
11' Ceiling

BED #3
12-6 x 11
9' Ceiling

59'-0"

PORCH
12-4 x 10
9' Ceiling

BED #4
12-6 x 11
9' Ceiling

## Plan #F04-130D-0371

Images provided by
designer/architect

| Dimensions: | 59' W x 59' D |
|---|---|
| Heated Sq. Ft.: | 1,668 |
| Bedrooms: 4 | Bathrooms: 2 |

Foundation: Slab standard; crawl
space or basement for a fee of
$150

| PDF File: | $885 |
|---|---|
| 5-Sets: | $1,010 |
| 8-Sets: | $1,085 |
| CAD File: | $1,135 |
| Upgrade to 2" x 6" Walls: | $150 |

*Pricing subject to change*

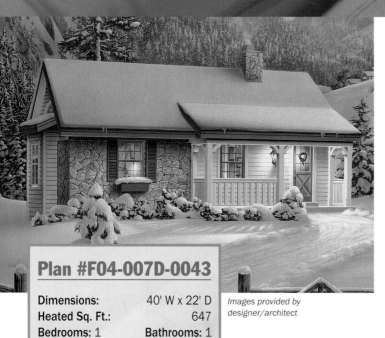

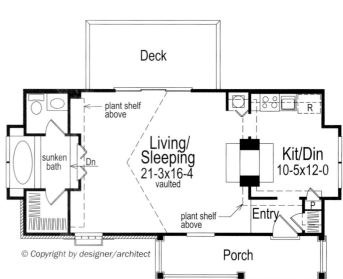

Deck

sunken
bath

plant shelf
above

Dn

Living/
Sleeping
21-3x16-4
vaulted

R

Kit/Din
10-5x12-0

plant shelf
above

Entry

P

© Copyright by designer/architect

Porch

## Plan #F04-007D-0043

Images provided by
designer/architect

| Dimensions: | 40' W x 22' D |
|---|---|
| Heated Sq. Ft.: | 647 |
| Bedrooms: 1 | Bathrooms: 1 |
| Foundation: | Crawl space |
| PDF File: | $600 |
| 5-Sets: | $650 |
| Reproducible Master: | $650 |
| 8-Sets: | $725 |
| Material List: | $125 |

*Pricing subject to change*

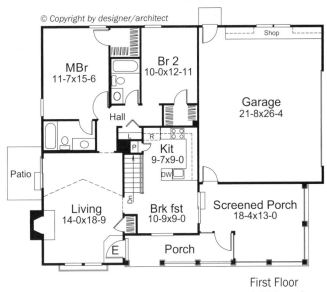

**MBr**
11-7x15-6

**Br 2**
10-0x12-11

Shop

Hall

**Garage**
21-8x26-4

Patio

**Kit**
9-7x9-0

**Living**
14-0x18-9

**Brk fst**
10-9x9-0

**Screened Porch**
18-4x13-0

E

**Porch**

First Floor
1,072 sq. ft.

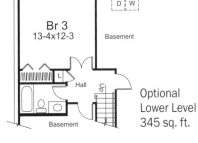

**Br 3**
13-4x12-3

Basement

Hall

Basement

Optional
Lower Level
345 sq. ft.

## Plan #F04-007D-0128

*Images provided by
designer/architect*

| | |
|---|---|
| Dimensions: | 52' W x 40'8" D |
| Heated Sq. Ft.: | 1,072 |
| Bedrooms: 2 | Bathrooms: 2 |
| Foundation: | Basement |
| PDF File: | $750 |
| 5-Sets: | $800 |
| 8-Sets: | $875 |
| CAD File: | $1,550 |
| Material List: | $125 |
| Upgrade to 2" x 6" Walls: | $150 |

*Pricing subject to change*

## Plan #F04-076D-0151

*Images provided by
designer/architect*

| | |
|---|---|
| Dimensions: | 45' W x 65'6" D |
| Heated Sq. Ft.: | 1,693 |
| Bedrooms: 3 | Bathrooms: 2½ |
| Foundation: Crawl space or slab, please specify when ordering | |
| 5-Sets: | $655 |
| 8-Sets: | $800 |
| PDF File: | $975 |
| CAD File: | $1,250 |

*Pricing subject to change*

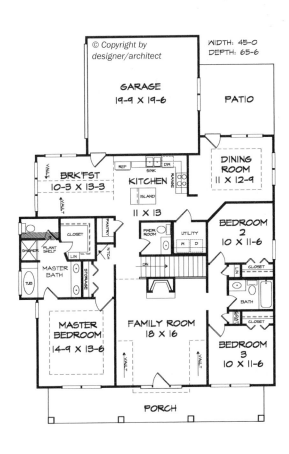

WIDTH: 45-0
DEPTH: 65-6

**GARAGE**
19-9 X 19-6

**PATIO**

**BRK'FST**
10-3 X 13-3

**KITCHEN**
11 X 13

**DINING ROOM**
11 X 12-9

**BEDROOM 2**
10 X 11-6

**MASTER BATH**

**MASTER BEDROOM**
14-9 X 13-6

**FAMILY ROOM**
18 X 16

**BEDROOM 3**
10 X 11-6

**PORCH**

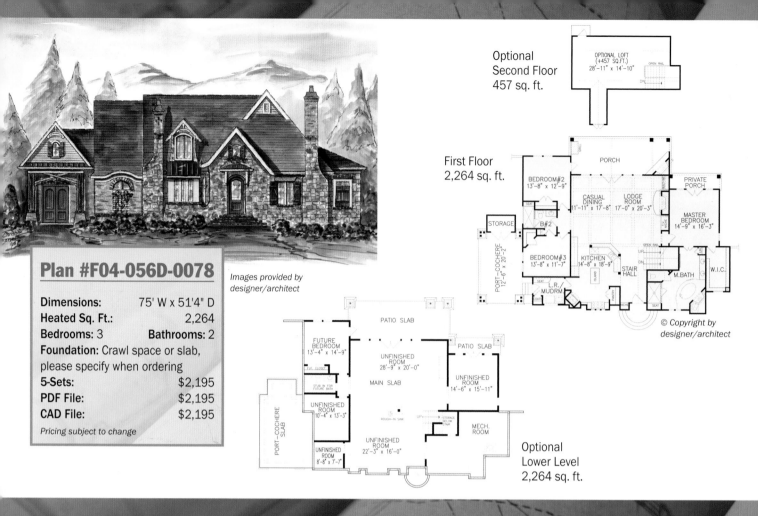

**Optional Second Floor** 457 sq. ft.

OPTIONAL LOFT (+457 SQ.FT.) 28'-11" x 14'-10"

**First Floor** 2,264 sq. ft.

© Copyright by designer/architect

**Optional Lower Level** 2,264 sq. ft.

## Plan #F04-056D-0078

*Images provided by designer/architect*

**Dimensions:** 75' W x 51'4" D
**Heated Sq. Ft.:** 2,264
**Bedrooms:** 3     **Bathrooms:** 2
**Foundation:** Crawl space or slab, please specify when ordering

| | |
|---|---|
| 5-Sets: | $2,195 |
| PDF File: | $2,195 |
| CAD File: | $2,195 |

*Pricing subject to change*

---

## Plan #F04-055D-0017

**Dimensions:** 51'6" W x 49'10" D
**Heated Sq. Ft.:** 1,525
**Bedrooms:** 3     **Bathrooms:** 2
**Foundation:** Slab or crawl space standard; basement or walk-out basement for a fee of $250

| | |
|---|---|
| 5-Sets: | $730 |
| 8-Sets: | $870 |
| PDF File: | $1,340 |
| CAD File: | $2,065 |
| Upgrade to 2" x 6" Walls: | $250 |

*Pricing subject to change*

*Images provided by designer/architect*

© Copyright by designer/architect

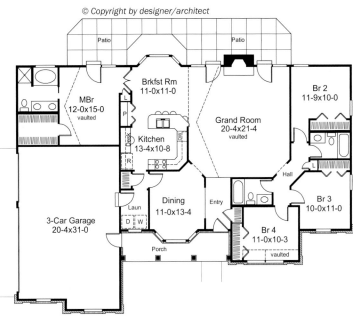

© Copyright by designer/architect

## Plan #F04-007D-0146

*Images provided by designer/architect*

| | |
|---|---|
| Dimensions: | 68' W x 49'8" D |
| Heated Sq. Ft.: | 1,929 |
| Bedrooms: 4 | Bathrooms: 3 |
| Foundation: Basement, slab or crawl space, please specify when ordering | |
| PDF File: | $900 |
| 5-Sets: | $950 |
| 8-Sets: | $1,025 |
| CAD File: | $1,800 |
| Material List: | $125 |
| Upgrade to 2" x 6" Walls: | $150 |

*Pricing subject to change*

## Plan #F04-065D-0384

*Images provided by designer/architect*

| | |
|---|---|
| Dimensions: | 60' W x 70' D |
| Heated Sq. Ft.: | 2,563 |
| Bedrooms: 3 | Bathrooms: 2½ |
| Foundation: | Basement |
| 5-Sets: | $795 |
| 8-Sets: | $880 |
| PDF File: | $1,075 |
| CAD File: | $1,620 |

*Pricing subject to change*

© Copyright by designer/architect

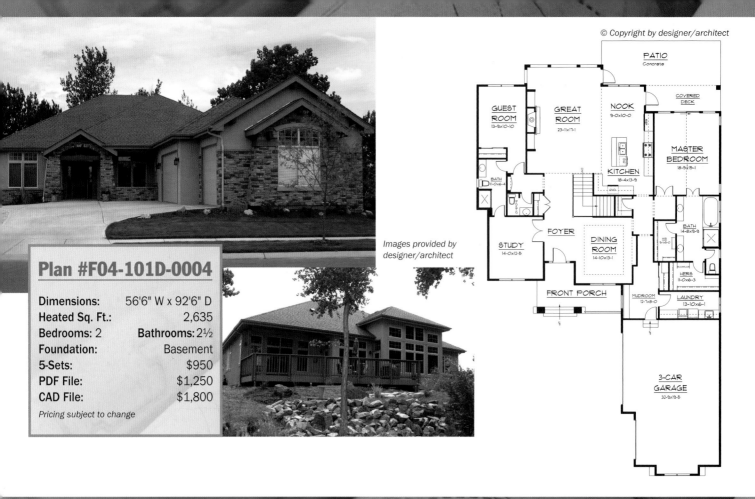

*Images provided by designer/architect*

## Plan #F04-101D-0004

| | |
|---|---|
| Dimensions: | 56'6" W x 92'6" D |
| Heated Sq. Ft.: | 2,635 |
| Bedrooms: 2 | Bathrooms: 2½ |
| Foundation: | Basement |
| 5-Sets: | $950 |
| PDF File: | $1,250 |
| CAD File: | $1,800 |

*Pricing subject to change*

*Images provided by designer/architect*

## Plan #F04-032D-0836

| | |
|---|---|
| Dimensions: | 38' W x 48' D |
| Heated Sq. Ft.: | 1,124 |
| Bedrooms: 2 | Bathrooms: 1 |
| Foundation: | Basement |
| Exterior Walls: | 2" x 6" |
| 5-Sets: | $785 |
| 8-Sets: | $815 |
| PDF File: | $930 |
| CAD File: | $1,500 |
| Material List: | $120 |

*Pricing subject to change*

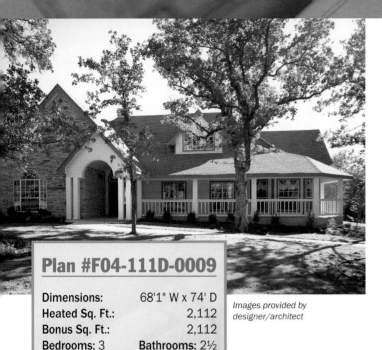

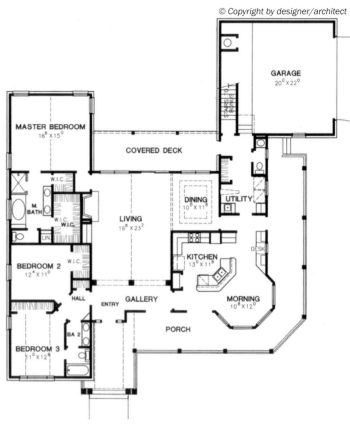

© Copyright by designer/architect

# Plan #F04-111D-0009

| | |
|---|---|
| Dimensions: | 68'1" W x 74' D |
| Heated Sq. Ft.: | 2,112 |
| Bonus Sq. Ft.: | 2,112 |
| Bedrooms: 3 | Bathrooms: 2½ |

Foundation: Basement, slab or crawl space, please specify when ordering

| | |
|---|---|
| 5-Sets: | $995 |
| 8-Sets: | $1,095 |
| PDF File: | $1,345 |
| CAD File: | $2,345 |

*Pricing subject to change*

*Images provided by designer/architect*

# Plan #F04-055D-0532

| | |
|---|---|
| Dimensions: | 37' W x 74'4" D |
| Heated Sq. Ft.: | 1,933 |
| Bedrooms: 3 | Bathrooms: 2 |

Foundation: Crawl space or slab, please specify when ordering

| | |
|---|---|
| 5-Sets: | $630 |
| 8-Sets: | $720 |
| PDF File: | $1,105 |
| CAD File: | $1,700 |

*Pricing subject to change*

*Images provided by designer/architect*

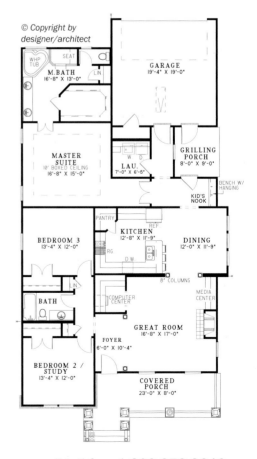

© Copyright by designer/architect

## Plan #F04-026D-1894

| | |
|---|---|
| **Dimensions:** | 68' W x 64' D |
| **Heated Sq. Ft.:** | 2,500 |
| **Bedrooms:** 3 | **Bathrooms:** 2 |

**Foundation:** Slab standard; crawl space or basement for a fee of $195; walk-out basement for a fee of $390

| | |
|---|---|
| **PDF File:** | $935 |
| **5-Sets:** | $1,010 |
| **8-Sets:** | $1,130 |
| **CAD File:** | $1,435 |
| **Upgrade to 2" x 6" Walls:** | $195 |

*Pricing subject to change*

*Images provided by designer/architect*

## Features

- The spacious great room enjoys views of the outdoor covered veranda that features an outdoor fireplace and kitchen
- The flex room is an ideal space for many purposes including a nursery, a home office, or even a library
- The owner's suite maintains a private location and enjoys a spa style bath with a double-bowl vanity, a corner whirlpool tub, an oversized walk-in shower, and a massive walk-in closet
- 3-car front entry garage

## Plan #F04-077D-0002

| | |
|---|---|
| **Dimensions:** | 72'8" W x 51' D |
| **Heated Sq. Ft.:** | 1,855 |
| **Bedrooms:** 3 | **Bathrooms:** 2½ |

**Foundation:** Basement, crawl space or slab, please specify when ordering

| | |
|---|---|
| **5-Sets:** | $1,015 |
| **PDF File:** | $1,125 |
| **Reproducible Master:** | $1,200 |
| **CAD File:** | $1,680 |
| **Material List:** | $130 |

*Pricing subject to change*

*Images provided by designer/architect*

## Features

- The great room boasts a 12' ceiling and a cozy corner gas fireplace
- The bayed breakfast area adjoins the kitchen that features a corner walk-in pantry
- The relaxing master bedroom includes a private bath with a walk-in closet, a garden tub and a walk-in separate shower
- 2-car side entry garage with storage

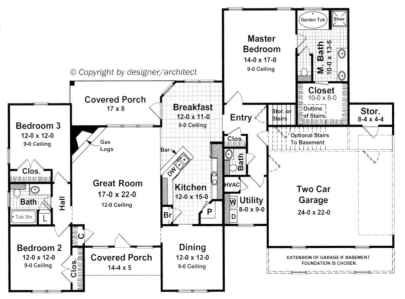

© Copyright by designer/architect

First Floor
1,855 sq. ft.

Optional
Second Floor
416 sq. ft.

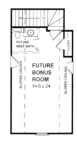

Optional
Second Floor
370 sq. ft.

FUTURE
HALF BATH

FUTURE
BONUS
ROOM
14-8 x 24

SLOPED CEILING

SLOPED CEILING

CLOSET

## Plan #F04-077D-0053

*Images provided by designer/architect*

| Dimensions: | 78' W x 49'6" D |
|---|---|
| Heated Sq. Ft.: | 1,852 |
| Bedrooms: 3 | Bathrooms: 2½ |

Foundation: Basement, crawl space or slab, please specify when ordering

| Exterior Walls: | 2" x 6" |
|---|---|
| 5-Sets: | $1,015 |
| PDF File: | $1,125 |
| Reproducible Master: | $1,200 |
| CAD File: | $1,680 |
| Material List: | $130 |

*Pricing subject to change*

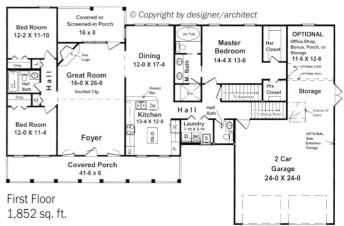

© Copyright by designer/architect

Bed Room
12-2 X 11-10

Covered or
Screened-in Porch
16 x 8

Gas
Logs

Clos.

Hall

Hall
Bath

Clos.

Bed Room
12-0 X 11-4

Great Room
16-0 X 26-0
Vaulted Clg.

Raised
Bar

Dining
12-0 X 17-4

Jet Tub

M. Bath

Shr

Master
Bedroom
14-4 X 13-6

Her
Closet

OPTIONAL
Office, Shop,
Bonus, Porch, or
Storage
11-6 X 12-6

OPTIONAL DOOR

OPTIONAL WALL

His
Closet

Storage

To Basement

To Bonus Room

Outline Of
Stairs

OPTIONAL
Side
Entrance
Garage

Foyer

Kitchen
13-4 X 12-8

ISLD.

BC

Laundry
7-10 X 5-10

D W S

Hall

Half
Bath

P

2 Car
Garage
24-0 X 24-0

Covered Porch
41-6 x 6

First Floor
1,852 sq. ft.

## Plan #F04-077D-0048

*Images provided by designer/architect*

| Dimensions: | 65' W x 50'10" D |
|---|---|
| Heated Sq. Ft.: | 1,800 |
| Bedrooms: 3 | Bathrooms: 2 |

Foundation: Slab, basement or crawl space, please specify when ordering

| 5-Sets: | $1,015 |
|---|---|
| PDF File: | $1,125 |
| Reproducible Master: | $1,200 |
| CAD File: | $1,680 |
| Material List: | $130 |

*Pricing subject to change*

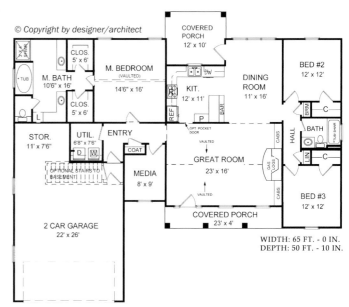

© Copyright by designer/architect

TUB

M. BATH
10'6" x 16'

CLOS.
5' x 6'

CLOS.
5' x 6'

M. BEDROOM
(VAULTED)
14'6" x 16'

COVERED
PORCH
12' x 10'

DW

KIT.
12' x 11'

REF

BAR

DINING
ROOM
11' x 16'

BED #2
12' x 12'

BRM

C

STOR.
11' x 7'6"

UTIL.
6'8" x 7'6"

D W

ENTRY

COAT

OPT. POCKET
DOOR

VAULTED

GREAT ROOM
23' x 16'

VAULTED

GAS
LOGS

CABS

HALL

BATH

TUB SHWR

LIN

C

CABS

OPTIONAL STAIRS TO
BASEMENT

MEDIA
8' x 9'

COVERED PORCH
23' x 4'

BED #3
12' x 12'

2 CAR GARAGE
22' x 26'

WIDTH: 65 FT. - 0 IN.
DEPTH: 50 FT. - 10 IN.

## Plan #F04-121D-0011

| | |
|---|---|
| Dimensions: | 68'4" W x 56' D |
| Heated Sq. Ft.: | 2,241 |
| Bedrooms: 4 | Bathrooms: 2½ |
| Foundation: | Basement |
| PDF File: | $900 |
| 5-Sets: | $950 |
| 8-Sets: | $1,025 |
| CAD File: | $1,800 |
| Material List: | $125 |
| Upgrade to 2" x 6" Walls: | $150 |

*Pricing subject to change*

*Images provided by designer/architect*

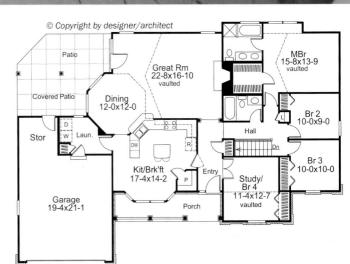

## Plan #F04-007D-0049

| | |
|---|---|
| Dimensions: | 68' W x 48'4" D |
| Heated Sq. Ft.: | 1,791 |
| Bedrooms: 4 | Bathrooms: 2 |
| Foundation: Basement, slab or crawl space, please specify when ordering | |
| PDF File: | $825 |
| 5-Sets: | $875 |
| 8-Sets: | $950 |
| CAD File: | $1,725 |
| Material List: | $125 |
| Upgrade to 2" x 6" Walls: | $150 |

*Pricing subject to change*

*Images provided by designer/architect*

## Plan #F04-013D-0053

| | |
|---|---|
| Dimensions: | 71'4" W x 74'8" D |
| Heated Sq. Ft.: | 2,461 |
| Bedrooms: 3 | Bathrooms: 3½ |
| Foundation: | Basement |
| PDF File: | $995 |
| 5-Sets: | $1,045 |
| 8-Sets: | $1,095 |
| CAD File: | $1,495 |

*Pricing subject to change*

*Images provided by designer/architect*

## Features

- A covered porch with elegant columns greets family and friends as they enter this delightful home
- The gourmet kitchen combines with the hearth room, nook and dining area, all of which feature dazzling angled windows
- The luxurious master suite has a large walk-in closet with conveniently separated hanging areas
- The master bath's built-in tub exudes peace and quiet and is a model of luxury situated in the bay window
- Additional amenities include the rear covered deck/screened porch for enjoying the outdoors in any weather, and the optional second floor that can be finished as needed
- 3-car side entry garage

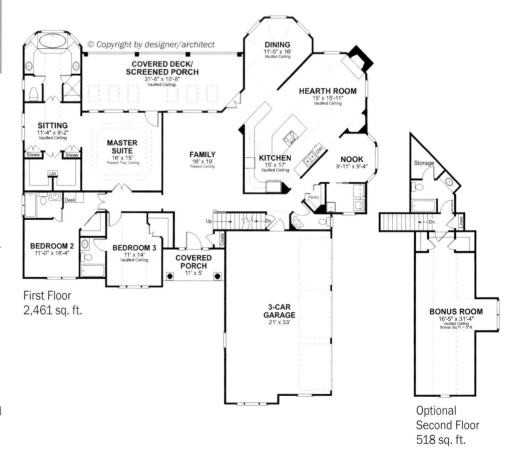

© Copyright by designer/architect

First Floor
2,461 sq. ft.

Optional
Second Floor
518 sq. ft.

## Plan #F04-026D-1889

| | |
|---|---|
| Dimensions: | 62' W x 48' D |
| Heated Sq. Ft.: | 1,763 |
| Bedrooms: 3 | Bathrooms: 3 |

Foundation: Basement standard; crawl space and slab for a fee of $195; walk-out basement for a fee of $390

| | |
|---|---|
| PDF File: | $855 |
| 5-Sets: | $930 |
| 8-Sets: | $1,050 |
| CAD File: | $1,355 |
| Upgrade to 2" x 6" Walls: | $195 |

*Pricing subject to change*

*Images provided by designer/architect*

### Features

- Stylish one-story home has spacious cathedral ceilings in the family and dining rooms
- The kitchen is designed for maximum efficiency and includes a center island and a large corner walk-in pantry
- The master bath is outfitted with a walk-in shower as well as a corner spa style tub
- Bedroom 3 enjoys a spacious walk-in closet for keeping things organized
- 3-car front entry garage

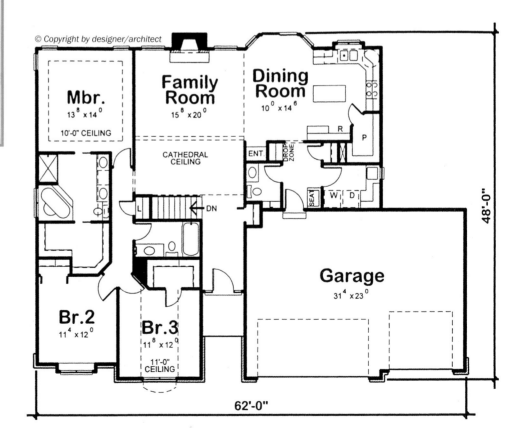

© Copyright by designer/architect

## Plan #F04-013D-0022

**Dimensions:** 66'2" W x 62' D
**Heated Sq. Ft.:** 1,992
**Bedrooms:** 4    **Bathrooms:** 2
**Foundation:** Basement, crawl space or slab, please specify when ordering

| | |
|---|---|
| PDF File: | $895 |
| 5-Sets: | $945 |
| 8-Sets: | $995 |
| CAD File: | $1,395 |
| Material List: | $125 |

*Pricing subject to change*

*Images provided by designer/architect*

## Features

- Interesting angled walls add drama to many of the living areas including the family room, the master bedroom and the breakfast area
- The rear covered porch includes a spa and an outdoor kitchen with a sink, a refrigerator, and a cooktop
- Enter the majestic master bath to find a dramatic oversized corner tub
- The bonus room above the garage has an additional 299 square feet of living area
- 2-car side entry garage

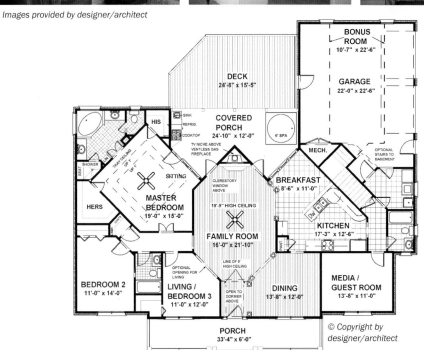

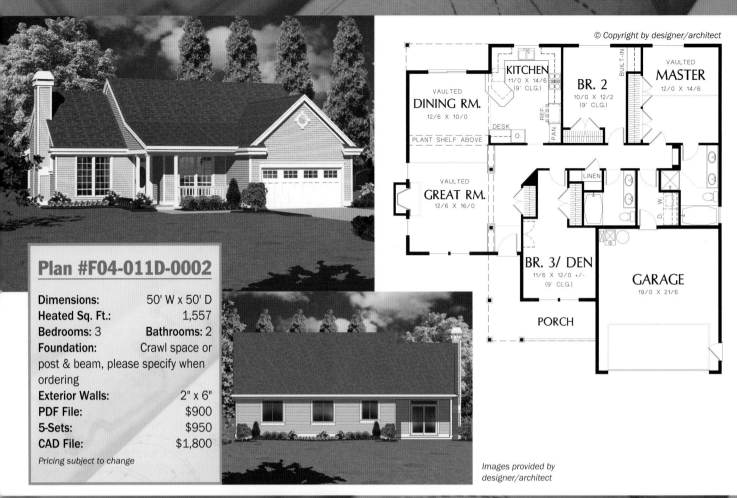

KITCHEN
11/0 X 14/6
(9' CLG.)

BR. 2
10/0 X 12/2
(9' CLG.)

BUILT-IN

VAULTED
MASTER
12/0 X 14/6

VAULTED
DINING RM.
12/6 X 10/0

DESK
REF.
PAN.

PLANT SHELF ABOVE

LINEN

VAULTED
GREAT RM.
12/6 X 16/0

W.
D.

BR. 3/ DEN
11/6 X 12/0 +/-
(9' CLG.)

GARAGE
19/0 X 21/6

PORCH

*Images provided by designer/architect*

## Plan #F04-011D-0002

| | |
|---|---|
| Dimensions: | 50' W x 50' D |
| Heated Sq. Ft.: | 1,557 |
| Bedrooms: 3 | Bathrooms: 2 |
| Foundation: | Crawl space or post & beam, please specify when ordering |
| Exterior Walls: | 2" x 6" |
| PDF File: | $900 |
| 5-Sets: | $950 |
| CAD File: | $1,800 |

*Pricing subject to change*

---

MBR.
10'-1 1/8" STEP CEILING
12'0"x13'0"

DIN. RM.
VAULTED CEILING
11'0"x11'0"

GRT. RM.
VAULTED CEILING
15'6"x17'4"

KIT.
VAULTED CEILING
9'6"x11'6"

LIN.

E.
VAULTED CEILING

DN.

BR. #3
9'-1 1/8" CEILING
9'8"x10'0"

BR. #2
9'-1 1/8" CEILING
9'8"x11'0"

9'8"x25'0"

3 CAR GARAGE
19'8"x20'8"

*Images provided by designer/architect*

## Plan #F04-051D-0711

| | |
|---|---|
| Dimensions: | 56' W x 50' D |
| Heated Sq. Ft.: | 1,351 |
| Bedrooms: 3 | Bathrooms: 2 |
| Foundation: | Basement |
| Exterior Walls: | 2" x 6" |
| 5-Sets: | $795 |
| 8-Sets: | $835 |
| PDF File: | $995 |
| CAD File: | $1,570 |

*Pricing subject to change*

## Plan #F04-084D-0051

*Images provided by designer/architect*

| | |
|---|---|
| **Dimensions:** | 51' W x 28' D |
| **Heated Sq. Ft.:** | 815 |
| **Bedrooms:** 1 | **Bathrooms:** 1 |

**Foundation:** Slab standard; basement or crawl space for a fee of $350

| | |
|---|---|
| **5-Sets:** | $800 |
| **8-Sets:** | $860 |
| **PDF File:** | $1,000 |
| **CAD File:** | $1,800 |
| **Material List:** | $65 |
| **Upgrade to 2" x 6" Walls:** | $255 |

*Pricing subject to change*

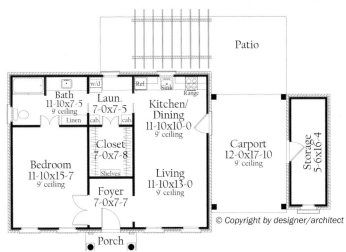

© Copyright by designer/architect

## Plan #F04-007D-0181

*Images provided by designer/architect*

| | |
|---|---|
| **Dimensions:** | 38' W x 52'8" D |
| **Heated Sq. Ft.:** | 1,140 |
| **Bedrooms:** 3 | **Bathrooms:** 2 |

**Foundation:** Basement, slab or crawl space, please specify when ordering

| | |
|---|---|
| **PDF File:** | $750 |
| **5-Sets:** | $800 |
| **Reproducible Master:** | $800 |
| **8-Sets:** | $875 |
| **Material List:** | $125 |

*Pricing subject to change*

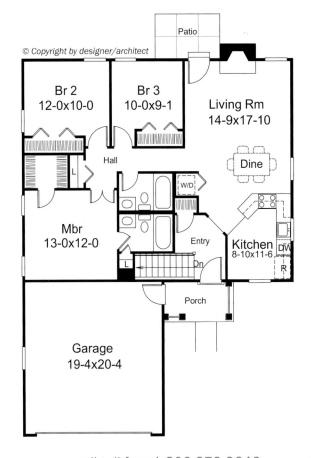

© Copyright by designer/architect

## Plan #F04-011S-0003

**Dimensions:** 164'8" W x 115'9" D
**Heated Sq. Ft.:** 5,628
**Bedrooms:** 5    **Bathrooms:** 5½
**Foundation:** Crawl space or post & beam standard; slab for a fee of $375
**Exterior Walls:** 2" x 6"
**PDF File:** $1,750
**5-Sets:** $1,825
**CAD File:** $3,400
*Pricing subject to change*

*Images provided by designer/architect*

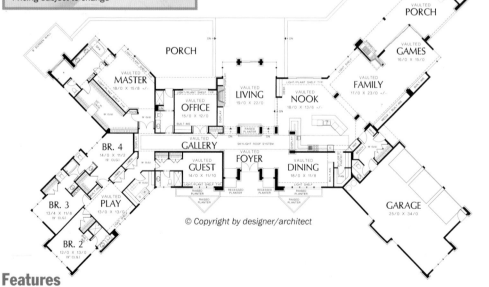

© Copyright by designer/architect

## Features

- This home's unique floor plan creates a sprawling exterior complete with screened porches, open patios, and an inviting pool, each an ideal spot for relaxing away the day
- Interesting angles continue in the vaulted master bedroom, while a wall of windows and a cozy fireplace add additional ambiance to this private space
- Planters, art niches, and stretches of natural light are numerous in this home
- With room to spare, it becomes easy to accomplish kitchen tasks and gather the family in this multi-functional kitchen and vaulted nook
- 3-car rear entry garage

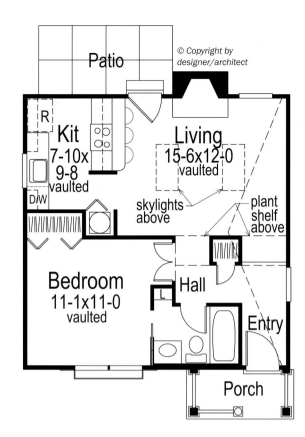

© Copyright by designer/architect

## Plan #F04-007D-0029

| | |
|---|---|
| Dimensions: | 24' W x 30' D |
| Heated Sq. Ft.: | 576 |
| Bedrooms: 1 | Bathrooms: 1 |
| Foundation: | Crawl space |
| PDF File: | $525 |
| 5-Sets: | $575 |
| Reproducible Master: | $575 |
| 8-Sets: | $650 |
| Material List: | $125 |

*Pricing subject to change*

*Images provided by designer/architect*

## Plan #F04-121D-0021

| | |
|---|---|
| Dimensions: | 65' W x 46'4" D |
| Heated Sq. Ft.: | 1,562 |
| Bedrooms: 3 | Bathrooms: 2 |
| Foundation: | Basement |
| PDF File: | $825 |
| 5-Sets: | $875 |
| 8-Sets: | $950 |
| CAD File: | $1,725 |
| Material List: | $125 |

*Pricing subject to change*

*Images provided by designer/architect*

© Copyright by designer/architect

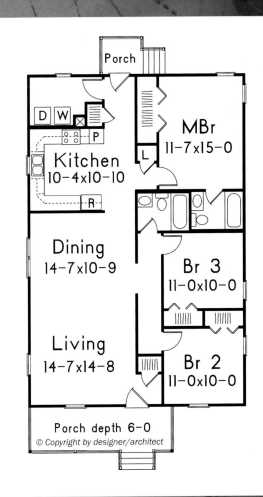

## Plan #F04-001D-0036

| | |
|---|---|
| Dimensions: | 30' W x 50' D |
| Heated Sq. Ft.: | 1,320 |
| Bedrooms: 3 | Bathrooms: 2 |
| Foundation: | Crawl space |
| PDF File: | $750 |
| 5-Sets: | $800 |
| Reproducible Master: | $800 |
| 8-Sets: | $875 |
| Material List: | $125 |

*Pricing subject to change*

*Images provided by designer/architect*

Kitchen 10-4x10-10
MBr 11-7x15-0
Dining 14-7x10-9
Br 3 11-0x10-0
Living 14-7x14-8
Br 2 11-0x10-0
Porch
Porch depth 6-0

© Copyright by designer/architect

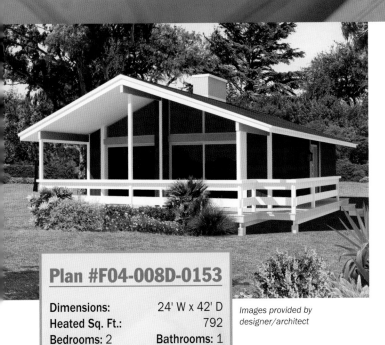

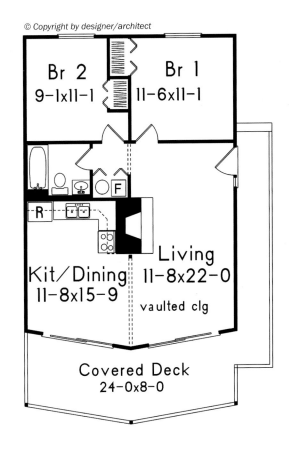

## Plan #F04-008D-0153

| | |
|---|---|
| Dimensions: | 24' W x 42' D |
| Heated Sq. Ft.: | 792 |
| Bedrooms: 2 | Bathrooms: 1 |
| Foundation: Slab or crawl space, please specify when ordering | |
| PDF File: | $675 |
| 5-Sets: | $725 |
| Reproducible Master: | $725 |
| 8-Sets: | $800 |
| Material List: | $125 |

*Pricing subject to change*

*Images provided by designer/architect*

© Copyright by designer/architect

Br 2 9-1x11-1
Br 1 11-6x11-1
Kit/Dining 11-8x15-9
Living 11-8x22-0 vaulted clg
Covered Deck 24-0x8-0

## Plan #F04-013D-0156

| | |
|---|---|
| Dimensions: | 63' W x 73' D |
| Heated Sq. Ft.: | 1,800 |
| Bedrooms: 3 | Bathrooms: 3 |
| Foundation: Crawl space standard; basement or slab for a fee of $250 | |
| PDF File: | $895 |
| 5-Sets: | $945 |
| 8-Sets: | $995 |
| CAD File: | $1,395 |

*Pricing subject to change*

*Images provided by designer/architect*

## Features

- Many lovely window accents are found throughout the home providing a warm glow and plenty of natural light
- Highly functional ceiling fans are located in the screen porch, angled master bedroom suite, and the family room
- Bedrooms #2 and #3 each contain ample closet space and immediate access to a full bath
- The bonus room above the garage has an additional 503 square feet of living space
- 3-car side entry garage with storage

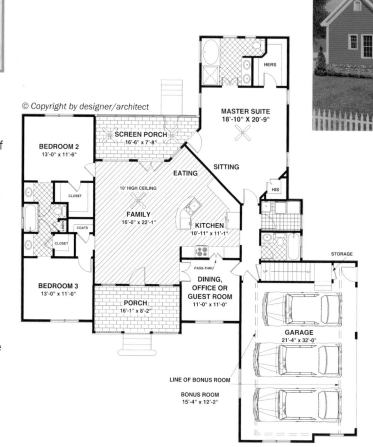

© Copyright by designer/architect

## Plan #F04-001D-0067

| | |
|---|---|
| **Dimensions:** | 48' W x 37'8" D |
| **Heated Sq. Ft.:** | 1,285 |
| **Bedrooms:** 3 | **Bathrooms:** 2 |

**Foundation:** Basement, slab or crawl space, please specify when ordering

| | |
|---|---|
| **PDF File:** | $750 |
| **5-Sets:** | $800 |
| **8-Sets:** | $875 |
| **CAD File:** | $1,550 |
| **Material List:** | $125 |
| **Upgrade to 2" x 6" Walls:** | $150 |

*Pricing subject to change*

*Images provided by designer/architect*

### Features

- This accommodating home has a charming country-style covered front porch
- The large storage area on the back of the home is a handy feature for lawn equipment
- The master bedroom includes a dressing area, a private bath, and a built-in bookcase for added character
- The kitchen features a pantry, a breakfast bar and a complete view to the dining area

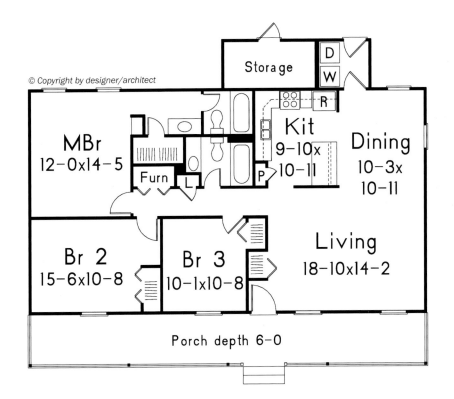

© Copyright by designer/architect

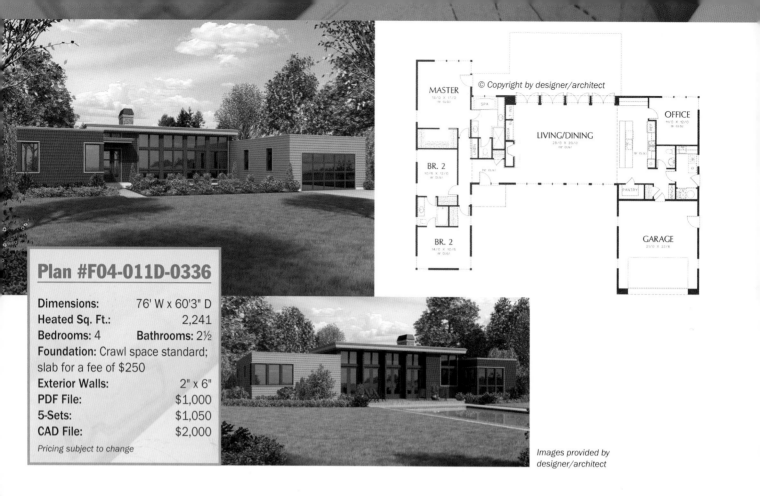

## Plan #F04-011D-0336

| | |
|---|---|
| Dimensions: | 76' W x 60'3" D |
| Heated Sq. Ft.: | 2,241 |
| Bedrooms: 4 | Bathrooms: 2½ |
| Foundation: Crawl space standard; slab for a fee of $250 | |
| Exterior Walls: | 2" x 6" |
| PDF File: | $1,000 |
| 5-Sets: | $1,050 |
| CAD File: | $2,000 |

*Pricing subject to change*

© Copyright by designer/architect

*Images provided by designer/architect*

## Plan #F04-020D-0370

*Images provided by designer/architect*

© Copyright by designer/architect

| | |
|---|---|
| Dimensions: | 68' W x 70' D |
| Heated Sq. Ft.: | 2,240 |
| Bedrooms: 3 | Bathrooms: 2 |
| Foundation: Slab or crawl space, please specify when ordering | |
| Exterior Walls: | 2" x 6" |
| PDF File: | $950 |
| 5-Sets: | $975 |
| 8-Sets: | $1,020 |
| CAD File: | $1,738 |
| Material List: | $90 |

*Pricing subject to change*

## Plan #F04-007D-0109

| | |
|---|---|
| Dimensions: | 35' W x 38' D |
| Heated Sq. Ft.: | 888 |
| Bedrooms: 2 | Bathrooms: 1 |
| Foundation: | Basement |
| PDF File: | $675 |
| 5-Sets: | $725 |
| 8-Sets: | $800 |
| CAD File: | $1,475 |
| Material List: | $125 |

*Pricing subject to change*

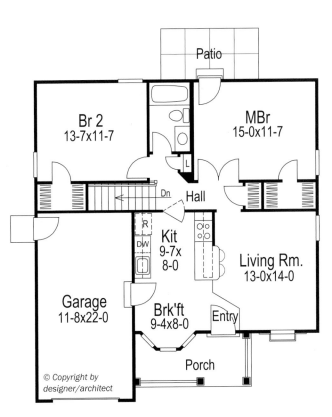

*Images provided by designer/architect*

© Copyright by designer/architect

---

## Plan #F04-011D-0001

| | |
|---|---|
| Dimensions: | 40' W x 58' D |
| Heated Sq. Ft.: | 1,275 |
| Bedrooms: 3 | Bathrooms: 2 |

Foundation: Joisted crawl space, post & beam, Trusjoist floor system or joisted continuous footing standard; basement or slab for a fee of $195

| | |
|---|---|
| Exterior Walls: | 2" x 6" |
| PDF File: | $800 |
| 5-Sets: | $825 |
| CAD File: | $1,600 |

*Pricing subject to change*

*Images provided by designer/architect*

© Copyright by designer/architect

## Plan #F04-011S-0018

| | |
|---|---|
| **Dimensions:** | 77' W x 65' D |
| **Heated Sq. Ft.:** | 4,600 |
| **Bedrooms:** 4 | **Bathrooms:** 3½ |
| **Foundation:** Partial crawl space/ walk-out basement | |
| **Exterior Walls:** | 2" x 6" |
| **PDF File:** | $1,550 |
| **5-Sets:** | $1,600 |
| **CAD File:** | $3,000 |

*Pricing subject to change*

*Images provided by designer/architect*

## Features

- A unique glass floor leads to the staircase and allows one to look down to the lower level below
- Plant shelves adorn this house in numerous places
- The differently designed kitchen has most of its emphasis on a gracious center island
- The master bedroom flows into an open bathroom with a spa tub and a double-bowl vanity
- 3-car front entry tandem garage or use the extra space as a workshop

First Floor
2,624 sq. ft.

Lower Level
1,976 sq. ft.

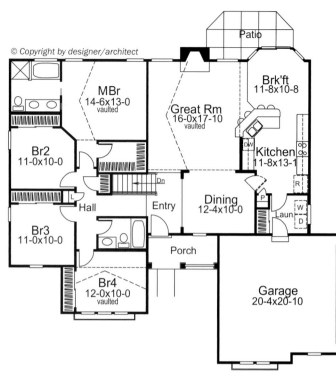

© Copyright by designer/architect

*Images provided by designer/architect*

## Plan #F04-007D-0067

| | |
|---|---|
| Dimensions: | 57' W x 52'2" D |
| Heated Sq. Ft.: | 1,761 |
| Bedrooms: 4 | Bathrooms: 2 |
| Foundation: | Basement |
| PDF File: | $825 |
| 5-Sets: | $875 |
| 8-Sets: | $950 |
| CAD File: | $1,725 |
| Material List: | $125 |

*Pricing subject to change*

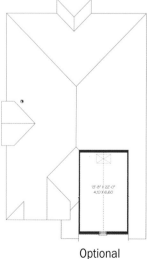

© Copyright by designer/architect

First Floor
1,634 sq. ft.

Optional
Second Floor
334 sq. ft.

## Plan #F04-032D-0735

| | |
|---|---|
| Dimensions: | 39'4" W x 64' D |
| Heated Sq. Ft.: | 1,634 |
| Bedrooms: 3 | Bathrooms: ½ |
| Foundation: | Floating slab |
| Exterior Walls: | 2" x 6" |
| 5-Sets: | $850 |
| 8-Sets: | $880 |
| PDF File: | $990 |
| CAD File: | $1,560 |
| Material List: | $130 |

*Pricing subject to change*

*Images provided by designer/architect*

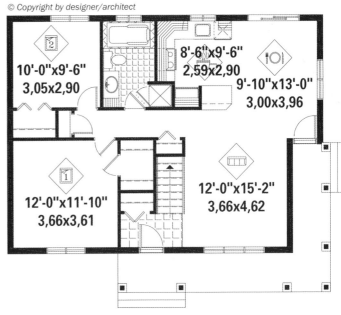

10'-0"x9'-6"
3,05x2,90

8'-6"x9'-6"
2,59x2,90

9'-10"x13'-0"
3,00x3,96

12'-0"x11'-10"
3,66x3,61

12'-0"x15'-2"
3,66x4,62

## Plan #F04-126D-0562

*Images provided by designer/architect*

| | |
|---|---|
| Dimensions: | 36' W x 26' D |
| Heated Sq. Ft.: | 894 |
| Bedrooms: 2 | Bathrooms: 1 |
| Foundation: | Basement |
| Exterior Walls: | 2" x 6" |
| 5-Sets: | $535 |
| 8-Sets: | $575 |
| PDF File: | $700 |
| CAD File: | $1,300 |
| Material List: | $90 |

*Pricing subject to change*

10'-4" X 10'-4"
3,10 X 3,10

14'-4" X 16'-8"
4,30 X 5,00

14'-8" X 16'-0"
4,40 X 4,80

12'-8" X 13'-4"
3,80 X 4,00

*Images provided by designer/architect*

## Plan #F04-032D-0613

| | |
|---|---|
| Dimensions: | 36' W x 38' D |
| Heated Sq. Ft.: | 1,217 |
| Bedrooms: 2 | Bathrooms: 1 |
| Foundation: | Basement |
| Exterior Walls: | 2" x 6" |
| 5-Sets: | $785 |
| 8-Sets: | $815 |
| PDF File: | $930 |
| CAD File: | $1,500 |
| Material List: | $120 |

*Pricing subject to change*

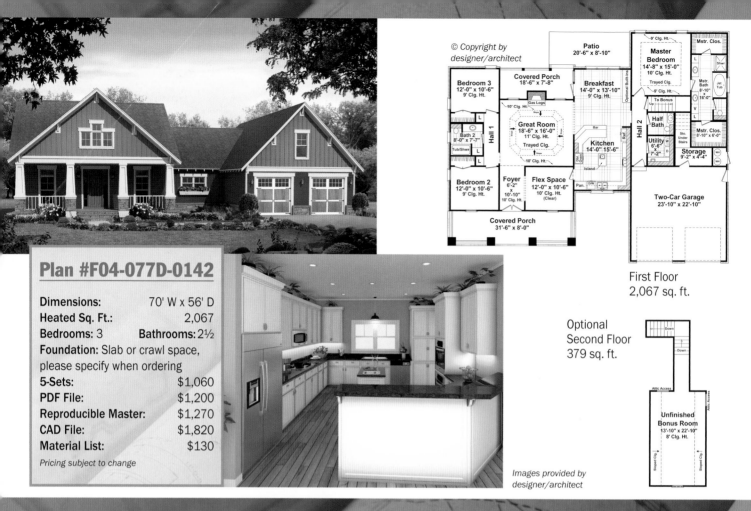

**Patio**
20'-6" x 8'-10"

**Covered Porch**
18'-6" x 7'-8"

**Master Bedroom**
14'-8" x 15'-0"
10' Clg. Ht.
Trayed Clg.

Mstr. Clos.

9' Clg. Ht.

**Bedroom 3**
12'-0" x 10'-6"
9' Clg. Ht.

**Breakfast**
14'-0" x 13'-10"
9' Clg. Ht.

Mstr. Bath
8'-10" x 16'-0"

Gas Logs

Optional Built-in

9'-0" Clg. Ht.

**Great Room**
18'-6" x 16'-0"
11' Clg. Ht.
Trayed Clg.

Bar

To Bonus
Up

Half Bath

**Bath 2**
8'-0" x 7'-7"

Tub/Show

**Kitchen**
14'-0" 15'-6"

Island

Hall 2

**Utility**
6'-6" x 7'-2"

Mstr. Clos.
5'-10" x 6'-0"

Sto. Under Stairs

**Storage**
9'-2" x 4'-4"

10'-0" Clg. Ht.

Hall 1

**Bedroom 2**
12'-0" x 10'-6"
9' Clg. Ht.

**Foyer**
6'-2" x 10'-0"
10' Clg. Ht.

**Flex Space**
12'-0" x 10'-6"
10' Clg. Ht.
(Clear)

Pan.

DW

Ref

**Two-Car Garage**
23'-10" x 22'-10"

**Covered Porch**
31'-6" x 8'-0"

**First Floor**
2,067 sq. ft.

**Optional Second Floor**
379 sq. ft.

Down

Down

Attic Access

Attic Access

**Unfinished Bonus Room**
13'-10" x 22'-0"
8' Clg. Ht.

Sloped Clg.

Sloped Clg.

*Images provided by designer/architect*

## Plan #F04-077D-0142

| | |
|---|---|
| **Dimensions:** | 70' W x 56' D |
| **Heated Sq. Ft.:** | 2,067 |
| **Bedrooms:** 3 | **Bathrooms:** 2½ |
| **Foundation:** Slab or crawl space, please specify when ordering | |
| **5-Sets:** | $1,060 |
| **PDF File:** | $1,200 |
| **Reproducible Master:** | $1,270 |
| **CAD File:** | $1,820 |
| **Material List:** | $130 |

*Pricing subject to change*

## Plan #F04-121D-0005

| | |
|---|---|
| **Dimensions:** | 65' W x 46'4" D |
| **Heated Sq. Ft.:** | 1,562 |
| **Bedrooms:** 3 | **Bathrooms:** 2 |
| **Foundation:** | Basement |
| **PDF File:** | $825 |
| **5-Sets:** | $875 |
| **8-Sets:** | $950 |
| **CAD File:** | $1,725 |
| **Material List:** | $125 |
| **Upgrade to 2" x 6" Walls:** | $150 |

*Pricing subject to change*

*Images provided by designer/architect*

Patio

**Brkfst**
10-8x11-7
Vaulted

**MBr**
14-3x13-3
Coffer Clg

**Great Rm**
15-9x16-0
Vaulted

**Kitchen**
10-8x11-9
Vaulted

DW

Dn

**Br 2**
11-0x10-2

**Br 3**
10-6x10-2

Foyer

**Dining**
10-1x11-4
Vaulted

Plant Shelf

R

P

**Laun/ Mud Rm**

W D

**Porch**
Vaulted

**Garage**
20-8x21-4

Images provided by designer/architect

## Plan #F04-011D-0330

| | |
|---|---|
| **Dimensions:** | 55' W x 58' D |
| **Heated Sq. Ft.:** | 2,000 |
| **Bedrooms:** 3 | **Bathrooms:** 2 |

**Foundation:** Joisted crawl space or post & beam standard; slab or basement for a fee of $250

| | |
|---|---|
| **Exterior Walls:** | 2" x 6" |
| **PDF File:** | $1,000 |
| **5-Sets:** | $1,050 |
| **CAD File:** | $2,000 |

*Pricing subject to change*

---

Optional
Second Floor
341 sq. ft.

First Floor
1,250 sq. ft.

## Plan #F04-030D-0018

| | |
|---|---|
| **Dimensions:** | 52'6" W x 45'8" D |
| **Heated Sq. Ft.:** | 1,250 |
| **Bedrooms:** 2 | **Bathrooms:** 2 |

**Foundation:** Crawl space, slab or basement, please specify when ordering

| | |
|---|---|
| **PDF File:** | $750 |
| **5-Sets:** | $800 |
| **8-Sets:** | $875 |
| **CAD File:** | $1,550 |

*Pricing subject to change*

Images provided by designer/architect

## Plan #F04-065D-0013

| | |
|---|---|
| Dimensions: | 67'6" W x 63'6" D |
| Heated Sq. Ft.: | 2,041 |
| Bedrooms: 3 | Bathrooms: 2 |
| Foundation: | Walk-out basement |
| 5-Sets: | $695 |
| 8-Sets: | $880 |
| PDF File: | $1,075 |
| Reproducible Master: | $1,075 |
| Material List: | $85 |

*Pricing subject to change*

*Images provided by designer/architect*

## Features

- The great room has direct access directly to the covered rear deck with ceiling fan above
- The private master bedroom has a beautiful octagon-shaped sitting area that opens and brightens the space
- Two secondary bedrooms share a full bath
- A wall of windows in the great room merges the interior with its exterior surroundings perfectly
- Dramatic stone and carpentry combine creating an extraordinary focal point as seen in the great room
- The optional lower level has an additional 1,942 square feet of living area
- 2-car side entry garage

## Plan #F04-047D-0146

| | |
|---|---|
| Dimensions: | 66'4" W x 80'8" D |
| Heated Sq. Ft.: | 2,713 |
| Bedrooms: 3 | Bathrooms: 3 |
| Foundation: | Slab |
| 5-Sets: | $910 |
| PDF File: | $1,120 |
| Reproducible Master: | $1,170 |
| CAD File: | $1,920 |

*Pricing subject to change*

*Images provided by designer/architect*

## Features

- This simple symmetrical facade is strikingly beautiful and draws the eye to the front door
- Stepping out onto the covered porch will transport you into a place of relaxation
- Accented by the corner fireplace, beautiful built-in shelves are perfect for storing media equipment or board games in the family room
- Large windows fill the breakfast nook with natural light, creating an airy atmosphere
- The foyer is illuminated by natural light and is topped with a decorative ceiling
- Framing - only concrete block available
- 3-car side entry garage

Optional
Second Floor
440 sq. ft.

First Floor
2,713 sq. ft.

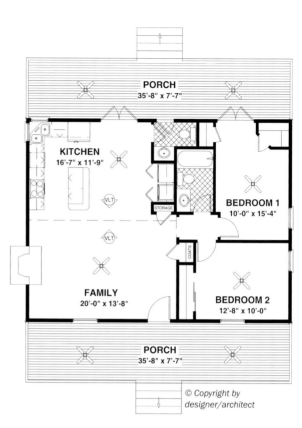

## Plan #F04-013D-0133

| | |
|---|---|
| Dimensions: | 36' W x 42'4" D |
| Heated Sq. Ft.: | 953 |
| Bedrooms: 2 | Bathrooms: 1½ |
| Foundation: | Crawl space |
| PDF File: | $795 |
| 5-Sets: | $845 |
| 8-Sets: | $895 |
| CAD File: | $1,095 |

*Pricing subject to change*

*Images provided by designer/architect*

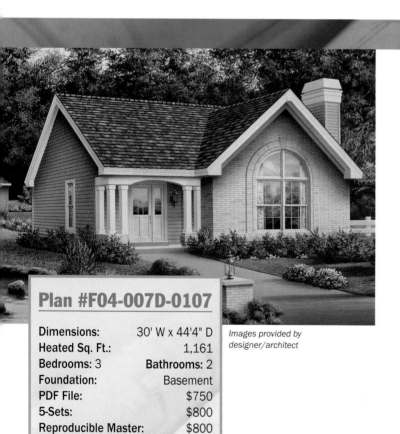

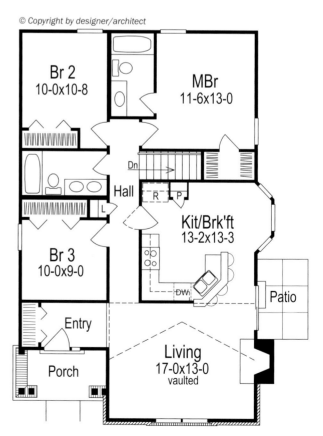

## Plan #F04-007D-0107

| | |
|---|---|
| Dimensions: | 30' W x 44'4" D |
| Heated Sq. Ft.: | 1,161 |
| Bedrooms: 3 | Bathrooms: 2 |
| Foundation: | Basement |
| PDF File: | $750 |
| 5-Sets: | $800 |
| Reproducible Master: | $800 |
| 8-Sets: | $875 |
| Material List: | $125 |

*Pricing subject to change*

*Images provided by designer/architect*

Images provided by designer/architect

© Copyright by designer/architect

DECK

DIN. RM.
13'4"x9'6"
9'-1 1/8" CEILING

GRT. RM.
VAULTED CEILING
18'4"x15'0"

KIT.
9'-1 1/8" CEILING
13'4"x13'6"

MBR.
10'-1 1/8" STEP CEILING
13'6"x15'0"

DEN
9'-1 1/8" CEILING
10'8"x13'8"

E.
VAULTED CEILING

BR. #2
9'-1 1/8" CEILING
11'8"x11'0"

2 CAR GARAGE
21'8"x22'0"

## Plan #F04-051D-0801

| | |
|---|---|
| Dimensions: | 54' W x 60'4" D |
| Heated Sq. Ft.: | 1,734 |
| Bedrooms: 2 | Bathrooms: 2 |
| Foundation: | Basement |
| Exterior Walls: | 2" x 6" |
| 5-Sets: | $823 |
| 8-Sets: | $865 |
| PDF File: | $1,032 |
| CAD File: | $1,630 |

*Pricing subject to change*

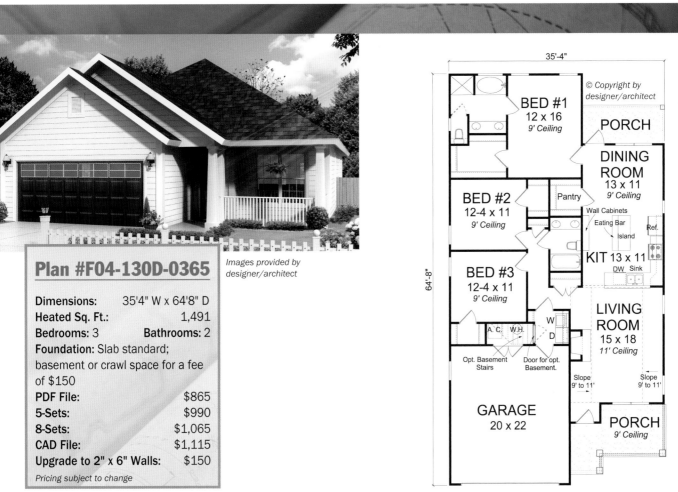

Images provided by designer/architect

## Plan #F04-130D-0365

| | |
|---|---|
| Dimensions: | 35'4" W x 64'8" D |
| Heated Sq. Ft.: | 1,491 |
| Bedrooms: 3 | Bathrooms: 2 |

Foundation: Slab standard; basement or crawl space for a fee of $150

| | |
|---|---|
| PDF File: | $865 |
| 5-Sets: | $990 |
| 8-Sets: | $1,065 |
| CAD File: | $1,115 |
| Upgrade to 2" x 6" Walls: | $150 |

*Pricing subject to change*

35'-4"

64'-8"

© Copyright by designer/architect

BED #1
12 x 16
9' Ceiling

PORCH

DINING ROOM
13 x 11
9' Ceiling

BED #2
12-4 x 11
9' Ceiling

Pantry

Wall Cabinets

Eating Bar

Island

Ref.

KIT 13 x 11
9' Ceiling

DW   Sink

BED #3
12-4 x 11
9' Ceiling

A.C.   W.H.

W
D

Opt. Basement Stairs

Door for opt. Basement.

GARAGE
20 x 22

LIVING ROOM
15 x 18
11' Ceiling

Slope 9' to 11'

Slope 9' to 11'

PORCH
9' Ceiling

## Plan #F04-101D-0059

| | |
|---|---|
| **Dimensions:** | 88'6" W x 67'6" D |
| **Heated Sq. Ft.:** | 2,196 |
| **Bedrooms:** 2 | **Bathrooms:** 2½ |

**Foundation:** Basement, daylight basement or walk-out basement, please specify when ordering

| | |
|---|---|
| **Exterior Walls:** | 2" x 6" |
| **5-Sets:** | $850 |
| **PDF File:** | $1,150 |
| **CAD File:** | $1,650 |

*Pricing subject to change*

*Images provided by designer/architect*

### Features

- This home was designed with 10' ceilings on both the first floor and the lower level making it extremely open and spacious

- The laundry and mud room merge to form a powerhouse of efficiency and organization including lockers, a closet and extra counterspace

- The L-shaped kitchen island offers plenty of seating and houses a double sink and the dishwasher

- 2-car front entry garage and a 1-car side entry garage

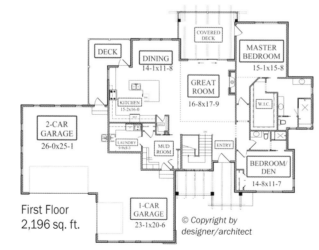

First Floor
2,196 sq. ft.

© Copyright by designer/architect

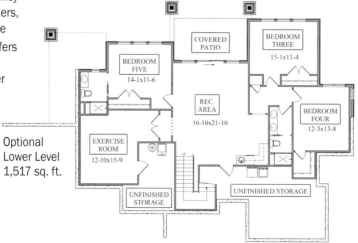

Optional
Lower Level
1,517 sq. ft.

## Plan #F04-047D-0083

| | |
|---|---|
| Dimensions: | 51' W x 74'4" D |
| Heated Sq. Ft.: | 2,293 |
| Bedrooms: 3 | Bathrooms: 2 |
| Foundation: | Slab |
| PDF File: | $975 |
| 5-Sets: | $1,025 |
| Reproducible Master: | $1,025 |
| CAD File: | $1,875 |

*Pricing subject to change*

### Features

- The family and dining rooms feature 12' ceilings for added openness
- The cozy breakfast nook area brings in an abundance of warm natural light
- The master bedroom enjoys private access onto the covered patio and a deluxe bath
- The angled floor plan draws the eye to the covered patio that is designed with a built-in fire pit
- 2-car side entry garage

*Images provided by designer/architect*

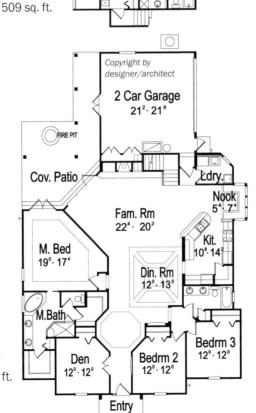

Optional
Second Floor
509 sq. ft.

**Balc.**

**Bonus/Bedrm 4**
21⁴ · 16⁴

*Copyright by designer/architect*

**2 Car Garage**
21² · 21⁸

**FIRE PIT**

**Cov. Patio**

**Ldry.**

**Nook**
5⁴ · 7⁴

**Fam. Rm**
22⁴ · 20²

**Kit.**
10⁸ · 14²

**M. Bed**
19⁰ · 17⁴

**Din. Rm**
12⁰ · 13⁰

**M.Bath**

First Floor
2,293 sq. ft.

**Den**
12⁰ · 12⁰

**Bedrm 2**
12⁰ · 12⁰

**Bedrm 3**
12⁰ · 12⁰

**Entry**

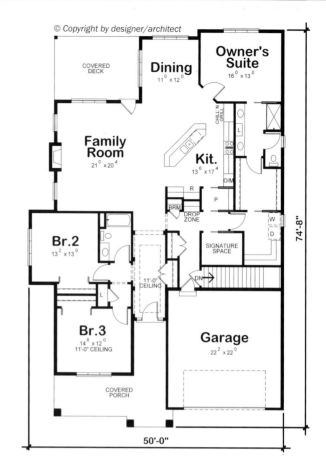

© Copyright by designer/architect

*Images provided by designer/architect*

## Plan #F04-026D-1906

| | |
|---|---|
| Dimensions: | 50' W x 74'8" D |
| Heated Sq. Ft.: | 2,326 |
| Bedrooms: 3 | Bathrooms: 2 |
| Foundation: Basement standard; slab or crawl space for a fee of $195 | |
| Exterior Walls: | 2" x 6" |
| PDF File: | $915 |
| 5-Sets: | $990 |
| 8-Sets: | $1,110 |
| CAD File: | $1,415 |

*Pricing subject to change*

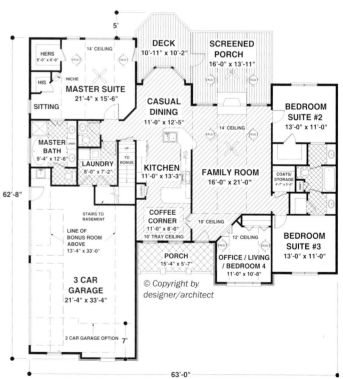

© Copyright by designer/architect

*Images provided by designer/architect*

## Plan #F04-013D-0164

| | |
|---|---|
| Dimensions: | 63' W x 62'8" D |
| Heated Sq. Ft.: | 2,000 |
| Bonus Sq. Ft.: | 495 |
| Bedrooms: 4 | Bathrooms: 2½ |
| Foundation: | Basement |
| PDF File: | $995 |
| 5-Sets: | $1,045 |
| 8-Sets: | $1,095 |
| CAD File: | $1,495 |

*Pricing subject to change*

## Plan #F04-032D-0813

| | |
|---|---|
| Dimensions: | 26' W x 26' D |
| Heated Sq. Ft.: | 686 |
| Bedrooms: 2 | Bathrooms: 1 |
| Foundation: | Monolithic slab |
| Exterior Walls: | 2" x 6" |
| 5-Sets: | $595 |
| 8-Sets: | $625 |
| PDF File: | $730 |
| CAD File: | $1,300 |
| Material List: | $100 |

*Pricing subject to change*

*Images provided by designer/architect*

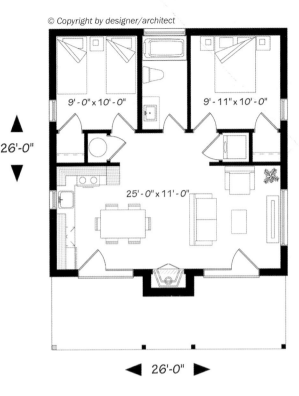

© Copyright by designer/architect

26'-0"

9' - 0" x 10' - 0"

9' - 11" x 10' - 0"

25' - 0" x 11' - 0"

26'-0"

---

## Plan #F04-139D-0038

| | |
|---|---|
| Dimensions: | 56'11" W x 59'9" D |
| Heated Sq. Ft.: | 2,368 |
| Bedrooms: 3 | Bathrooms: 2½ |
| Foundation: Crawl space standard; basement or slab for a fee of $450 | |
| Exterior Walls: | 2" x 6" |
| 5-Sets: | $1,245 |
| PDF File: | $1,320 |
| CAD File: | $2,995 |

*Pricing subject to change*

*Images provided by designer/architect*

Optional Second Floor 491 sq. ft.

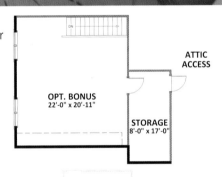

ATTIC ACCESS

OPT. BONUS
22'-0" x 20'-11"

STORAGE
8'-0" x 17'-0"

First Floor 2,368 sq. ft.

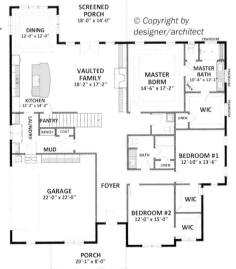

© Copyright by designer/architect

SCREENED PORCH
18'-0" x 14'-0"

DINING
12'-0" x 12'-0"

VAULTED FAMILY
18'-2" x 17'-2"

MASTER BDRM
14'-6" x 17'-2"

MASTER BATH
10'-4" x 12'-1"

KITCHEN
12'-2" x 14'-2"

WIC

PANTRY

BENCH  COAT

LAUNDRY

MUD

BATH

LINEN

BEDROOM #1
12'-10" x 13'-6"

GARAGE
22'-0" x 22'-0"

FOYER

WIC

BEDROOM #2
12'-0" x 15'-0"

WIC

PORCH
20'-1" x 8'-0"

## Plan #F04-126D-0162

| | |
|---|---|
| Dimensions: | 24' W x 37' D |
| Heated Sq. Ft.: | 888 |
| Bedrooms: 2 | Bathrooms: 1 |
| Foundation: | Basement |
| Exterior Walls: | 2" x 6" |
| 5-Sets: | $535 |
| 8-Sets: | $575 |
| PDF File: | $700 |
| CAD File: | $1,300 |
| Material List: | $90 |

*Pricing subject to change*

*Images provided by designer/architect*

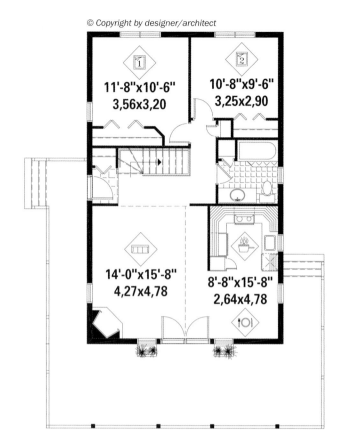

© Copyright by designer/architect

## Plan #F04-007D-0168

| | |
|---|---|
| Dimensions: | 89'10" W x 40'2" D |
| Heated Sq. Ft.: | 1,814 |
| Bedrooms: 3 | Bathrooms: 2 |
| Foundation: | Basement |
| PDF File: | $750 |
| 5-Sets: | $800 |
| Reproducible Master: | $800 |
| 8-Sets: | $875 |
| Material List: | $125 |

*Pricing subject to change*

*Images provided by designer/architect*

© Copyright by designer/architect

First Floor
737 sq. ft.

© Copyright by designer/architect

*Images provided by designer/architect*

Lower Level
658 sq. ft.

## Plan #F04-011D-0292

| | |
|---|---|
| Dimensions: | 36' W x 35' D |
| Heated Sq. Ft.: | 1,395 |
| Bedrooms: 3 | Bathrooms: 2 |
| Foundation: | Walk-out basement |
| Exterior Walls: | 2" x 6" |
| PDF File: | $800 |
| 5-Sets: | $825 |
| CAD File: | $1,600 |

*Pricing subject to change*

© Copyright by designer/architect

## Plan #F04-076D-0258

| | |
|---|---|
| Dimensions: | 45'6" W x 53' D |
| Heated Sq. Ft.: | 1,797 |
| Bedrooms: 3 | Bathrooms: 2½ |
| Foundation: | Slab |
| 5-Sets: | $655 |
| 8-Sets: | $800 |
| PDF File: | $975 |
| CAD File: | $1,250 |

*Pricing subject to change*

*Images provided by designer/architect*

## Plan #F04-026D-1891

| | |
|---|---|
| Dimensions: | 56' W x 72' D |
| Heated Sq. Ft.: | 2,407 |
| Bedrooms: | 1 |
| Bathrooms: | 1 full, 2 half |

**Foundation:** Basement standard; slab or crawl space for a fee of $195; walk-out basement for a fee of $390

| | |
|---|---|
| Exterior Walls: | 2" x 6" |
| PDF File: | $925 |
| 5-Sets: | $1,000 |
| 8-Sets: | $1,120 |
| CAD File: | $1,425 |

*Pricing subject to change*

*Images provided by designer/architect*

## Features

- The den can easily be used as a home office or guest bedroom as it has its own private half bath

- The eating area and great room share a fireplace that warms both of the rooms nicely

- The kitchen features a corner pantry, a large island, and a curved seating space

- The master bedroom comes with an impressive stepped ceiling, an alcove for a dresser, two closets and a bath with all the amenities

- Entering through the garage the homeowner's have a drop zone, storage closet, half bath and convenient access to a large laundry room with plenty of counter space

- 3-car front entry garage

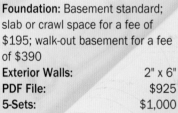

© Copyright by designer/architect

# bonus rooms&basements
## finding flexibility within your home

You found it – the perfect dream home! It has the exact number of bedrooms and bathrooms. The open floor plan is great. The kitchen is spacious, the mud room ideal, and the storage is awesome. You even have a bonus room. Now, what to do with that space? Here lies the beauty of this space – you can do whatever you like! From newlyweds to families of five, the bonus room holds numerous possibilities for every homeowner to customize their design as they see fit. Many one-story homes today are designed with bonus or flex spaces that give families that wiggle room when additional space is needed. Let your imagination run wild! There are so many opportunities to make this your area for fun, fitness, work or relaxation; you name it.

### Think Big
Maximize your home's fun quotient by finishing your flex or bonus space for a big time fun spot everyone will love! Better yet, your basement may be below ground, but there's nothing sub-par about these ideas!

*Page 134, top, left: Plan #055D-0202, houseplansandmore.com; above: Plan #091S-0001, houseplansandmore.com; Page 135, top: Plan #F04-011S-0018 on page 116; Bonus room playroom, istockphoto.com; Plan #F04-055D-0748 on page 8; Plan #101S-0019, houseplansandmore.com.*

## THE PLAY ROOM

Every mom wishes she had a place where she could put those extra toys, keeping them from clashing with her living room décor, or ending up under her feet while she tries to fix dinner. So why not put that bonus room to good use as a designated play room? Organizational systems of cubbies, baskets, and shelves will keep an unruly collection of toys organized, while providing enough space to enjoy playing with them. Bean bag chairs and play rugs in bright colors keep the room fun and functional. You could even break the room down into stations – an art area with chalkboard paint walls for your budding Van Gogh, a reading corner with special pillows and lighting, or a block table for the young architect. Keep this room child-friendly and fun and your kids will flock there, all while keeping the mess out of the rest of the house.

## THE HOME THEATER

To turn your bonus room into your own personal theater experience, you need surprisingly few items. A quality television, proper media players, and surround sound are the best setup. Now that your theater is functional it's time to personalize your movie watching experience. Are you going to put in oversized reclining chairs and couches, or movie theater seats? Will you put in dimming ambient lights? How about a popcorn machine? After all, the primary reason you have a home theater is to enjoy cinema entertainment in unsurpassed comfort. Some homeowners with serious theater systems choose to have professional input and installation. Whether home designed or professionally outfitted, the home theater is a bonus room design enjoyed by all.

## THE FAMILY GATHERING SPOT

Often called a recreation or game room, this family gathering spot is the place where family can get together and relax. Filled with games, movies, and perhaps a snack area or wet bar, this bonus room use is great for families that need an informal space to hang out in that doesn't necessarily need to be kept perfect like the highly visible great room. Keep this space cozy and inviting for making family memories.

## THE HOME GYM

We all know someone who has purchased home workout equipment only to realize that the plan was not thought out. Bulky equipment is a pain to set up and take down everyday, so it often goes unused. If the equipment is left out, those machines always manage to take up awkward amounts of space. Even small free weights often find themselves in the way, causing stubbed toes and storage woes. Turning your bonus room into a home gym, or exercise room creates a designated space for all that equipment, plus it allows options of customized flooring or built-in sound systems. It will definitely make exercising less of a chore since you won't have to leave the house!

## THE HOME OFFICE

If you choose to work from home, there is no more valuable a space than a bonus room that's been turned into a home office. Remember that your home office is a reflection of you and the work you produce. Make it a priority to keep the space efficient and eye-appealing with necessary storage, noise buffers, and organizational systems. Keeping this room working for you makes working from home a pleasant affair and ensures the bonus room is never a wasted space.

# double your square footage ✛ customize your basement into something special

*M*any of today's one-story homes like the ones featured in this book are designed with an optional lower level. Offering flexibility if additional square footage is needed or desired, finishing a lower level can instantly increase a home's square footage providing added bedrooms, gathering space, or whatever you need to make your home more functional and work for you. Gone are the days of a home's basement being only used as a place for old boxes. The basements, or lower levels of today are nothing in comparison. Basement storage is being transformed into finished family spaces. The most popular options are best broken into specialized areas. From gaming to movie theaters, much like a bonus or flex room, your basement can be designed to your unique desires.

*Page 136, top, left: Plan #055D-0817, houseplansandmore.com; top, middle: home gym, istockphotos.com; Page 135, top: Plan #026D-1408, houseplansandmore.com; Plan #F04-051D-0187 on page 142; Page 137, top: Plan #071S-0001, houseplansandmore.com; middle: Plan #072S-0003, houseplansandmore.com; bottom: Plan #F01-101D-0047 on page 162.*

_need ideas?_

## GAME ON

What you do with your dedicated game room depends on the game to be played. Families may choose to have a special table for game play, with shelves installed to organize their extensive board game collections. Poker, or Texas Hold'em are popular and if you love to play, then a personalized table, chips, and cards would be great additions to this space. Pool tables, air hockey, shuffleboard, and even full-scale arcade games are also available for purchase, allowing fans to recreate their favorite gaming experiences – without worrying about their high scores being challenged!

## MAKE THE MOST OF THE MEDIA

As family lifestyles become more hectic, the free time they spend together is often wanted at home. The availability of flat screen smart televisions, surround sound (often wireless), and multiple video, audio, gaming systems and apps allow any media experience to be enjoyed at full capacity without ever leaving home. Specialized lighting can add the appropriate ambiance when movie watching or having gaming tournaments with just a click of the remote.

## LOUNGING AROUND

For some families, extra space is best outfitted with the amenities needed to relax. Cozy furniture, warm lighting, blankets and bookshelves create a desirable place to retreat to while enjoying one another's company.

Many families choose to mix and match the different suggestions, creating zones of activity within the basement. Additionally, refreshment centers are becoming more popular in finished basements, adding to the level of comfort. These can be uniquely designed, ranging from full-scale kitchens to specialized wet bars. Wine cellars and humidors are also popular in many households. Keep in mind that with refreshments usually come bathrooms. Full baths, saunas, hot tubs, and even guest rooms are prevalent in basements when resources allow.

When it comes to decorating and creating a specific atmosphere, it may be best to consider a theme. This works particularly well for dedicated rooms. If you are choosing to outfit your basement for multiple uses, stick to something that will be enjoyed by everyone without overshadowing any particular area. Your basement is one more opportunity to show how creative you are – so, don't hold back!

Attempt to use as much of the space as you can. Vertical shelves are great for visible, neat storage, while also giving you further places to display pictures and other treasures while also promoting a feeling of spaciousness with their height.

*Page 138, top: Plan #013S-0011, houseplansandmore.com; bottom: Plan # 065D-0361, houseplansandmore.com; Page 139, top: Plan #091D-0476, houseplansandmore.com; middle: Plan #F04-101D-0052 on page 60; bottom: Plan #F04-101D-0056 on page 270.*

## Hot Tip

Make your finished basement feel like an extension of your main level. Use the same finishes and remove the doors that separate each floor and now you have twice the house with twice the personality and comfort!

## HIT THE FLOOR

Flooring is important, and the basement will likely be exposed to heavy traffic flow. Durability and comfort are both vital in addition to stain resistance and sound proofing. Cork flooring is growing in popularity for these reasons. Another popular choice is luxury vinyl laminate, or ceramic tile. Both of these options can look exactly like stone or wood flooring, but are entirely waterproof, perfect for damper environments like basements and areas where there will be plenty of entertaining and the chance for frequent spills.

## LET THERE BE LIGHT

Recessed lighting eliminates overhead and wasting floor space, but can be expensive. Sconces are another idea to prevent wasting precious entertainment space, but try to include as much natural light as possible to avoid the feeling of being underground. Today, many areas have code requirements for egress windows in basements, these windows are larger than their traditional counterparts and allow much more natural light to filter into the space. They alleviate the feeling of a dark, damp basement instantly, and they also allow any bedroom designed into a basement space to be considered a true bedroom when you plan to resell your home. Per code, a bedroom must have a proper escape method if there's a fire, and an egress window is large enough for just that.

## MAKE IT MULTI-TASK

Some homeowners like the idea of multiple uses but really desire the peace of reading a book without overhearing the poker game going on across the room. Don't give up the hope of having both a flexible and functional recreation room. Curtain rails and bi-fold doors/walls can be installed, sectioning off areas in use or opening up the room to its greatest space potential, perfect for privacy or parties.

As you ponder finishing your basement with a festive and fun game room, or a tranquil spa and meditation area, keep in mind the space allowed as well as your budget, time constrictions and future needs. Measure the area and plan for traffic flow and adequate seating. It will be beneficial to pick a large space and plot the exact layout you desire. Homeowners are often surprised to find that a simple ping-pong table can take up a third of a room's floor space when unfolded. It is essential to have a defined plan for what amenities you definitely need to include in your new basement, in addition to where they will be located. Then, discuss your desires with your contractor. They can re-evaluate your design, ensuring the availability of your preferences. Although tempting, avoid purchasing items until your contractor has agreed to a layout. If you already own specific items, inform your contractor of their existence so those components are not ruled out when adjustments are made. With a little creativity, your former damp, dark basement will become the family's favorite gathering place, or the much-needed comfortable guest or living quarters you've always wanted.

## Plan #F04-051D-0670

| | |
|---|---|
| Dimensions: | 125'8" W x 76' D |
| Heated Sq. Ft.: | 3,109 |
| Bedrooms: 2 | Bathrooms: 2½ |
| Foundation: | Basement |
| Exterior Walls: | 2" x 6" |
| 5-Sets: | $1,001 |
| 8-Sets: | $1,042 |
| Reproducible Master: | $1,254 |

*Pricing subject to change*

### Features

- This luxurious home has a spacious open floor plan perfect when entertaining on a daily basis, or on special occasions

- The central great room and kitchen flow together perfectly and an enormous bayed dining area is also nearby

- There's plenty of outdoor living spaces including a sun room, covered porch and deck

- The bayed master bedroom has a lovely private bath and a huge walk-in closet for the homeowners

- 3-car front entry garage

*Images provided by designer/architect*

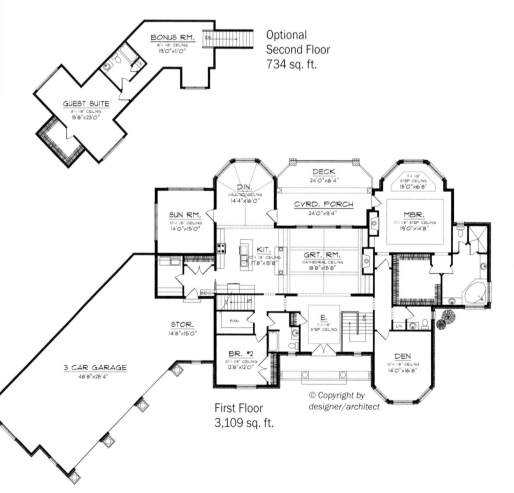

Optional Second Floor 734 sq. ft.

First Floor 3,109 sq. ft.

© Copyright by designer/architect

## Plan #F04-032D-0390

| | |
|---|---|
| Dimensions: | 32' W x 42' D |
| Heated Sq. Ft.: | 1,072 |
| Bedrooms: 2 | Bathrooms: 1 |
| Foundation: | Basement |
| Exterior Walls: | 2" x 6" |
| 5-Sets: | $725 |
| 8-Sets: | $755 |
| PDF File: | $870 |
| CAD File: | $1,440 |
| Material List: | $110 |

*Pricing subject to change*

*Images provided by designer/architect*

## Features

- The family gathering space is highlighted by a warm fireplace, lovely window accents and vast spaciousness

- The luxurious bath has a corner whirlpool tub for pampering, a separate shower and the nearby bedrooms have generously sized closets

- The bonus room above the garage has an additional 231 square feet of living area

- 1-car front entry detached garage

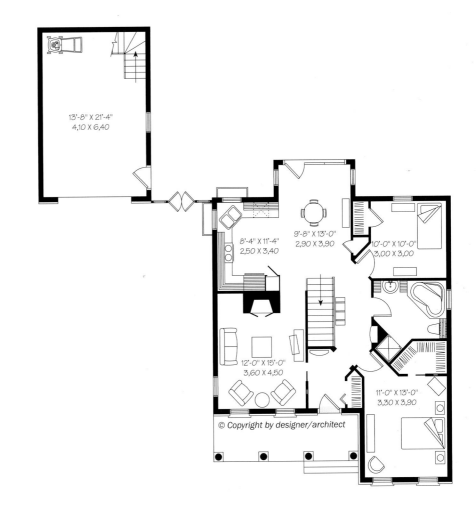

© Copyright by designer/architect

## Plan #F04-051D-0187

| | |
|---|---|
| **Dimensions:** | 65' W x 58' D |
| **Heated Sq. Ft.:** | 3,777 |
| **Bedrooms:** 4 | **Bathrooms:** 3½ |
| **Foundation:** | Walk-out basement |
| **Exterior Walls:** | 2" x 6" |
| **5-Sets:** | $1,600 |
| **8-Sets:** | $1,740 |
| **PDF File:** | $1,960 |
| **CAD File:** | $3,340 |

*Pricing subject to change*

### Features

- A dramatic entry has been created with the help of rich wood details, contrasting wall color and wrought iron ornamentation
- Enter the home to find this heavenly great room filled with light from the stunning window wall
- The master bedroom provides the ultimate relaxation with a deluxe bath and walk-in closet to keep everything organized
- A walk-in pantry and snack bar peninsula add efficiency to the kitchen that opens to the great room and cozy nook
- The lower level is comprised of two secondary bedrooms, a recreation room and a wet bar
- 3-car front entry garage

*Images provided by designer/architect*

© Copyright by designer/architect

First Floor
2,049 sq. ft.

Lower Level
1,728 sq. ft.

## Plan #F04-077D-0138

*Images provided by designer/architect*

| | |
|---|---|
| Dimensions: | 61' W x 47'4" D |
| Heated Sq. Ft.: | 1,509 |
| Bedrooms: 3 | Bathrooms: 2 |

Foundation: Slab, basement or crawl space, please specify when ordering

| | |
|---|---|
| 1-Sets: | $ 950 |
| 5-Sets: | $1,015 |
| PDF File: | $1,125 |
| Reproducible Master: | $1,200 |
| Material List: | $130 |

*Pricing subject to change*

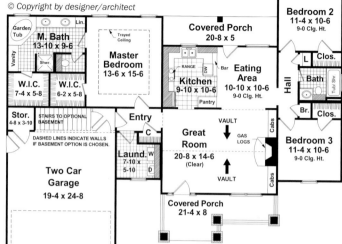

© Copyright by designer/architect

## Plan #F04-011D-0307

| | |
|---|---|
| Dimensions: | 40' W x 57' D |
| Heated Sq. Ft.: | 1,529 |
| Bedrooms: 3 | Bathrooms: 2 |

Foundation: Joisted crawl space or post & beam standard; slab for a fee of $225

| | |
|---|---|
| Exterior Walls: | 2" x 6" |
| PDF File: | $900 |
| 5-Sets: | $950 |
| CAD File: | $1,800 |

*Pricing subject to change*

*Images provided by designer/architect*

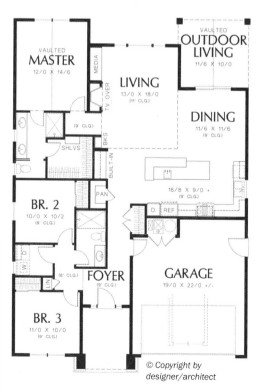

© Copyright by designer/architect

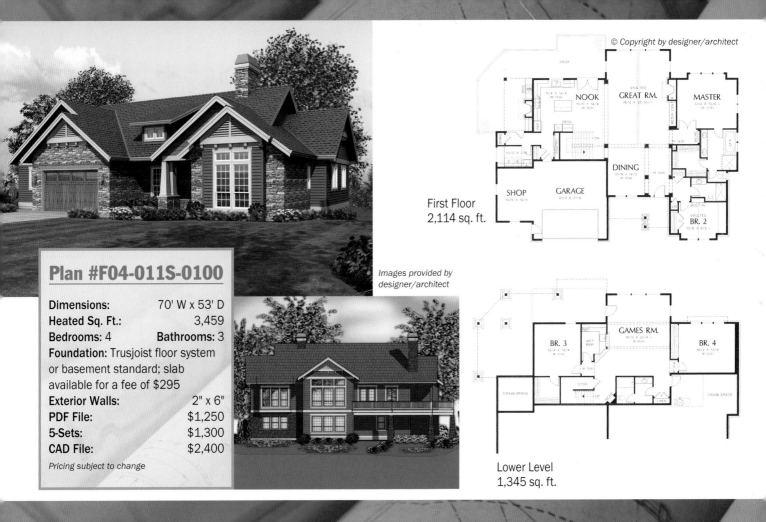

First Floor
2,114 sq. ft.

*Images provided by designer/architect*

Lower Level
1,345 sq. ft.

## Plan #F04-011S-0100

| | |
|---|---|
| Dimensions: | 70' W x 53' D |
| Heated Sq. Ft.: | 3,459 |
| Bedrooms: 4 | Bathrooms: 3 |
| Foundation: Trusjoist floor system or basement standard; slab available for a fee of $295 | |
| Exterior Walls: | 2" x 6" |
| PDF File: | $1,250 |
| 5-Sets: | $1,300 |
| CAD File: | $2,400 |

*Pricing subject to change*

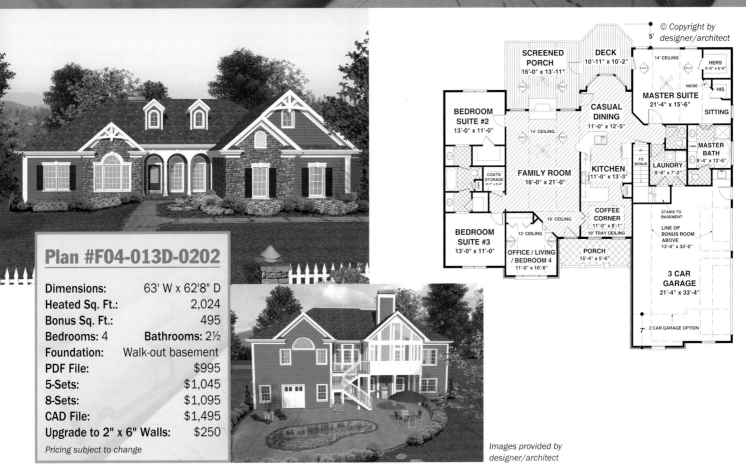

*Images provided by designer/architect*

## Plan #F04-013D-0202

| | |
|---|---|
| Dimensions: | 63' W x 62'8" D |
| Heated Sq. Ft.: | 2,024 |
| Bonus Sq. Ft.: | 495 |
| Bedrooms: 4 | Bathrooms: 2½ |
| Foundation: | Walk-out basement |
| PDF File: | $995 |
| 5-Sets: | $1,045 |
| 8-Sets: | $1,095 |
| CAD File: | $1,495 |
| Upgrade to 2" x 6" Walls: | $250 |

*Pricing subject to change*

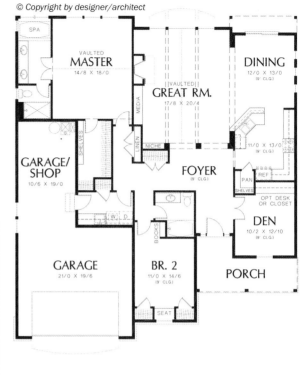

© Copyright by designer/architect

## Plan #F04-011D-0076

| | |
|---|---|
| Dimensions: | 52' W x 58' D |
| Heated Sq. Ft.: | 1,975 |
| Bedrooms: 2 | Bathrooms: 2 |
| Foundation: Joisted crawl space, post & beam, or TrusJoist floor system standard; slab for fee of $225 | |
| PDF File: | $900 |
| 5-Sets: | $950 |
| CAD File: | $1,800 |

*Pricing subject to change*

*Images provided by designer/architect*

*Images provided by designer/architect*

© Copyright by designer/architect

## Plan #F04-070D-0750

| | |
|---|---|
| Dimensions: | 61' W x 73'4" D |
| Heated Sq. Ft.: | 2,195 |
| Bedrooms: 3 | Bathrooms: 2½ |
| Foundation: | Basement |
| 1-Set: | $760 |
| PDF File: | $860 |
| 5-Sets: | $960 |
| 8-Sets: | $1,060 |

*Pricing subject to change*

© Copyright by designer/architect

Images provided by designer/architect

## Plan #F04-011D-0013

| | |
|---|---|
| **Dimensions:** | 60' W x 50' D |
| **Heated Sq. Ft.:** | 2,001 |
| **Bedrooms: 3** | **Bathrooms: 2** |

**Foundation:** Joisted crawl space, post & beam, or TrusJoist floor system standard; slab or basement for fee of $250

| | |
|---|---|
| **Exterior Walls:** | 2" x 6" |
| **PDF File:** | $1,000 |
| **5-Sets:** | $1,050 |
| **CAD File:** | $2,000 |

*Pricing subject to change*

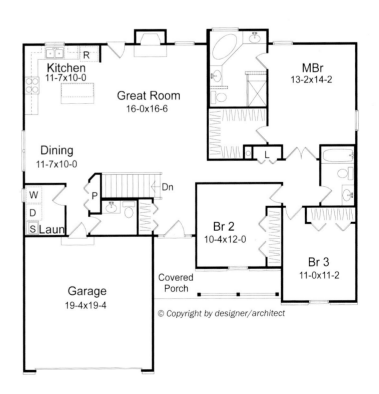

*Images provided by designer/architect*

© Copyright by designer/architect

## Plan #F04-058D-0172

| | |
|---|---|
| **Dimensions:** | 51' W x 50'4" D |
| **Heated Sq. Ft.:** | 1,635 |
| **Bedrooms: 3** | **Bathrooms: 2½** |

**Foundation:** Basement standard; slab for a fee of $250

| | |
|---|---|
| **5-Sets:** | $505 |
| **8-Sets:** | $575 |
| **PDF File:** | $575 |
| **CAD File:** | $675 |
| **Material List:** | $80 |

*Pricing subject to change*

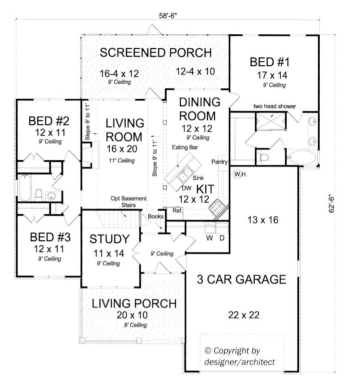

58'-6"

| SCREENED PORCH | | BED #1 |
|---|---|---|

**SCREENED PORCH**
16-4 x 12    12-4 x 10
9' Ceiling

**BED #1**
17 x 14
9' Ceiling

two head shower

**BED #2**
12 x 11
9' Ceiling

**LIVING ROOM**
16 x 20
11' Ceiling

**DINING ROOM**
12 x 12
9' Ceiling

Eating Bar

Pantry

Slope 9' to 11'

Slope 9' to 11'

Sink    W.H.

DW

**KIT**
12 x 12

Opt Basement Stairs

Ref.

Books

13 x 16

62'-6"

**BED #3**
12 x 11

**STUDY**
11 x 14
9' Ceiling

9' Ceiling

W   D

**LIVING PORCH**
20 x 10
9' Ceiling

**3 CAR GARAGE**
22 x 22

© Copyright by designer/architect

## Plan #F04-130D-0370

*Images provided by designer/architect*

| | |
|---|---|
| Dimensions: | 58'6" W x 62'6" D |
| Heated Sq. Ft.: | 1,788 |
| Bedrooms: 3 | Bathrooms: 2 |
| Foundation: | Slab standard; crawl space or basement for a fee of $150 |
| PDF File: | $885 |
| 5-Sets: | $1,010 |
| 8-Sets: | $1,085 |
| CAD File: | $1,135 |
| Upgrade to 2" x 6" Walls: | $150 |

*Pricing subject to change*

*Images provided by designer/architect*

**SCREENED PORCH**
15'4" x 13'10"
VLT

**DECK**
11'0" x 7'6"

14' CEILING

**SITTING**

**BEDROOM 3**
13'0" x 11'0"

**BRKFST**
11'0" x 10'10"

**MASTER SUITE**
21'4" x 15'0"

8' HIGH OPENING

DW

**FAMILY ROOM**
16'0" x 24'1"

VLT

**KITCHEN**
13'8" x 9'6"

PANTRY

13'-10" CEILING

LINEN

LINEN   COATS

10' CEILING

OPTIONAL STAIRS TO BASEMENT

**BEDROOM 2**
13'0" x 11'0"

VLT

13'-4" CEILING

**DINING**
11'0" x 12'0"

TRAY CEILING

9' CEILING

**3 CAR GARAGE**
21'4" x 29'10"

**LIVING**
11'0" x 12'0"

**PORCH**
15'4" x 5'4"

2 CAR GARAGE OPTION

© Copyright by designer/architect

## Plan #F04-013D-0159

| | |
|---|---|
| Dimensions: | 63' W x 57'2" D |
| Heated Sq. Ft.: | 1,992 |
| Bedrooms: 3 | Bathrooms: 2½ |
| Foundation: | Slab, basement or crawl space, please specify when ordering |
| PDF File: | $895 |
| 5-Sets: | $945 |
| 8-Sets: | $995 |
| CAD File: | $1,395 |
| Material List: | $125 |

*Pricing subject to change*

## Plan #F04-011D-0006

| | |
|---|---|
| Dimensions: | 70' W x 51' D |
| Heated Sq. Ft.: | 1,873 |
| Bedrooms: 3 | Bathrooms: 2 |

Foundation: Crawl space, post & beam, or TrusJoist floor system standard; slab or basement for a fee of $225

| | |
|---|---|
| Exterior Walls: | 2" x 6" |
| PDF File: | $900 |
| 5-Sets: | $950 |
| CAD File: | $1,800 |

*Pricing subject to change*

*Images provided by designer/architect*

© Copyright by designer/architect

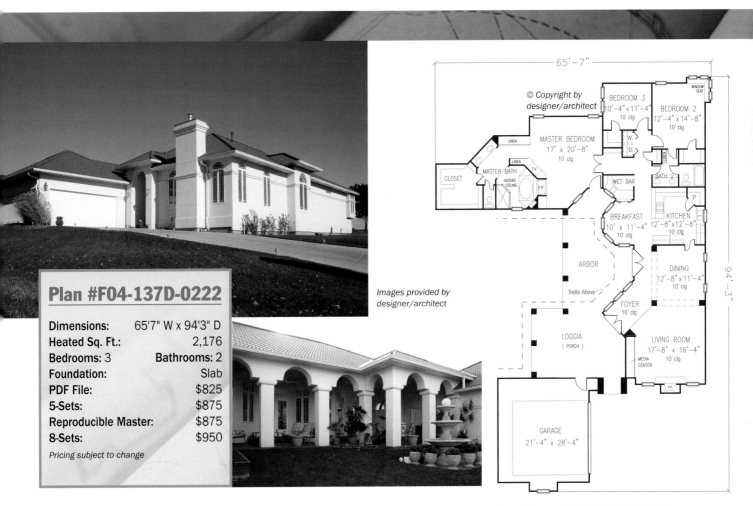

## Plan #F04-137D-0222

| | |
|---|---|
| Dimensions: | 65'7" W x 94'3" D |
| Heated Sq. Ft.: | 2,176 |
| Bedrooms: 3 | Bathrooms: 2 |
| Foundation: | Slab |
| PDF File: | $825 |
| 5-Sets: | $875 |
| Reproducible Master: | $875 |
| 8-Sets: | $950 |

*Pricing subject to change*

*Images provided by designer/architect*

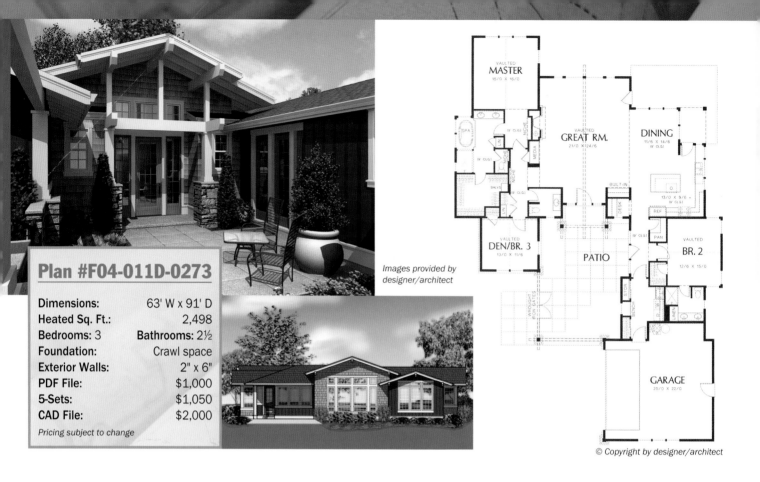

## Plan #F04-011D-0273

| | |
|---|---|
| Dimensions: | 63' W x 91' D |
| Heated Sq. Ft.: | 2,498 |
| Bedrooms: 3 | Bathrooms: 2½ |
| Foundation: | Crawl space |
| Exterior Walls: | 2" x 6" |
| PDF File: | $1,000 |
| 5-Sets: | $1,050 |
| CAD File: | $2,000 |

*Pricing subject to change*

Images provided by designer/architect

© Copyright by designer/architect

## Plan #F04-007D-0174

| | |
|---|---|
| Dimensions: | 82'4" W x 49'4" D |
| Heated Sq. Ft.: | 2,322 |
| Bedrooms: 4 | Bathrooms: 3 |

Foundation: Basement, slab or crawl space, please specify when ordering

| | |
|---|---|
| PDF File: | $900 |
| 5-Sets: | $950 |
| 8-Sets: | $1,025 |
| CAD File: | $1,800 |
| Material List: | $125 |

*Pricing subject to change*

Images provided by designer/architect

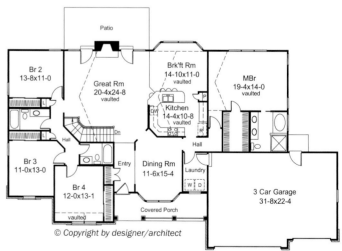

© Copyright by designer/architect

## Plan #F04-013D-0169

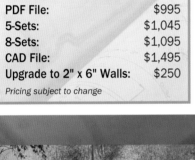

*Images provided by designer/architect*

| Dimensions: | 63' W x 65'8" D |
|---|---|
| Heated Sq. Ft.: | 2,000 |
| Bonus Sq. Ft.: | 503 |
| Bedrooms: 3 | Bathrooms: 3½ |
| Foundation: Slab standard; basement for a fee of $250 | |
| PDF File: | $995 |
| 5-Sets: | $1,045 |
| 8-Sets: | $1,095 |
| CAD File: | $1,495 |
| Upgrade to 2" x 6" Walls: | $250 |

*Pricing subject to change*

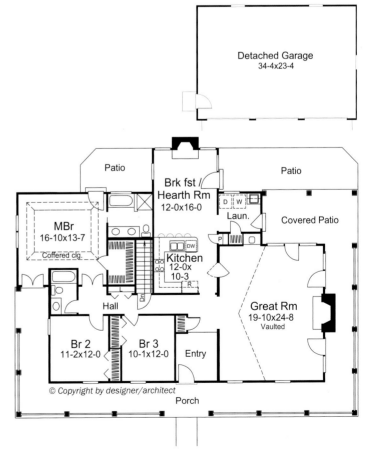

## Plan #F04-007D-0124

*Images provided by designer/architect*

| Dimensions: | 65' W x 51' D |
|---|---|
| Heated Sq. Ft.: | 1,944 |
| Bedrooms: 3 | Bathrooms: 2 |
| Foundation: | Basement |
| PDF File: | $900 |
| 5-Sets: | $950 |
| 8-Sets: | $1,025 |
| CAD File: | $1,800 |
| Material List: | $125 |
| Upgrade to 2" x 6" Walls: | $150 |

*Pricing subject to change*

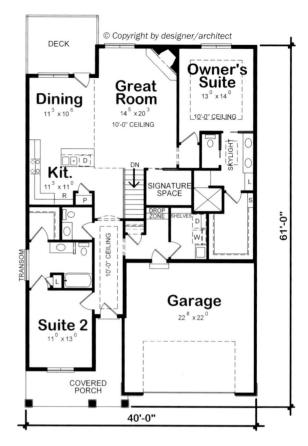

© Copyright by designer/architect

DECK

Dining
11³ x 10⁶

Great Room
14⁵ x 20³
10'-0" CEILING

Owner's Suite
13⁰ x 14⁰
10'-0" CEILING

Kit.
11³ x 11⁰

SKYLIGHT

SIGNATURE SPACE

DROP ZONE

SHELVES

DN

TRANSOM

10'-0" CEILING

Suite 2
11⁰ x 13⁰

Garage
22⁸ x 22⁰

COVERED PORCH

40'-0"

61'-0"

## Plan #F04-026D-1907

Images provided by designer/architect

| Dimensions: | 40' W x 61' D |
|---|---|
| Heated Sq. Ft.: | 1,676 |
| Bedrooms: 2 | Bathrooms: 2½ |

Foundation:
Basement standard; crawl space or slab for fee of $195

| Exterior Walls: | 2" x 6" |
|---|---|
| PDF File: | $845 |
| 5-Sets: | $995 |
| 8-Sets: | $1,040 |
| CAD File: | $1,345 |

*Pricing subject to change*

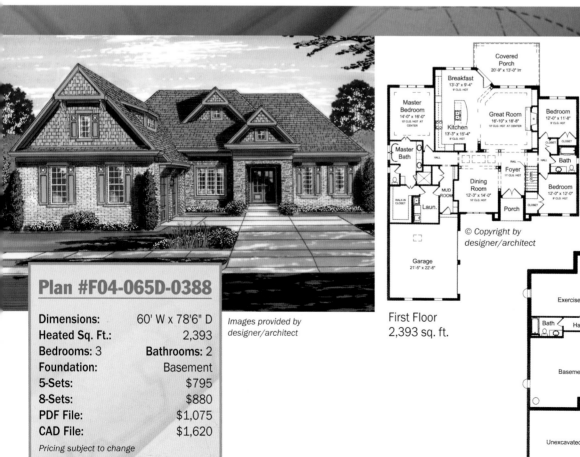

Covered Porch
20'-9" x 13'-0" Irr

Breakfast
13'-3" x 9'-4"
9' CLG. HGT

Master Bedroom
14'-0" x 16'-0"
9' CLG. HGT AT CENTER

Kitchen
13'-3" x 15'-4"
9' CLG. HGT

Great Room
16'-10" x 18'-8"
12' CLG. HGT AT CENTER

Bedroom
12'-0" x 11'-8"
9' CLG. HGT

Master Bath

Dining Room
12'-3" x 14'-0"
10' CLG. HGT

Foyer
11' CLG. HGT

Bedroom
12'-0" x 12'-0"
9' CLG. HGT

WALK-IN CLOSET

MUD ROOM

Laun.

Porch

Bath

Garage
21'-5" x 22'-8"

© Copyright by designer/architect

First Floor
2,393 sq. ft.

Unexcavated

Exercise

Media Area

Billiards

Bath

Hall

Rec. Room

Basement

Unex.

Unexcavated

Optional Lower Level
1,477 sq. ft.

## Plan #F04-065D-0388

Images provided by designer/architect

| Dimensions: | 60' W x 78'6" D |
|---|---|
| Heated Sq. Ft.: | 2,393 |
| Bedrooms: 3 | Bathrooms: 2 |
| Foundation: | Basement |
| 5-Sets: | $795 |
| 8-Sets: | $880 |
| PDF File: | $1,075 |
| CAD File: | $1,620 |

*Pricing subject to change*

## Plan #F04-155D-0041

| | |
|---|---|
| Dimensions: | 54' W x 49'4" D |
| Heated Sq. Ft.: | 1,800 |
| Bedrooms: 3 | Bathrooms: 2 |

Foundation: Crawl space or slab, please specify when ordering

| | |
|---|---|
| 5-Sets: | $730 |
| 8-Sets: | $870 |
| PDF File: | $1,340 |
| CAD File: | $2,065 |
| Upgrade to 2" x 6" Walls: | $250 |

*Pricing subject to change*

*Images provided by designer/architect*

## Plan #F04-007D-0110

*Images provided by designer/architect*

| | |
|---|---|
| Dimensions: | 37'4" W x 46'8" D |
| Heated Sq. Ft.: | 1,169 |
| Bedrooms: 3 | Bathrooms: 2 |
| Foundation: | Basement |
| PDF File: | $750 |
| 5-Sets: | $800 |
| Reproducible Master: | $800 |
| 8-Sets: | $875 |
| Material List: | $125 |

*Pricing subject to change*

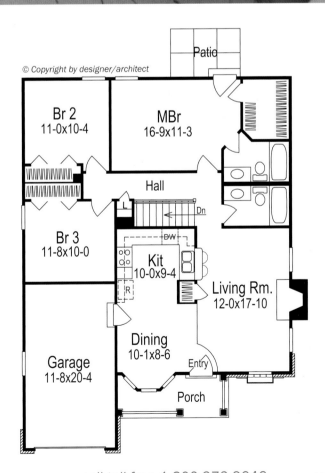

## Plan #F04-007D-0120

| | |
|---|---|
| Dimensions: | 63'8" W x 55'4" D |
| Heated Sq. Ft.: | 1,914 |
| Bedrooms: 4 | Bathrooms: 3 |
| Foundation: | Basement |
| PDF File: | $825 |
| 5-Sets: | $875 |
| Reproducible Master: | $875 |
| 8-Sets: | $950 |
| Material List: | $125 |

*Pricing subject to change*

*Images provided by designer/architect*

© Copyright by designer/architect

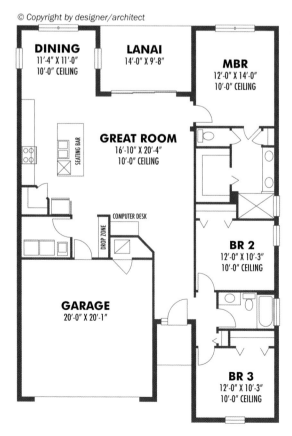

## Plan #F04-116D-0029

| | |
|---|---|
| Dimensions: | 40' W x 58' D |
| Heated Sq. Ft.: | 1,584 |
| Bedrooms: 3 | Bathrooms: 2 |
| Foundation: | Slab |
| Exterior Walls: | Concrete Block |
| 5-Sets: | $980 |
| 8-Sets: | $1,070 |
| PDF File: | $1,200 |
| CAD File: | $2,030 |

*Pricing subject to change*

*Images provided by designer/architect*

© Copyright by designer/architect

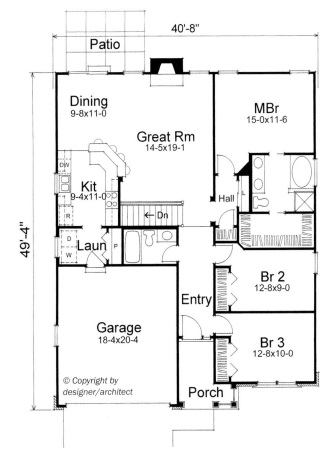

## Plan #F04-147D-0001

| | |
|---|---|
| Dimensions: | 40'8" W x 49'4" D |
| Heated Sq. Ft.: | 1,472 |
| Bedrooms: 3 | Bathrooms: 2 |

Foundation: Basement, slab or crawl space, please specify when ordering

| | |
|---|---|
| PDF File: | $675 |
| 5-Sets: | $725 |
| Reproducible Master: | $725 |
| 8-Sets: | $800 |

*Pricing subject to change*

*Images provided by designer/architect*

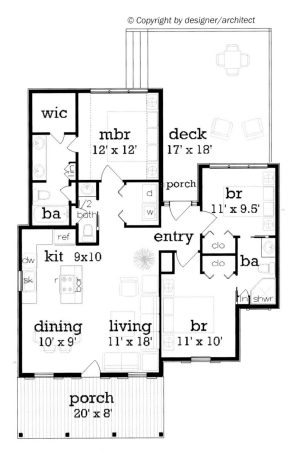

## Plan #F04-020D-0351

*Images provided by designer/architect*

| | |
|---|---|
| Dimensions: | 36' W x 46' D |
| Heated Sq. Ft.: | 1,086 |
| Bedrooms: 3 | Bathrooms: 2½ |

Foundation: Crawl space standard; slab for a fee of $100

| | |
|---|---|
| Exterior Walls: | 2" x 6" |
| PDF File: | $750 |
| 5-Sets: | $795 |
| 8-Sets: | $840 |
| CAD File: | $1,508 |

*Pricing subject to change*

## Plan #F04-076D-0238

| | |
|---|---|
| Dimensions: | 91'5" W x 79' D |
| Heated Sq. Ft.: | 2,925 |
| Bedrooms: 4 | Bathrooms: 3½ |
| Foundation: Slab or crawl space, please specify when ordering | |
| 5-Sets: | $875 |
| 8-Sets: | $1,125 |
| PDF File: | $1,325 |
| CAD File: | $1,650 |

*Pricing subject to change*

### Features

- The front porch features an arched opening with vaulted ceiling above
- On either side of the vaulted foyer is a dining room and a study/bedroom with private dressing area and shared bath
- The open kitchen contains ample counter space with an island sink and bar top
- The rear of this home allows for plenty of exterior views from both the wall of windows in the family and breakfast rooms
- The master suite is graced by a luxurious bath and a walk-in closet
- The utility room comes complete with cabinets, a sink, direct access to the master bedroom walk-in closet and also the garage entrance that includes a bench, a closet and a drop zone
- 2-car side entry garage

*Images provided by designer/architect*

© Copyright by designer/architect

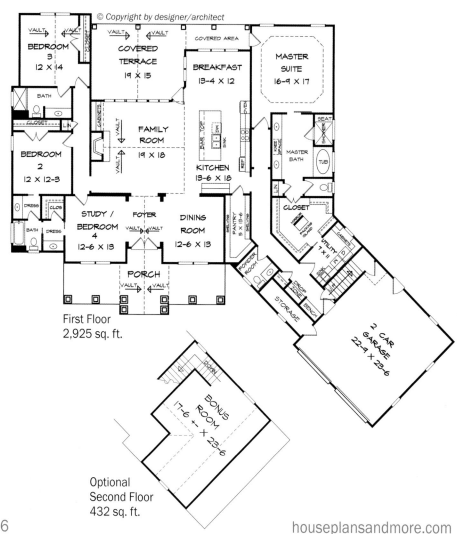

First Floor
2,925 sq. ft.

Optional
Second Floor
432 sq. ft.

## Plan #F04-055D-0193

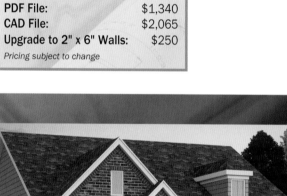

Dimensions: 63'10" W x 72'2" D
Heated Sq. Ft.: 2,131
Bedrooms: 3    Bathrooms: 2½
Foundation: Slab or crawl space, standard; basement for a fee of $250

| | |
|---|---|
| 5-Sets: | $730 |
| 8-Sets: | $870 |
| PDF File: | $1,340 |
| CAD File: | $2,065 |
| Upgrade to 2" x 6" Walls: | $250 |

*Pricing subject to change*

*Images provided by designer/architect*

## Plan #F04-026D-1937

Dimensions: 40' W x 62' D
Heated Sq. Ft.: 1,742
Bedrooms: 2    Bathrooms: 2
Foundation: Basement standard; crawl space or slab for a fee of $195

| | |
|---|---|
| Exterior Walls: | 2" x 6" |
| PDF File: | $795 |
| 5-Sets: | $905 |
| 8-Sets: | $1,085 |
| CAD File: | $1,295 |
| Upgrade to 2" x 6" Walls: | $195 |

*Pricing subject to change*

*Images provided by designer/architect*

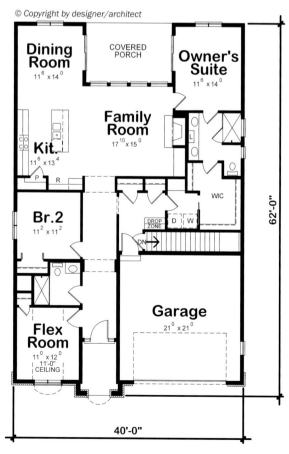

houseplansandmore.com

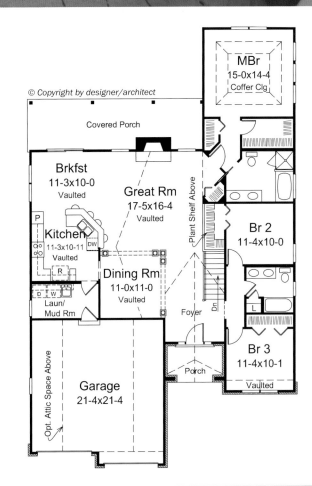

© Copyright by designer/architect

## Plan #F04-121D-0035

| | |
|---|---|
| Dimensions: | 45'8" W x 72'4" D |
| Heated Sq. Ft.: | 1,759 |
| Bedrooms: 3 | Bathrooms: 2 |
| Foundation: | Basement |
| PDF File: | $750 |
| 5-Sets: | $800 |
| 8-Sets: | $875 |
| CAD File: | $1,550 |
| Material List | $125 |

*Pricing subject to change*

*Images provided by designer/architect*

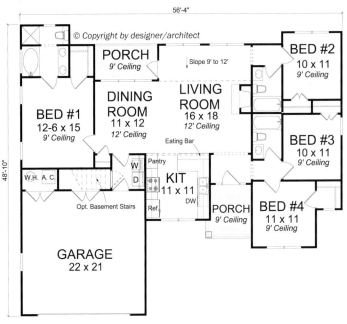

© Copyright by designer/architect

## Plan #F04-130D-0364

| | |
|---|---|
| Dimensions: | 56'4" W x 48'10" D |
| Heated Sq. Ft.: | 1,488 |
| Bedrooms: 4 | Bathrooms: 3 |

Foundation: Slab standard; basement or crawl space for a fee of $150

| | |
|---|---|
| PDF File: | $865 |
| 5-Sets: | $990 |
| 8-Sets: | $1,065 |
| CAD File: | $1,115 |
| Upgrade to 2" x 6" Walls: | $150 |

*Pricing subject to change*

*Images provided by designer/architect*

**Bonus Room**
12-2 x 22-4
8-0 CLG. HT.

**Optional Second Floor**
316 sq. ft.

**First Floor**
1,888 sq. ft.

**Two Car Garage**
21-6 x 22-4

**Covered Porch**
20-0 x 8-0

WH | Stor.

Storage

Half Bath

**Bedroom 3**
12-6 x 11-0
(Clear)
9-0 CLG. HT.

**Eating**
10-0 x 14-6
9-0 CLG. HT.

**Kitchen**
9-4 x 14-6

Eating Bar Island

**Flex Space**
11-0 x 11-6
9-0 CLG. HT.

Clos.

L

Hall

C

C

**Bath 2**

Tub/Shower

Hall

W | D

**Utility**
7-8 x 6-8

**Closet**
9-6 x 6-2

L

**Great Room**
17-6 x 18-6
(Clear)
10-0 CLG. HT.

Gas Logs

**Master Bedroom**
11-8 x 14-6
10-0 CLG. HT.

**Mstr. Bath**
9-6 x 15-0

Jet Tub

**Bedroom 2**
12-6 x 11-0
9-0 CLG. HT.

C

9-0 CLG. HT.

L

Shwr

**Covered Porch**
31-0 x 6-0

© Copyright by designer/architect

## Plan #F04-077D-0122

| | |
|---|---|
| Dimensions: | 55' W x 70' D |
| Heated Sq. Ft.: | 1,888 |
| Bedrooms: 3 | Bathrooms: 2½ |

Foundation: Slab or crawl space standard; basement for a fee of $250

| | |
|---|---|
| 5-Sets: | $1,015 |
| PDF File: | $1,125 |
| Reproducible Master: | $1,200 |
| CAD File: | $1,680 |
| Material List: | $130 |

*Pricing subject to change*

*Images provided by designer/architect*

## Plan #F04-130D-0362

| | |
|---|---|
| Dimensions: | 16' W x 24'8" D |
| Heated Sq. Ft.: | 395 |
| Bedrooms: 1 | Bathrooms: 1 |

Foundation: Slab standard; crawl space or basement for a fee of $150

| | |
|---|---|
| PDF File: | $825 |
| 5-Sets: | $1,050 |
| 8-Sets: | $1,125 |
| CAD File: | $1,150 |
| Upgrade to 2" x 6" Walls: | $150 |

*Pricing subject to change*

*Images provided by designer/architect*

16'-0"

© Copyright by designer/architect

French

**BED #1**
10 x 12
*8' Ceiling*

To A/C Above

24'-8"

Stack W/D

Ref.

**LIVING ROOM**
15-4 x 12

Slope

Slope

Sink

DW

Covered Stoop

## Plan #F04-055D-0199

| | |
|---|---|
| Dimensions: | 73'6" W x 80'6" D |
| Heated Sq. Ft.: | 2,951 |
| Bedrooms: 4 | Bathrooms: 3 |

Foundation: Slab or crawl space standard; basement or walk-out basement for a fee of $250

| | |
|---|---|
| 5-Sets: | $830 |
| 8-Sets: | $1,020 |
| PDF File: | $1,560 |
| CAD File: | $2,400 |

*Pricing subject to change*

*Images provided by designer/architect*

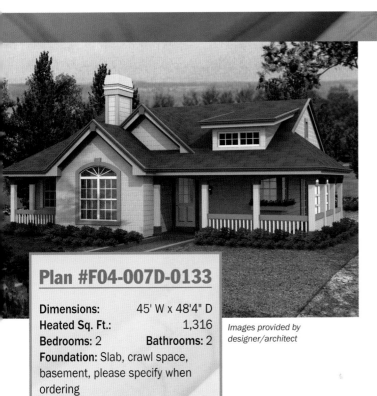

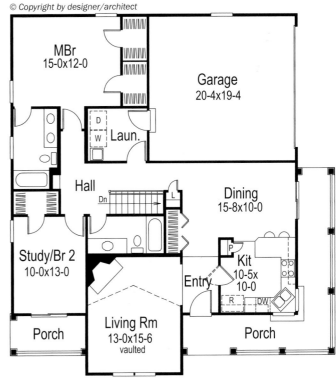

## Plan #F04-007D-0133

| | |
|---|---|
| Dimensions: | 45' W x 48'4" D |
| Heated Sq. Ft.: | 1,316 |
| Bedrooms: 2 | Bathrooms: 2 |

Foundation: Slab, crawl space, basement, please specify when ordering

| | |
|---|---|
| PDF File: | $750 |
| 5-Sets: | $800 |
| Reproducible Master: | $800 |
| 8-Sets: | $875 |
| Material List: | $125 |

*Pricing subject to change*

*Images provided by designer/architect*

## Plan #F04-101D-0047

| | |
|---|---|
| **Dimensions:** | 99' W x 81' D |
| **Heated Sq. Ft.:** | 2,478 |
| **Bedrooms:** 2 | **Bathrooms:** 2½ |
| **Foundation:** | Walk-out basement |
| **Exterior Walls:** | 2" x 6" |
| **5-Sets:** | $950 |
| **PDF File:** | $1,250 |
| **CAD File:** | $1,800 |

*Pricing subject to change*

*Images provided by designer/architect*

## Features

- The architectural style of this home has interesting features and great curb appeal

- The master bedroom features double walk-in closets, separate tub and shower and double bowl vanity

- Open living at its finest with the combination of great room, kitchen and dining for a relaxed casual atmosphere

- Directly off the foyer is a study that is private and could easily be converted to a home office

- The optional lower level features a craft area, sitting area, family room, and two additional bedrooms and a bath

- Oversized 5-car front entry tandem garage, 2-car side entry garage

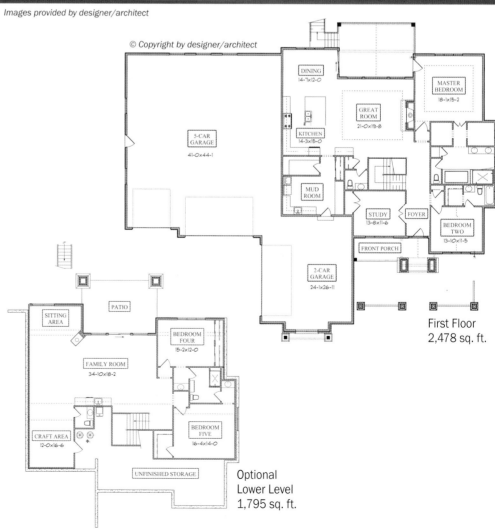

© Copyright by designer/architect

First Floor
2,478 sq. ft.

Optional
Lower Level
1,795 sq. ft.

Images provided by designer/architect

## Plan #F04-130D-0333

| | |
|---|---|
| Dimensions: | 65'6" W x 61' D |
| Heated Sq. Ft.: | 2,265 |
| Bedrooms: 4 | Bathrooms: 2½ |

Foundation: Slab standard; crawl space or basement for a fee of $150

| | |
|---|---|
| PDF File: | $955 |
| 5-Sets: | $1,180 |
| 8-Sets: | $1,255 |
| CAD File: | $1,205 |
| Upgrade to 2" x 6" Walls: | $150 |

*Pricing subject to change*

© Copyright by designer/architect

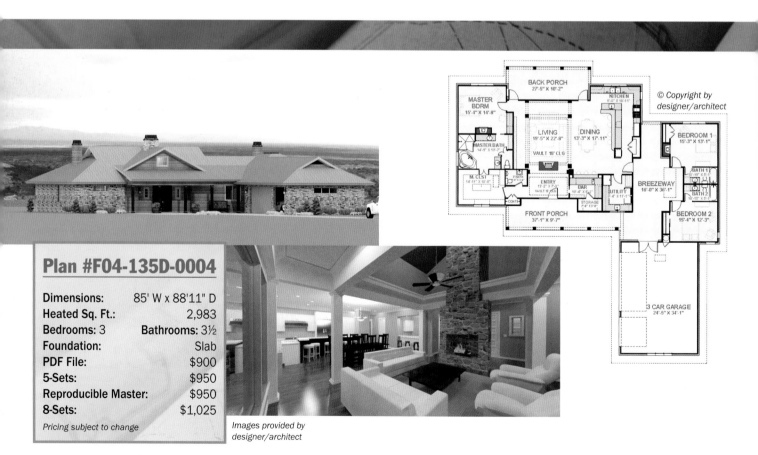

## Plan #F04-135D-0004

| | |
|---|---|
| Dimensions: | 85' W x 88'11" D |
| Heated Sq. Ft.: | 2,983 |
| Bedrooms: 3 | Bathrooms: 3½ |
| Foundation: | Slab |
| PDF File: | $900 |
| 5-Sets: | $950 |
| Reproducible Master: | $950 |
| 8-Sets: | $1,025 |

*Pricing subject to change*

Images provided by designer/architect

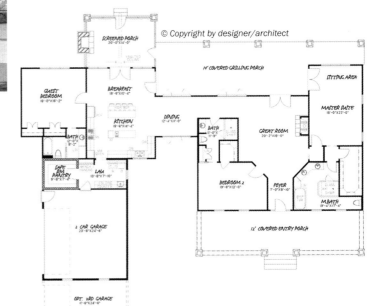

*Images provided by designer/architect*

© Copyright by designer/architect

## Plan #F04-155D-0004

Dimensions: 97'10" W x 72'10" D
Heated Sq. Ft.: 2,921
Bedrooms: 3      Bathrooms: 3
Foundation: Slab or crawl space, please specify when ordering

| | |
|---|---|
| 5-Sets: | $880 |
| 8-Sets: | $1,095 |
| PDF File: | $1,685 |
| CAD File: | $2,595 |

*Pricing subject to change*

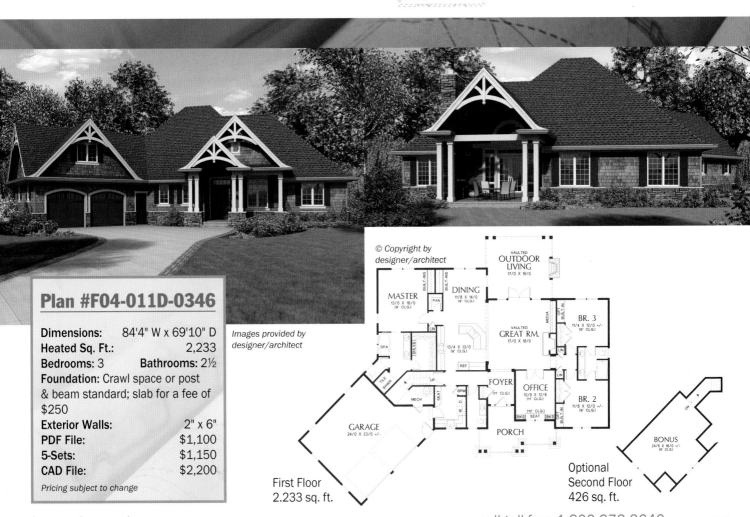

© Copyright by designer/architect

## Plan #F04-011D-0346

Dimensions: 84'4" W x 69'10" D
Heated Sq. Ft.: 2,233
Bedrooms: 3      Bathrooms: 2½
Foundation: Crawl space or post & beam standard; slab for a fee of $250
Exterior Walls: 2" x 6"

| | |
|---|---|
| PDF File: | $1,100 |
| 5-Sets: | $1,150 |
| CAD File: | $2,200 |

*Pricing subject to change*

*Images provided by designer/architect*

First Floor
2,233 sq. ft.

Optional
Second Floor
426 sq. ft.

## Plan #F04-121D-0010

| Dimensions: | 37'6" W x 52' D |
|---|---|
| Heated Sq. Ft.: | 1,281 |
| Bedrooms: 3 | Bathrooms: 2 |
| Foundation: | Basement |
| PDF File: | $750 |
| 5-Sets: | $800 |
| 8-Sets: | $875 |
| CAD File: | $1,550 |
| Material List: | $125 |

*Pricing subject to change*

*Images provided by designer/architect*

### Features

- The functional vaulted kitchen is close to the garage for easy unloading of groceries and features an angled raised counter perfect for a casual dining option

- The vaulted great room and dining area combine, maximizing the interior for an open, airy feel

- The vaulted master bedroom enjoys a sizable walk-in closet and its own private bath with a large double-bowl vanity

- 2 car front entry garage

© Copyright by designer/architect

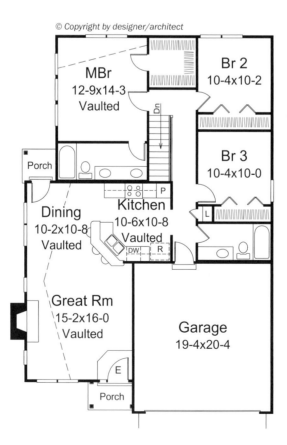

houseplansandmore.com

## Plan #F04-101D-0060

Images provided by designer/architect

| | |
|---|---|
| **Dimensions:** | 129'6" W x 109'4" D |
| **Heated Sq. Ft.:** | 4,774 |
| **Bedrooms:** 2 | **Bathrooms:** 3½ |
| **Foundation:** | Walk-out basement |
| **Exterior Walls:** | 2" x 6" |
| **5-Sets:** | $2,100 |
| **PDF File:** | $2,950 |
| **CAD File:** | $3,550 |

*Pricing subject to change*

## Features

- An amazing home with turrets and castle-like features
- A grand receiving area opens to the formal dining room and the staircase to the lower level
- The great room, kitchen and casual dining area combine for family living at its best
- 6-car front entry tandem garage

First Floor
4,774 sq. ft.

© Copyright by designer/architect

Optional
Lower Level
4,137 sq. ft.

## Plan #F04-007D-0117

| | |
|---|---|
| Dimensions: | 76'8" W x 57'6" D |
| Heated Sq. Ft.: | 2,695 |
| Bedrooms: 3 | Bathrooms: 2½ |
| Foundation: | Basement |
| PDF File: | $975 |
| 5-Sets: | $1,025 |
| 8-Sets: | $1,100 |
| CAD File: | $1,875 |
| Material List: | $125 |
| Upgrade to 2" x 6" Walls: | $150 |

*Pricing subject to change*

*Images provided by designer/architect*

## Plan #F04-026D-1910

| | |
|---|---|
| Dimensions: | 52' W x 50' D |
| Heated Sq. Ft.: | 1,719 |
| Bedrooms: 3 | Bathrooms: 2 |

Foundation: Slab standard;
basement or crawl space for a fee
of $195; walk-out basement for a
fee of $390

| | |
|---|---|
| PDF File: | $855 |
| 5-Sets: | $930 |
| 8-Sets: | $1,050 |
| CAD File: | $1,355 |
| Upgrade to 2" x 6" Walls: | $195 |

*Pricing subject to change*

*Images provided by designer/architect*

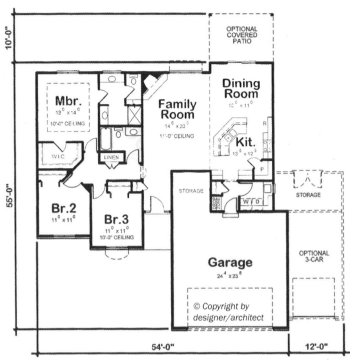

## Plan #F04-026D-1875

| | |
|---|---|
| Dimensions: | 54' W x 55' D |
| Heated Sq. Ft.: | 1,568 |
| Bedrooms: 3 | Bathrooms: 2 |

Foundation: Slab standard; basement or crawl space for a fee of $195; walk-out basement for a fee of $390

| | |
|---|---|
| PDF File: | $835 |
| 5-Sets: | $910 |
| 8-Sets: | $1,030 |
| CAD File: | $1,335 |
| Upgrade to 2" x 6" Walls: | $195 |

*Pricing subject to change*

*Images provided by designer/architect*

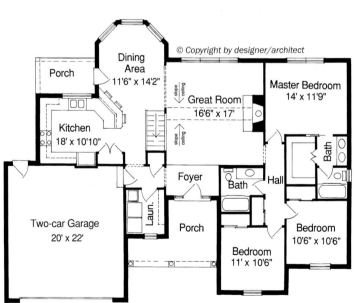

## Plan #F04-065D-0010

| | |
|---|---|
| Dimensions: | 60' W x 47' D |
| Heated Sq. Ft.: | 1,508 |
| Bedrooms: 3 | Bathrooms: 2 |

Foundation: Basement or crawl space, please specify when ordering

| | |
|---|---|
| 5-Sets: | $695 |
| 8-Sets: | $799 |
| PDF File: | $945 |
| Reproducible Master: | $945 |
| Material List: | $75 |

*Pricing subject to change*

*Images provided by designer/architect*

## Plan #F04-065D-0103

**Dimensions:** 64'-2" W x 44'2" D
**Heated Sq. Ft.:** 1,860
**Bedrooms:** 3    **Bathrooms:** 2
**Foundation:** Basement or walk-out basement, please specify when ordering

| | |
|---|---|
| **5-Sets:** | $695 |
| **8-Sets:** | $799 |
| **PDF File:** | $945 |
| **Reproducible Master:** | $945 |
| **Material List:** | $75 |

*Pricing subject to change*

*Images provided by designer/architect*

## Features

- This stunning ranch home with Country French accents features trendy stonework as well as striking shingled siding
- An open and airy feel has been achieved by blending the great room into the breakfast area and allowing only a decorative column to designate the formal dining room from the foyer and great room
- Cozy up to the fireplace and watch your favorite television show from the built-in TV alcove in the great room
- Unbelievable woodwork has been used to create the remarkable decorative ceiling in the formal dining room
- 2-car front entry garage

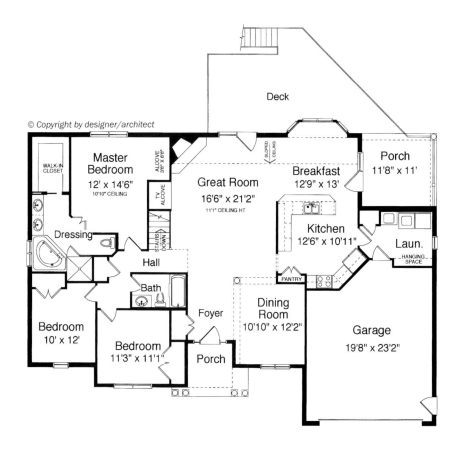

© Copyright by designer/architect

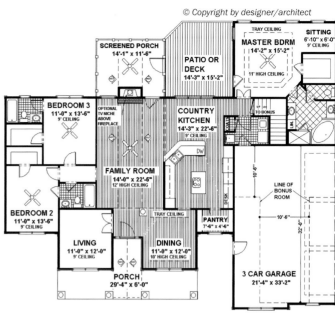

© Copyright by designer/architect

**SCREENED PORCH** 14'-1" x 11'-6"

**PATIO OR DECK** 14'-3" x 15'-2"

TRAY CEILING

**MASTER BDRM** 14'-2" x 15'-2"

**SITTING** 6'-10" x 6'-0" 9' CEILING

11' HIGH CEILING

**BEDROOM 3** 11'-0" x 13'-6" 9' CEILING

OPTIONAL TV NICHE ABOVE FIREPLACE

**COUNTRY KITCHEN** 14'-3" x 22'-6" 9' CEILING

TO BONUS

LINEN

**FAMILY ROOM** 14'-0" x 22'-6" 12' HIGH CEILING

DW

DESK

**BEDROOM 2** 11'-0" x 13'-6" 9' CEILING

TRAY CEILING

**PANTRY** 7'-6" x 4'-6"

LINE OF BONUS ROOM

10'-6"

10'-6"

32'-0"

**LIVING** 11'-0" x 12'-0" 9' CEILING

**DINING** 11'-0" x 12'-0" 10' HIGH CEILING

**3 CAR GARAGE** 21'-4" x 33'-2"

**PORCH** 29'-4" x 6'-0"

## Plan #F04-013D-0025

| | |
|---|---|
| Dimensions: | 70'2" W x 59' D |
| Heated Sq. Ft.: | 2,097 |
| Bonus Sq. Ft.: | 452 |
| Bedrooms: 3 | Bathrooms: 3 |
| Foundation: Basement, crawl space or slab, please specify when ordering | |
| PDF File: | $995 |
| 5-Sets: | $1,045 |
| 8-Sets: | $1,095 |
| CAD File: | $1,495 |
| Material List: | $125 |
| *Pricing subject to change* | |

*Images provided by designer/architect*

*Images provided by designer/architect*

## Plan #F04-020D-0357

| | |
|---|---|
| Dimensions: | 54' W x 48' D |
| Heated Sq. Ft.: | 1,565 |
| Bedrooms: 3 | Bathrooms: 2 |
| Foundation: Crawl space standard; basement for a fee of $100 | |
| Exterior Walls: | 2" x 6" |
| PDF File: | $850 |
| 5-Sets: | $875 |
| 8-Sets: | $920 |
| CAD File: | $1,638 |
| *Pricing subject to change* | |

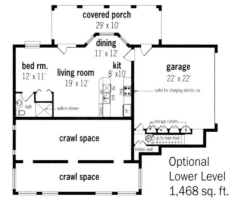

**covered porch** 29' x 10'

**dining** 11' x 12'

**bed rm.** 12' x 11'

**living room** 19' x 12'

**kit** 8' x 10'

**garage** 22' x 22'

outlet for charging electric car

walk-in shower

storage closets

**crawl space**

**crawl space**

hidden vault

up to main level

Optional Lower Level 1,468 sq. ft.

**porch** 29' x 10'

© Copyright by designer/architect

**eating**

wrap-a-round bar

**bedroom** 11' x 10' 9' ceilings

**living** 18' x 15' 11' tray ceilings

**master suite** 15' x 15'

vaulted ceilings with half circle window transom at end of gable roof

sloped ceilings

books

book shelves below counter

5'X3' clo

**bedroom** 14' x 11' 9' ceilings

**foyer** 12' x 5' 11' ceilings

**dining** 12' x 12' 11' ceilings

**util** 9' x 7'

wic 10' x 6' 24' of hanging space

bath 10' x 8' 9'-clg

above toilet

**porch** 34' x 8' 9' ceilings

First Floor 1,565 sq. ft.

© Copyright by designer/architect

## Plan #F04-011D-0286

Images provided by designer/architect

| | |
|---|---|
| Dimensions: | 50' W x 59' D |
| Heated Sq. Ft.: | 1,800 |
| Bedrooms: 3 | Bathrooms: 3 |

Foundation: Joisted crawl space, post & beam, joisted continuous footing or TrusJoist floor system standard; slab for a fee of $225

| | |
|---|---|
| Exterior Walls: | 2" x 6" |
| PDF File: | $900 |
| 5-Sets: | $950 |
| CAD File: | $1,800 |

*Pricing subject to change*

## Plan #F04-070D-0747

Images provided by designer/architect

| | |
|---|---|
| Dimensions: | 56'4" W x 56'8" D |
| Heated Sq. Ft.: | 1,903 |
| Bedrooms: 3 | Bathrooms: 2½ |
| Foundation: | Basement |
| PDF File: | $800 |
| 5-Sets: | $900 |
| 8-Sets: | $1,000 |

*Pricing subject to change*

© Copyright by designer/architect

© Copyright by designer/architect

*Images provided by designer/architect*

## Plan #F04-065D-0188

| | |
|---|---|
| Dimensions: | 51'8" W x 47' D |
| Heated Sq. Ft.: | 1,488 |
| Bedrooms: 3 | Bathrooms: 2 |
| Foundation: | Basement |
| 5-Sets: | $695 |
| 8-Sets: | $799 |
| PDF File: | $945 |
| Reproducible Master: | $945 |
| Material List: | $75 |

*Pricing subject to change*

Floor plan labels: Deck, Bath, Master Bedroom 12'-0" x 17'-0", Laun., Bedroom 11'-4" x 12'-0", Dining 12'-3" x 13'-11", Kitchen 9'-2" x 13'-11" 8'-1" CEIL. HGT. (TYP.), WALK-IN CLOSET, Bath, Great Room 18'-0" x 15'-4", Den/Bedroom 10'-0" x 11'-9", Foyer, Garage 20'-0" x 20'-10", Porch

---

© Copyright by designer/architect

*Images provided by designer/architect*

## Plan #F04-155D-0003

| | |
|---|---|
| Dimensions: | 82'10" W x 76'11" D |
| Heated Sq. Ft.: | 2,647 |
| Bedrooms: 4 | Bathrooms: 2½ |
| Foundation: | Slab or crawl space standard; basement or walk-out basement for a fee of $250 |
| 5-Sets: | $1,100 |
| 8-Sets: | $1,200 |
| PDF File: | $1,850 |
| CAD File: | $2,845 |

*Pricing subject to change*

First Floor
2,647 sq. ft.

Optional
Second Floor
514 sq. ft.

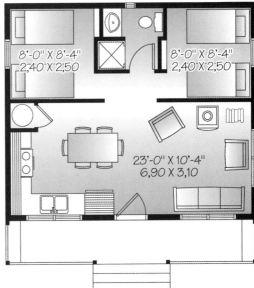

© Copyright by designer/architect

8'-0" X 8'-4"
2,40 X 2,50

8'-0" X 8'-4"
2,40 X 2,50

23'-0" X 10'-4"
6,90 X 3,10

## Plan #F04-032D-0709

*Images provided by designer/architect*

| | |
|---|---|
| Dimensions: | 24' W x 20' D |
| Heated Sq. Ft.: | 480 |
| Bedrooms: 2 | Bathrooms: 1 |
| Foundation: | Pier |
| Exterior Walls: | 2" x 6" |
| 5-Sets: | $595 |
| 8-Sets: | $625 |
| PDF File: | $730 |
| CAD File: | $1,300 |
| Material List: | $100 |

*Pricing subject to change*

© Copyright by designer/architect

OUTDOOR LIVING
18/0 X 14/0
(11' CLG.)

MASTER
13/0 X 17/0
(9' CLG.)

DINING
12/6 X 13/0
(11' CLG.)

LIVING
17/0 X 18/0
(11' CLG.)

SPA

PAN

13/8 X 10/8
(11' CLG.)

FLEX RM
16/0 X 11/6
(9' CLG.)

BENCH

W D

REF

FOYER
(9' CLG.)

LINEN

BR. 3
12/0 X 11/6
(9' CLG.)

GARAGE
19/0 X 21/0

BR. 2
10/6 X 14/0
(9' CLG.)

## Plan #F04-011D-0348

*Images provided by designer/architect*

| | |
|---|---|
| Dimensions: | 50' W x 73' D |
| Heated Sq. Ft.: | 2,175 |
| Bedrooms: 4 | Bathrooms: 2½ |
| Foundation: | Crawl space or post & beam standard; slab for a fee of $250 |
| Exterior Walls: | 2" x 6" |
| PDF File: | $1,000 |
| 5-Sets: | $1,050 |
| CAD File: | $2,000 |

*Pricing subject to change*

## Plan #F04-101D-0057

| | |
|---|---|
| Dimensions: | 58' W x 90' D |
| Heated Sq. Ft.: | 2,037 |
| Bedrooms: 1 | Bathrooms: 1½ |
| Foundation: | Walk-out basement |
| Exterior Walls: | 2" x 6" |
| 5-Sets: | $850 |
| PDF File: | $1,150 |
| CAD File: | $1,650 |

*Pricing subject to change*

## Features

- Enjoy the outdoors on both levels of this home with upper and lower covered patios and decks
- The front porch opens to an entry hall with formal dining and a staircase to the lower level nearby
- The large U-shaped kitchen features space for casual dining as well as a wet bar for entertaining
- The master bedroom is in a wing to itself and features a stepped ceiling, a luxurious bath, and a large walk-in closet
- The lower level offers two additional bedrooms with baths, an office, an open recreation space as well as a safe room and unfinished storage
- 3-car side entry garage

*Images provided by designer/architect*

First Floor
2,037 sq. ft.

© Copyright by designer/architect

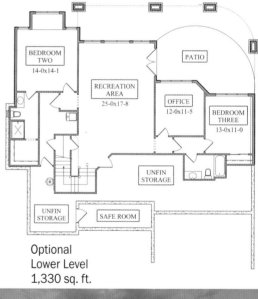

Optional
Lower Level
1,330 sq. ft.

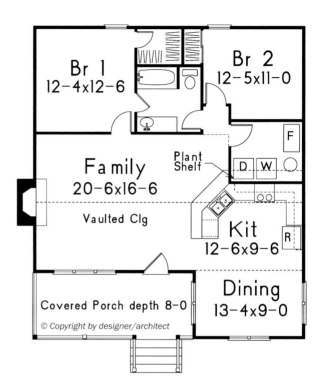

## Plan #F04-058D-0012

| | |
|---|---|
| Dimensions: | 36' W x 38' D |
| Heated Sq. Ft.: | 1,143 |
| Bedrooms: 2 | Bathrooms: 1 |
| Foundation: | Crawl space |
| 5-Sets: | $480 |
| PDF File: | $500 |
| 8-Sets: | $550 |
| CAD File: | $625 |
| Material List: | $70 |
| Upgrade to 2" x 6" Walls: | $75 |

*Pricing subject to change*

*Images provided by designer/architect*

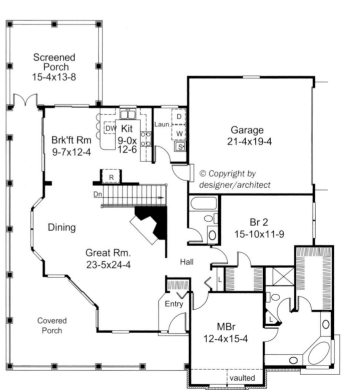

## Plan #F04-007D-0172

| | |
|---|---|
| Dimensions: | 56'4" W x 61'4" D |
| Heated Sq. Ft.: | 1,646 |
| Bedrooms: 2 | Bathrooms: 2 |
| Foundation: Basement, slab or crawl space, please specify when ordering | |
| PDF File: | $825 |
| 5-Sets: | $875 |
| 8-Sets: | $950 |
| CAD File: | $1,725 |
| Material List: | $125 |

*Pricing subject to change*

*Images provided by designer/architect*

Garage
23-4x23-4

© Copyright by designer/architect

Patio

© Copyright by designer/architect

MBr
14-1x12-10
Coffer
Opt Vault

Kit
8-2x
12-6

Dining
11-9x12-6
Vaulted

Great Rm
20-3x15-0
Vaulted

Br 2
11-6x10-4

Br 3
10-2x10-4

Porch

## Plan #F04-121D-0025

| | |
|---|---|
| Dimensions: | 50' W x 34'6" D |
| Heated Sq. Ft.: | 1,368 |
| Bedrooms: 3 | Bathrooms: 2 |
| Foundation: | Basement |
| PDF File: | $675 |
| 5-Sets: | $725 |
| 8-Sets: | $800 |
| CAD File: | $1,475 |
| Material List: | $125 |

*Pricing subject to change*

*Images provided by designer/architect*

GARAGE
21-3 X 20-6

© Copyright by designer/architect

COVERED AREA

UTILITY

KITCHEN / BRK'FST
17-3 X 12

PANT

FAMILY ROOM
18 X 16

DINING ROOM
14-3 X 12-9

PWDR
ROOM

MASTER
BATH

CLOSET

BEDROOM 3
11-6 X 11

LINEN

DRESS

BATH

MASTER
BEDROOM
15-3 X 14-6

FOYER

BEDROOM 2
11-6 X 11

PORCH

CLOSET

## Plan #F04-076D-0263

| | |
|---|---|
| Dimensions: | 37'6" W x 76'6" D |
| Heated Sq. Ft.: | 1,815 |
| Bedrooms: 3 | Bathrooms: 2½ |
| Foundation: | Slab |
| 5-Sets: | $655 |
| 8-Sets: | $800 |
| PDF File: | $975 |
| CAD File: | $1,250 |

*Pricing subject to change*

*Images provided by designer/architect*

## Plan #F04-076D-0218

| | |
|---|---|
| **Dimensions:** | 91'9" W x 81'7" D |
| **Heated Sq. Ft.:** | 2,818 |
| **Bedrooms:** 3 | **Bathrooms:** 2½ |

**Foundation:** Basement, crawl space or slab, please specify when ordering

| | |
|---|---|
| **5-Sets:** | $850 |
| **8-Sets:** | $1,100 |
| **PDF File:** | $1,300 |
| **CAD File:** | $1,600 |

*Pricing subject to change*

*Images provided by designer/architect*

## Features

- The master bedroom is one to remember with its tray ceiling and vaulted bath featuring a separate tub, a shower, two vanities and two walk-in closets
- The grand family room features an 11' coffered ceiling, a fireplace flanked by built-in cabinets, and a view to the covered terrace
- Decorative columns accent the formal dining room
- The secondary bedrooms each have walk-in closets, private dressing areas, and share a bath
- The focal point of the kitchen is the large sink topped island with seating
- The covered grilling terrace is handy right next to the kitchen
- 2-car side entry garage

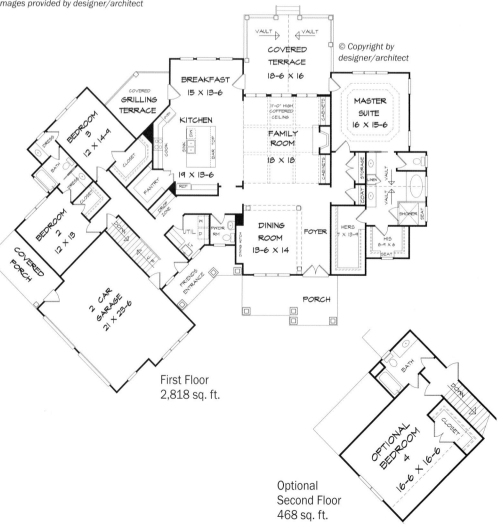

First Floor
2,818 sq. ft.

Optional
Second Floor
468 sq. ft.

Images provided by designer/architect

# Plan #F04-084D-0052

| | |
|---|---|
| **Dimensions:** | 38'6" W x 48'6" D |
| **Heated Sq. Ft.:** | 1,170 |
| **Bedrooms:** 2 | **Bathrooms:** 2 |

**Foundation:** Slab standard; crawl space or basement for a fee of $350

| | |
|---|---|
| **5-Sets:** | $800 |
| **8-Sets:** | $860 |
| **PDF File:** | $1,000 |
| **CAD File:** | $1,800 |
| **Material List:** | $65 |
| **Upgrade to 2" x 6" Walls:** | $255 |

*Pricing subject to change*

## Features

- The large covered side porch offers plans for an optional trellis patio
- The laundry closet is conveniently located by the bedrooms
- High ceilings in this home offer a feeling of spaciousness throughout
- The master bedroom features a walk-in closet and a private bath with a shower
- In the kitchen, the angled snack bar overlooks the dining space and offers additional seating
- 1-car front entry garage

© Copyright by designer/architect

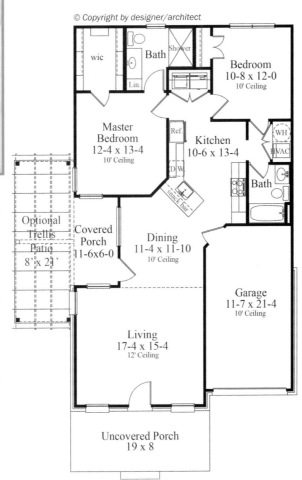

# the *Social* kitchen

You have just put the finishing touches on a beautiful table centerpiece, and the spread of hors d'oeuvres and the other delectable culinary treats for your gathering. The utmost attention to detail has been made to the great room, dining area and all the gathering places in your home. You want to make sure your guests feel pampered, comfortable, and completely at ease. But, no matter how inviting your living space may be, why does it always seem everyone ends up gathering in the kitchen?

Kitchens seem to be magnets for everyone who enters a home. Maybe it's the flurry of activity always taking place there, or the scrumptious aromas that fill the air making guests want to investigate what possibly could be cooking. Whatever the reason, kitchens are everyone's favorite gathering spots in the home. So, instead of fighting it, give in and make your kitchen a socially inviting place that is comfortable, fun and also allows you to get everything done even if people are lingering about. There are many ways to create social spots that keep everyone in the kitchen, while allowing him or her to feel welcome and comfortable in participating in the activities.

Thankfully, today's floor plans are taking this into consideration now more than ever. Most homes being designed today utilize an open floor plan that easily integrates the kitchen into the gathering spaces seamlessly. So, no longer is the kitchen hidden behind a swinging door. It's actually a stunning focal point filled with many design elements that enhance the entire gathering area including seating, dining space and other amenities.

*Page 182 top: Plan #F04-026D-1891 on page 132, Crown V Photography LLC; bottom: Plan #032D-0667, houseplansandmore.com; Page 183 top: Kohler Crevasse sink, kohler.com; Plan #F04-101D-0052 on page 60, Damon Searles, photographer.*

The kitchen is the center of your home; where you do the most work, where you entertain friends, where you gather as a family, and where life happens. It is hands-down the busiest area of the home and needs to be carefully planned for function as well as style.

A home's kitchen tends to be a place that quickly turns into a dumping ground. With the daily mail, homework projects, laundry, food storage and office work finding its way there, the kitchen can often have an identity crisis since there are so many different activities being carried out in the same space. Well, these habits will never change most likely, so instead of letting them aggravate you, embrace them and learn how to incorporate all of your family's favorite activities into this one wonderful place within your home.

One way to create an inviting feeling with function within your kitchen is to create a chopping and chatting spot. Whether it's a breakfast bar counter, an island, workbench or table, guests and family will need a spot that can function as a place for dining, prepping a meal, or finishing the homework that's due tomorrow. A decent space for gathering around will become a beacon and will keep everyone right where the action is, but out of the cooking space. An important thing to remember when creating this special gathering spot is that you don't want to crowd your kitchen with too many tables, or an island that is too oversized. It shouldn't affect the natural traffic flow, or act as a barrier at all. So, pick a piece of furniture, or a space that facilitates function, storage and possibly workspace, plus a spot where people feel they can just hang out and not be in the chef's way.

Another important factor to include when creating a social kitchen is to make sure there is plenty of seating. Use stools, benches and other seating options to offer plenty of places for your guest to "pop a squat." Of course, you may be thinking that your dining table has chairs and that should be enough, but think of other types of seating that can be tucked away (under a counter, for example) and can remain out of sight. That is also why the idea of a bench is great. It can provide a handy place to drop things the minute you come in the door, plus when company arrive, it's an instant spot for chatting with the chef. Everyone enjoys gathering in the kitchen and enjoying chips and dip, while watching the cook finish up their meal time tasks. Having some comfortable stools, benches, and other seating options will ensure your guests remain comfortable for their entire stay. Even better, stick with wood, plastic or other low-maintenance options for this seating and if spills occur, clean up will be a breeze.

Adding a variety of lighting in the kitchen is another way to make this space feel inviting, warm and comfortable for all those who enter it. Add lighting under the cabinets, recessed lighting into the ceiling and over tables and work zones so that all the bases are covered. That way, when the family cozies up around the table playing games, you can just light the table area and its nearby surroundings for a warmer feel. Plus, light sources can really play with the mood of the space.

So, when entertaining, use soft, low lighting and when cooking or prepping, turn up the lighting so it's safer for everyone involved with these tasks. Even soft candlelight on a countertop or dining table adds warmth and dimension to the space making it feel intimate and less institutional.

A great way to inexpensively allow you to change the amount of light in your kitchen is to install dimmer switches on many of the light sources. That way, the light above the sink can be bright enough for kitchen tasks at mealtime and then turned down much lower and used as a night light after everyone has gone off to bed. Dimmers allow great versatility and keep you from having an overabundance of lighting that may make your kitchen feel too busy, distracting or tense.

A kitchen filled entirely of glass cabinetry would be a little distressing don't you think? With all those kitchen gadgets being seen by everyone who came into the space, all of the clutter would make for a busy space that would be unnerving for most. But, strategically placing a couple of glass front cabinets in your kitchen can really become a focal point. If you have a great collection of brightly colored vases or old-fashioned pitchers, glass front cabinets give you the perfect opportunity to display away. Not only will they add some great character to your kitchen interior, but they will surely become conversation starters.

Just remember that less is more. Select just a few key items to be seen in these cabinets and avoid the temptation of showing a huge collection. It will make your kitchen instantly cluttered and less interesting than just giving them a glimpse of your special collection.

Making some minor adjustments with the layout, seating options, lighting, and cabinetry can add scores of points when family and guests gather in your kitchen. Instead of trying to find ways to keep everyone out while you cook away, invite them in and let the party begin!

*Page 184 top, right: Plan #071S-0001, houseplansandmore.com; top, left: Plan 101S-0015, houseplansandmore.com, Warren Diggles Photography; middle: Plan #24S-0023, houseplansandmore.com; Plan #032D-0427, houseplansandmore.com; Page 185: Plan #082S-0004, houseplansandmore.com.*

# your dream kitchen wish list

If you're designing the ultimate kitchen, trying to make your kitchen more functional for entertaining, or building a new home and trying to remember the things to take into consideration with a kitchen layout, it is important to remember that it is one of the best home investments you can make so make sure it meets all your needs right from the start.

The three main appliances in the kitchen are the sink, the refrigerator, and the stove. Make sure you arrange them so the workspace flows.

**SINK OR SWIM** Of the three appliances, the sink gets the most use. Place it in an area of the kitchen that is visually appealing to its user. So, don't push it up against a wall without a view. Place it in front of a window with a view to the outdoors, or in an island that overlooks the other areas of the home. It is also important to place the dishwasher to either side of the sink so that loading dishes is convenient. Many kitchens have a second sink, one for preparing food and another for dishes. Some kitchens also feature a second dishwasher, one for gently washing breakables and another for power scrubbing pots and pans.

**SHUT THE FRIDGE** When it comes to the refrigerator there are many basic options such as brand, color, size and finish. But, also think about the various styles including a freezer/fridge combination, side-by-side doors, a top and bottom door style, a style with an ice and water dispenser in the door, a smart fridge with technology that allows you to see what's inside it from your smart phone, and now the fun retro refrigerators meant to make a bold decorating statement and be a focal point. Also showing resurgence, refrigerators with the same cabinet style treatment added to the door so they don't stand out in your kitchen, are becoming quite popular again. Shiny stainless steel finishes are becoming less popular as the new appliances being introduced have a matte finish. Whatever option you choose make sure you leave plenty of room for the doors to open completely. If the fridge is placed near a wall make sure the doors and drawers open freely without hitting the wall. It is a good idea to check with the manufacturer for specific installation dimensions. And, becoming extremely popular especially if a kitchen is small are counter the depth refrigerators. These slightly smaller sized models offer a seamless look to your kitchen that feels custom since the appliance doesn't stick out further than the countertops. It easily adds square footage to your kitchen without it being obvious.

**TOO HOT IN THE KITCHEN** The options available for stoves go way beyond gas or electric. There are cooktops, double ovens, oven and microwave combinations, burners and griddle tops, convection and even warming drawers. When making a decision it is important to think about the type of cooking you plan to do and how much space you have to work with. The cooking surface needs to be planned to allow for workspace that is easily accessible and safe.

The selection process isn't over just yet...now, it's time to think about cabinets, shelving, countertops, pantry units, closets, a planning center, electronics, a center island, and eating space!

## cabinets, shelving & countertops

You can never have enough storage and this is especially true when it comes to the kitchen and all of the gadgets that need to be stored. Most common are cabinets with closed fronts but also available are open cabinets where plates can be stored on end and open fronts where objects are quickly within reach. It is also a good idea to consider cabinets that go all the way up to the ceiling. The top shelf can easily be reached with a step stool and can hold the items that are not used on a daily basis. Countertops need to be durable and accent the cabinetry. There can be built-in items such as cutting boards and seamless sinks. There are many surfaces available and the biggest decision will be how long you want it to last and how much you want to spend. Granite has long been a favorite, but many new homeowners are also opting for quartz, concrete, or recycled glass countertops.

## pantries, storage walls, & closets

Pantries are a great way to store all of your food in one place. They are typically wider than a standard cabinet and have additional shelves for storage. If space allows, a built-in pantry closet is a wonderful addition to any kitchen. These can be placed in the general vicinity of the kitchen and custom shelving can be added to meet your storage needs. Storage walls in kitchens are very popular now too, and typically linger in the area near the stove. Often shelves are mounted on a wall near the stove and include spices, measuring cups, oils, vinegars and other cooking essentials. Or, kitchen storage walls are found on another wall often floor-to-ceiling and include an assortment of china, ceramic bowls, glassware and other items that look nice displayed together. Both decorative and functional, these kitchen walls can really show off your personality, while providing the extra storage always needed in the kitchen.

## planning and/or technology center

Growing in popularity, the planning or technology center is basically a simplified "home office" located in the kitchen or adjacent to it. It can consist of a desk with surrounding cabinets and storage, space for a computer or ipad®, a charging station with additional USB ports, an area to organize bills and other important papers, cubbies or bins for every family member to stay organized, and a family schedule.

## kitchen electronics

There are so many items that are used in the kitchen that need to be plugged in, make sure there are plenty of electrical outlets so you don't have to run extension cords. Mockett® simplifies the need for electrical outlets everywhere in the kitchen with this pop-up kitchen outlet design. Simply, click it and it ascends from the countertops to reveal additional outlets that can be used when additional seldom used appliances are needed.

## kitchen island

An island in the kitchen can function as an eating bar, additional workspace, or can house the cooktop or sink. Whatever the function, it usually ends up being the focal point of the kitchen and can be accented with dramatic lighting, or hanging kitchen racks that will creatively hold your pots and pans while reclaiming valuable cabinet space. Designing it with different colors than the other cabinets and countertops is a popular trend and makes it even more of a focal point.

## eating space

This can be a nook, breakfast bar, banquette or island and for many families on the go it is where most of the meals are served. If you plan on having an eat-in kitchen, make sure there is enough stools so everyone has a place to sit.

If you're trying to design or plan the layout of a new kitchen the options are a little overwhelming, but it is important to remember that it needs to be well-organized and efficient, as well as beautiful since it is everyone's favorite spot. After all, it is the place you live, entertain and most importantly – cook! From cabinetry to appliances, it is important to create the perfect gathering space so that the chef, as well as family and friends, are always happy when they enter.

## Plan #F04-076D-0255

| | |
|---|---|
| **Dimensions:** | 68'4" W x 63'7" D |
| **Heated Sq. Ft.:** | 2,435 |
| **Bedrooms:** 4 | **Bathrooms:** 2½ |

**Foundation:** Basement, crawl space or slab, please specify when ordering

| | |
|---|---|
| **5-Sets:** | $875 |
| **8-Sets:** | $1,125 |
| **PDF File:** | $1,325 |
| **CAD File:** | $1,650 |

*Pricing subject to change*

*Images provided by designer/architect*

### Features

- Upon entering the foyer, you'll have access to two formal area, the study and the formal dining room
- The casual family room has an 11' ceiling, a cozy fireplace that can be seen form the kitchen island, and a trio of windows with views of the patio
- The split bedroom floor plan has two bedrooms that share a bath, but each has their own dressing area and walk-in closet
- The private master suite enjoys a spacious bath with a separate spa style tub and walk-in shower, and a huge double-door walk-in closet
- 2-car side entry garage

Optional
Second Floor
447 sq. ft.

First Floor
2,435 sq. ft.

© Copyright by designer/architect

## Plan #F04-135D-0006

| | |
|---|---|
| Dimensions: | 95'5" W x 47'6" D |
| Heated Sq. Ft.: | 2,058 |
| Bedrooms: 4 | Bathrooms: 2½ |
| Foundation: | Crawl space |
| PDF File: | $825 |
| 5-Sets: | $875 |
| Reproducible Master: | $875 |
| 8-Sets: | $950 |

Pricing subject to change

Images provided by designer/architect

## Features

- The massive front entry is vaulted for a grand feeling
- The living/dining area is a huge open space perfect for gathering and it's only steps from the open floor plan of the kitchen that features a large island
- The master bedroom has its own private bath, a cedar closet, a linen closet and a sizable walk-in closet offering plenty of storage options
- Three secondary bedrooms are placed on the opposite side of the home and share a conveniently located bath
- 2-car detached side entry garage

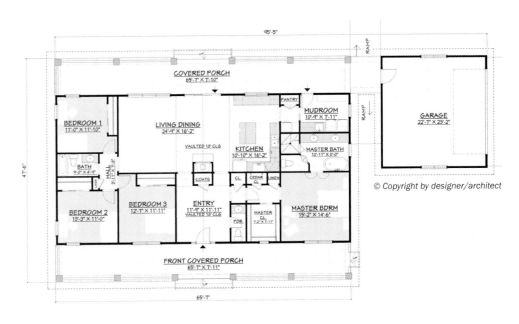

© Copyright by designer/architect

## Plan #F04-072D-1111

| | |
|---|---|
| Dimensions: | 72' W x 54' D |
| Heated Sq. Ft.: | 1,728 |
| Bedrooms: 2 | Bathrooms: 2 |
| Foundation: | Walk-out basement |
| Exterior Walls: | 2" x 6" |
| PDF File: | $750 |
| 5-Sets: | $800 |
| 8-Sets: | $875 |
| CAD File: | $1,550 |

*Pricing subject to change*

*Images provided by designer/architect*

### Features

- The second bedroom can easily be converted into an office with ample shelf space
- You will love the master bath equipped with a large walk-in closet, a relaxing shower, and a spa-style tub
- The kitchen has a breakfast island perfect for family gatherings
- The optional lower level offers an additional 1,005 square feet of living area
- The master bedroom is a place of rest and rejuvenation
- French doors allow the bedroom #2/office to transition between open and private space
- 3-car side entry garage

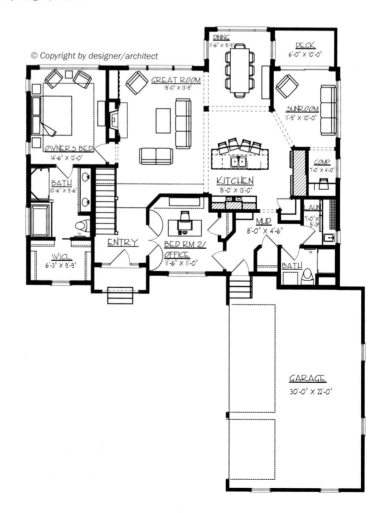

© Copyright by designer/architect

## Plan #F04-011D-0225

| | |
|---|---|
| Dimensions: | 48' W x 64' D |
| Heated Sq. Ft.: | 1,891 |
| Bedrooms: 3 | Bathrooms: 2 |

Foundation: Joisted crawl space or post & beam standard; basement or slab for a fee of $250

| | |
|---|---|
| Exterior Walls: | 2" x 6" |
| PDF File: | $900 |
| 5-Sets: | $950 |
| CAD File: | $1,800 |

*Pricing subject to change*

Images provided by designer/architect

© Copyright by designer/architect

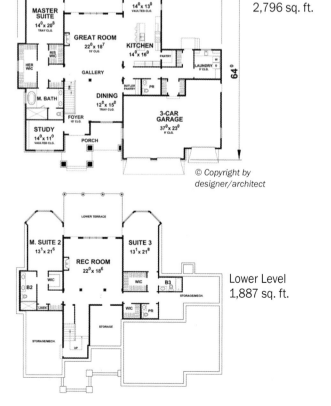

## Plan #F04-026D-1935

Images provided by designer/architect

| | |
|---|---|
| Dimensions: | 78' W x 64' D |
| Heated Sq. Ft.: | 2,796 |
| Bedrooms: 1 | Bathrooms: 1½ |
| Foundation: | Basement |
| Exterior Walls: | 2" x 6" |
| PDF File: | $905 |
| 5-Sets: | $1,015 |
| 8-Sets: | $1,195 |
| CAD File: | $1,405 |

*Pricing subject to change*

First Floor
2,796 sq. ft.

© Copyright by designer/architect

Lower Level
1,887 sq. ft.

## Plan #F04-088D-0719

| | |
|---|---|
| Dimensions: | 48' W x 40' D |
| Heated sq. ft.: | 2,350 |
| Bedrooms: 2 | Bathrooms: 2½ |
| Foundation: | Slab |
| Exterior Walls: | 2" x 6" |
| 5-Sets: | $775 |
| 8-Sets: | $850 |
| PDF File: | $1,000 |
| CAD File: | $1,000 |

*Pricing subject to change*

*Images provided by designer/architect*

**First Floor**
**1,808 sq. ft.**

DECK AREA

MASTER SUITE 15'10" X 16'

GREAT ROOM 19' X 26'8"

DINING 12'6" X 10'

WALK-IN CLOSET

DOWN

KITCHEN 12'6"X 12'8"

PANTRY

DEN 10' X 12'

GUEST/OFFICE 10' X 12'

ENTRY PORCH 20' X 8'

**Lower Level**
**542 sq. ft.**

OFFICE/STUDY 14'1 X 12'6

2 CAR GARAGE

UTILTIY 9'7" X 10'5"

LAUNDRY CHUTE

UP

© Copyright by designer/architect

---

## Plan #F04-130D-0369

| | |
|---|---|
| Dimensions: | 52' W x 65'10" D |
| Heated sq. ft.: | 1,810 |
| Bedrooms: 3 | Bathrooms: 2 |

Foundation: Slab standard; crawl space or basement for a fee of $150

| | |
|---|---|
| PDF File: | $905 |
| 5-Sets: | $1,030 |
| 8-Sets: | $1,105 |
| CAD File: | $1,155 |
| Upgrade to 2" x 6" Walls: | $150 |

*Pricing subject to change*

*Images provided by designer/architect*

52'-0"

BED #1 16 x14 *9' Ceiling*

PORCH

DINING ROOM 13-4 x 12 *9' Ceiling*

W D

Books

Glass Doors

Lin

Shoes

Tall Cabinets

Eating Bar

Island

Ref.

GARAGE 20 x 37

BED #2 12 x 11 *9' Ceiling*

Pantry

KIT 13-4 x 11-3 *9' Ceiling*

DW Sink

65'-10"

Books

42" High Wall

Slope 9' to 11'

Opt Basement Stairs

BED #3 12 x 11 *9' Ceiling*

LIVING ROOM 17 x 20 *11' Ceiling*

Slope 9' to 11'

© Copyright by designer/architect

STUDY 12 x 13 *9' Ceiling*

PORCH 13-8 x 10 *9' Ceiling*

First Floor
2,889 sq. ft.

Lower Level
2,165 sq. ft.

© Copyright by designer/architect

## Plan #F04-155D-0035

**Dimensions:** 95'7" W x 95'8" D
**Heated sq. ft.:** 5,054
**Bedrooms:** 4    **Bathrooms:** 4½
**Foundation:** Basement or walk-out basement, please specify when ordering
**5-Sets:** $1,550
**8-Sets:** $1,800
**PDF File:** $2,765
**CAD File:** $4,255
**Upgrade to 2" x 6" Walls:** $250
*Pricing subject to change*

*Images provided by designer/architect*

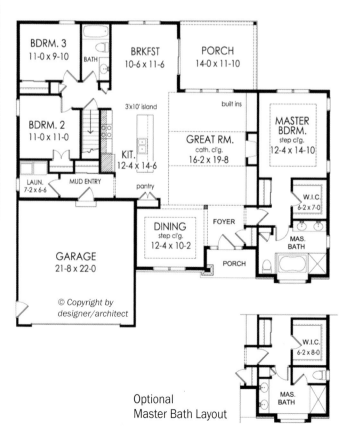

© Copyright by designer/architect

BDRM. 3
11-0 x 9-10

BATH

BRKFST
10-6 x 11-6

PORCH
14-0 x 11-10

built ins

BDRM. 2
11-0 x 11-0

3'x10' island

MASTER BDRM.
step cl'g.
12-4 x 14-10

GREAT RM.
cath. cl'g.
16-2 x 19-8

KIT.
12-4 x 14-6

LAUN.
7-2 x 6-6

MUD ENTRY

pantry

W.I.C.
6-2 x 7-0

DINING
step cl'g.
12-4 x 10-2

FOYER

MAS. BATH

GARAGE
21-8 x 22-0

PORCH

W.I.C.
6-2 x 8-0

Optional
Master Bath Layout

MAS. BATH

## Plan #F04-070D-0746

*Images provided by designer/architect*

**Dimensions:** 57' W x 53'4" D
**Heated sq. ft.:** 1,873
**Bedrooms:** 3    **Bathrooms:** 2
**Foundation:** Basement
**PDF File:** $800
**5-Sets:** $900
**8-Sets:** $1,000
*Pricing subject to change*

## Plan #F04-027D-0006

| | |
|---|---|
| **Dimensions:** | 63' W x 57'8" D |
| **Heated sq. ft.:** | 2,076 |
| **Bedrooms:** 3 | **Bathrooms:** 2 |

**Foundation:** Basement or walk-out basement, please specify when ordering

| | |
|---|---|
| **PDF File:** | $825 |
| **5-Sets:** | $875 |
| **8-Sets:** | $950 |
| **CAD File:** | $1,725 |
| **Material List:** | $125 |

*Pricing subject to change*

*Images provided by designer/architect*

© Copyright by designer/architect

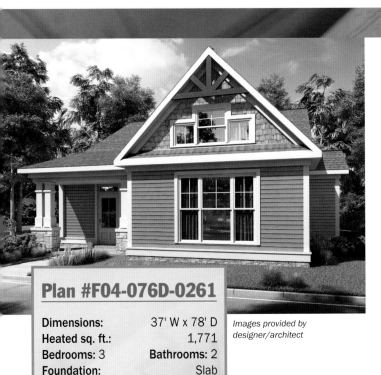

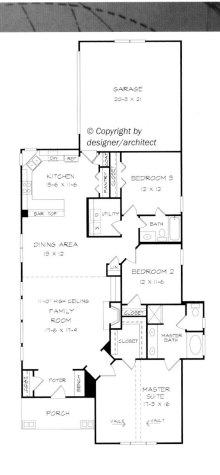

## Plan #F04-076D-0261

| | |
|---|---|
| **Dimensions:** | 37' W x 78' D |
| **Heated sq. ft.:** | 1,771 |
| **Bedrooms:** 3 | **Bathrooms:** 2 |
| **Foundation:** | Slab |
| **5-Sets:** | $655 |
| **8-Sets:** | $800 |
| **PDF File:** | $975 |
| **CAD File:** | $1,250 |

*Pricing subject to change*

*Images provided by designer/architect*

© Copyright by designer/architect

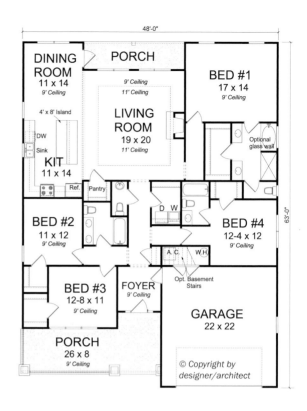

## Plan #F04-130D-0337

| | |
|---|---|
| Dimensions: | 48' W x 63' D |
| Heated sq. ft.: | 2,107 |
| Bedrooms: 4 | Bathrooms: 3 |

Foundation: Slab standard; crawl space or basement for a fee of $150

| | |
|---|---|
| PDF File: | $925 |
| 5-Sets: | $1,150 |
| CAD File: | $1,175 |
| 8-Sets: | $1,225 |
| Upgrade to 2" x 6" Walls: | $150 |

*Pricing subject to change*

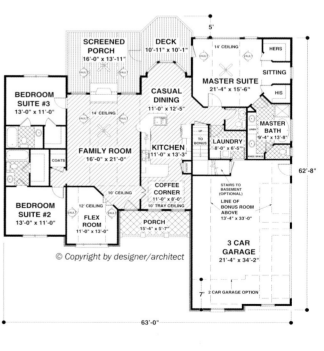

## Plan #F04-013D-0168

| | |
|---|---|
| Dimensions: | 63' W x 65' D |
| Heated sq. ft.: | 2,000 |
| Bonus sq. ft.: | 2,000 |
| Bedrooms: 4 | Bathrooms: 2½ |
| Foundation: | Basement |
| PDF File: | $995 |
| 5-Sets: | $1,045 |
| 8-Sets: | $1,095 |
| CAD File: | $1,495 |
| Upgrade to 2" x 6" Walls: | $150 |

*Pricing subject to change*

## Plan #F04-070D-0748

| | |
|---|---|
| Dimensions: | 58' W x 51'4" D |
| Heated sq. ft.: | 1,959 |
| Bedrooms: 3 | Bathrooms: 2½ |
| Foundation: | Basement |
| PDF File: | $800 |
| 5-Sets: | $900 |
| 8-Sets: | $1,000 |

*Pricing subject to change*

*Images provided by designer/architect*

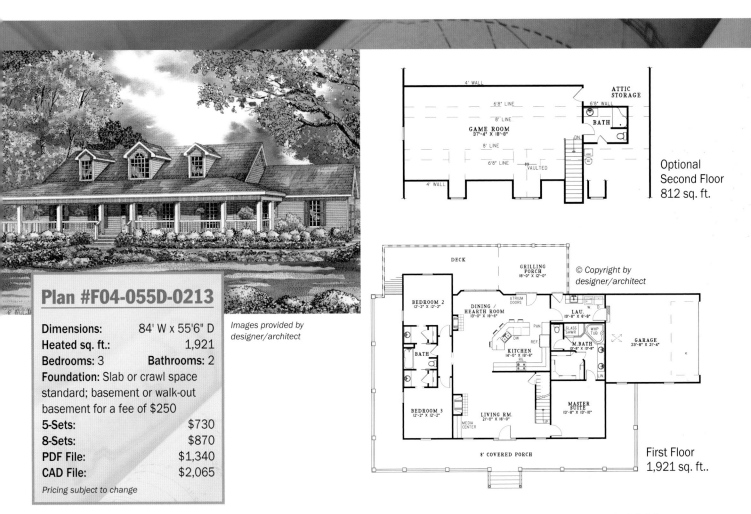

## Plan #F04-055D-0213

| | |
|---|---|
| Dimensions: | 84' W x 55'6" D |
| Heated sq. ft.: | 1,921 |
| Bedrooms: 3 | Bathrooms: 2 |

Foundation: Slab or crawl space standard; basement or walk-out basement for a fee of $250

| | |
|---|---|
| 5-Sets: | $730 |
| 8-Sets: | $870 |
| PDF File: | $1,340 |
| CAD File: | $2,065 |

*Pricing subject to change*

*Images provided by designer/architect*

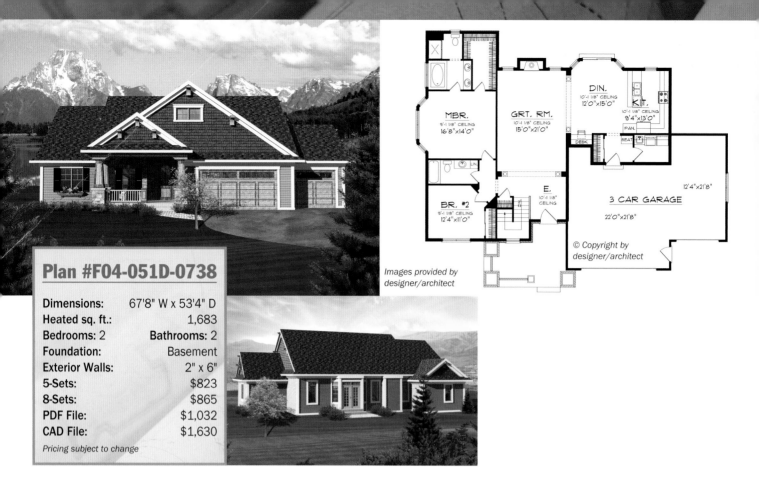

## Plan #F04-051D-0738

| | |
|---|---|
| Dimensions: | 67'8" W x 53'4" D |
| Heated sq. ft.: | 1,683 |
| Bedrooms: 2 | Bathrooms: 2 |
| Foundation: | Basement |
| Exterior Walls: | 2" x 6" |
| 5-Sets: | $823 |
| 8-Sets: | $865 |
| PDF File: | $1,032 |
| CAD File: | $1,630 |

*Pricing subject to change*

Images provided by designer/architect

© Copyright by designer/architect

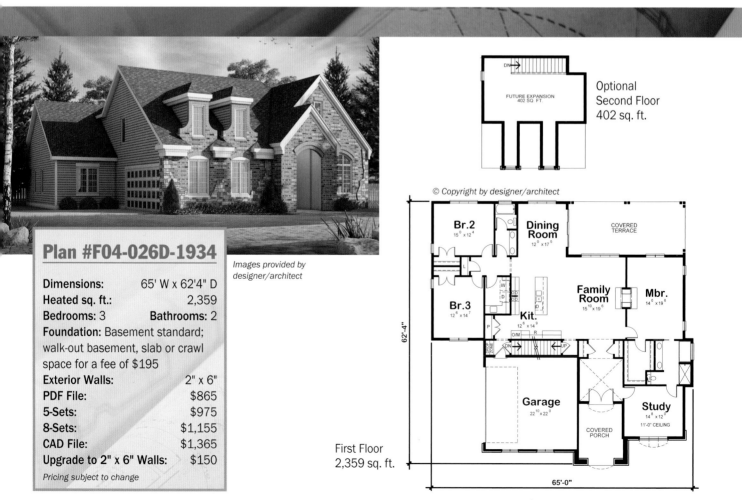

## Plan #F04-026D-1934

Images provided by designer/architect

| | |
|---|---|
| Dimensions: | 65' W x 62'4" D |
| Heated sq. ft.: | 2,359 |
| Bedrooms: 3 | Bathrooms: 2 |
| Foundation: Basement standard; walk-out basement, slab or crawl space for a fee of $195 | |
| Exterior Walls: | 2" x 6" |
| PDF File: | $865 |
| 5-Sets: | $975 |
| 8-Sets: | $1,155 |
| CAD File: | $1,365 |
| Upgrade to 2" x 6" Walls: | $150 |

*Pricing subject to change*

Optional Second Floor 402 sq. ft.

© Copyright by designer/architect

First Floor 2,359 sq. ft.

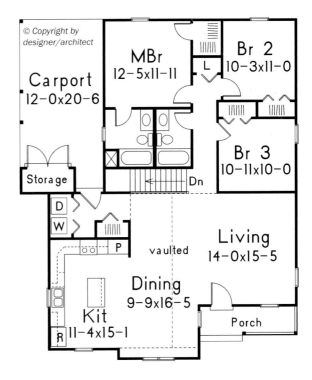

© Copyright by designer/architect

*Images provided by designer/architect*

Carport
12-0x20-6

Storage

D
W

MBr
12-5x11-11

L

Br 2
10-3x11-0

Br 3
10-11x10-0

Dn

Living
14-0x15-5

vaulted

Dining
9-9x16-5

Porch

Kit
11-4x15-1

P

R

## Plan #F04-001D-0035

| Dimensions: | 40' W x 47'4" D |
|---|---|
| Heated sq. ft.: | 1,396 |
| Bedrooms: 3 | Bathrooms: 2 |

Foundation: Basement or crawl space, please specify when ordering

| PDF File: | $675 |
|---|---|
| 5-Sets: | $725 |
| Reproducible Master: | $725 |
| 8-Sets: | $800 |
| Material List: | $125 |

*Pricing subject to change*

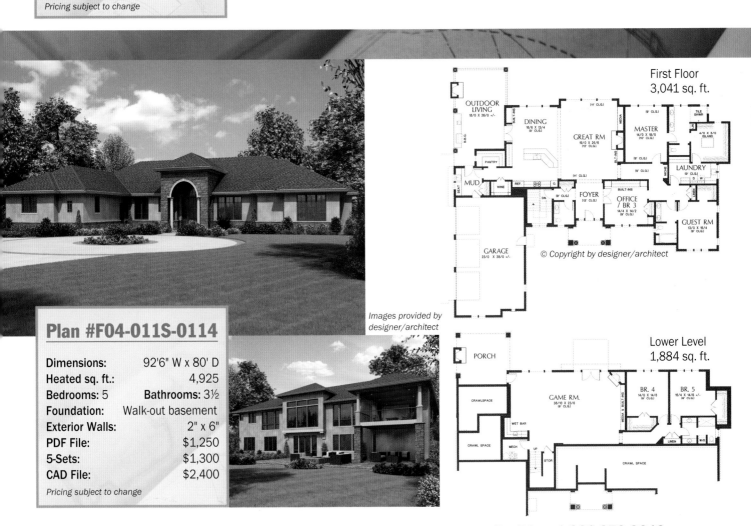

*Images provided by designer/architect*

First Floor
3,041 sq. ft.

OUTDOOR LIVING
18/0 X 26/0 +/-

DINING
15/6 X 13/4
(9' CLG)

GREAT RM
19/0 X 26/6
(12' CLG)

MASTER
14/0 X 18/0
(10' CLG)

TILE SHWR

PANTRY

MUD

WINE

REF.

FOYER

OFFICE / BR 3
14/4 X 14/2
(9' CLG)

BUILT-INS

LAUNDRY

GARAGE
23/0 X 38/0 +/-

GUEST RM
13/0 X 15/4
(9' CLG)

© Copyright by designer/architect

PORCH

Lower Level
1,884 sq. ft.

GAME RM.
38/10 X 23/6
(9' CLG)

CRAWLSPACE

WET BAR

CRAWL SPACE

MECH

UP

STOR

CRAWL SPACE

BR. 4
14/0 X 14/6
(9' CLG)

BR. 5
15/4 X 14/6
(9' CLG)

LINEN

## Plan #F04-011S-0114

| Dimensions: | 92'6" W x 80' D |
|---|---|
| Heated sq. ft.: | 4,925 |
| Bedrooms: 5 | Bathrooms: 3½ |
| Foundation: | Walk-out basement |
| Exterior Walls: | 2" x 6" |
| PDF File: | $1,250 |
| 5-Sets: | $1,300 |
| CAD File: | $2,400 |

*Pricing subject to change*

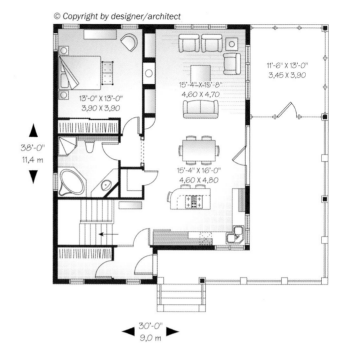

© Copyright by designer/architect

13'-0" X 13'-0"
3,90 X 3,90

15'-4"-X-15'-8"
4,60 X 4,70

11'-6" X 13'-0"
3,45 X 3,90

15'-4" X 16'-0"
4,60 X 4,80

38'-0"
11,4 m

30'-0"
9,0 m

## Plan #F04-032D-0801

*Images provided by designer/architect*

| | |
|---|---|
| Dimensions: | 30' W x 38' D |
| Heated sq. ft.: | 1,070 |
| Bedrooms: 1 | Bathrooms: 1 |
| Foundation: | Basement |
| Exterior Walls: | 2" x 6" |
| 5-Sets: | $725 |
| 8-Sets: | $755 |
| PDF File: | $870 |
| CAD File: | $1,440 |
| Material List: | $110 |

*Pricing subject to change*

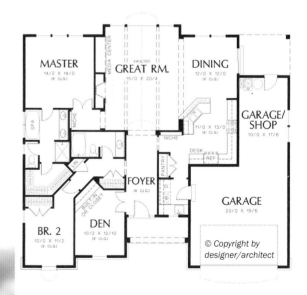

MASTER
14/2 X 14/0
(9' CLG.)

GREAT RM.
15/0 X 20/4
VAULTED

DINING
12/0 X 12/0
(9' CLG.)

GARAGE/
SHOP
10/0 X 17/6

11/0 X 13/0
(9' CLG.)

FOYER
(9' CLG.)

GARAGE
20/0 X 19/6

BR. 2
10/0 X 11/2
(9' CLG.)

DEN
10/2 X 12/10
(9' CLG.)

© Copyright by designer/architect

## Plan #F04-011D-0008

| | |
|---|---|
| Dimensions: | 55' W x 48' D |
| Heated sq. ft.: | 1,728 |
| Bedrooms: 2 | Bathrooms: 2 |

Foundation: Joisted crawl space, TrusJoist floor system or post & beam standard; slab or basement for a fee of $225

| | |
|---|---|
| Exterior Walls: | 2" x 6" |
| PDF File: | $900 |
| 5-Sets: | $950 |
| CAD File: | $1,800 |

*Pricing subject to change*

*Images provided by designer/architect*

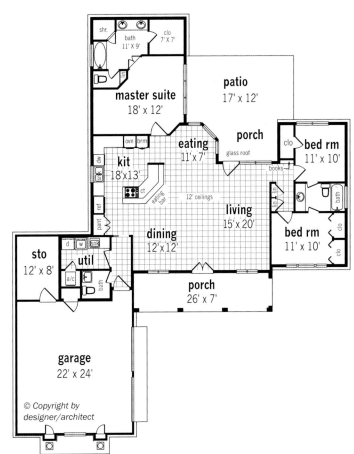

© Copyright by designer/architect

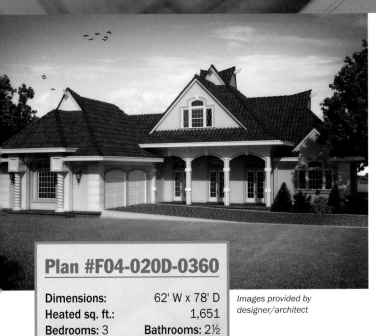

## Plan #F04-020D-0360

| Dimensions: | 62' W x 78' D |
|---|---|
| Heated sq. ft.: | 1,651 |
| Bedrooms: 3 | Bathrooms: 2½ |
| Foundation: | Slab |
| Exterior Walls: | 2" x 6" |
| PDF File: | $850 |
| 5-Sets: | $875 |
| 8-Sets: | $920 |
| CAD File: | $1,638 |

*Pricing subject to change*

*Images provided by designer/architect*

© Copyright by designer/architect

## Plan #F04-032D-0909

| Dimensions: | 44'8" W x 48' D |
|---|---|
| Heated sq. ft.: | 1,459 |
| Bedrooms: 2 | Bathrooms: 1 |
| Foundation: | Basement |
| Exterior Walls: | 2" x 6" |
| 5-Sets: | $785 |
| 8-Sets: | $815 |
| PDF File: | $930 |
| CAD File: | $1,500 |

*Pricing subject to change*

*Images provided by designer/architect*

**Optional Second Floor**
288 sq. ft.

BONUS ROOM ABOVE GARAGE
12'-0" X 24'-0"

© Copyright by designer/architect

2 CAR GARAGE
24'-0" X 24'-0"

MUD ROOM
10'-0" X 6'-0"

STORAGE
10'-0" X 10'-0"

PORCH NO. 2
46'-0" X 6'-0"

DINING AREA
14'-0" X 17'-0"

LAUNDRY

WALK-IN CLO.

BEDROOM NO. 3
14'-0" X 15'-0"

VENTLESS GAS FIREPLACE

GREAT ROOM
24'-0" X 24'-0"
11' TRAY CEILING

PANTRY

MASTER BATH
14'-0" X 7'-0"

BATH 2

KITCHEN
14'-0" X 18'-0"

MASTER BEDROOM
18'-0" X 20'-0"

BEDROOM NO. 2
14'-0" X 15'-0"

BATH 3

BEDROOM NO. 4
14'-0" X 10'-0"

FOYER

SITTING ROOM
14'-0" X 8'-0"

PORCH NO. 1
70'-0" X 6'-0"

**First Floor**
3,029 sq. ft.

Images provided by designer/architect

## Plan #F04-028D-0022

| | |
|---|---|
| Dimensions: | 70' W x 80' D |
| Heated sq. ft.: | 3,029 |
| Bedrooms: 4 | Bathrooms: 3 |

Foundation: Slab or crawl space, please specify when ordering

| | |
|---|---|
| 5-Sets: | $960 |
| 8-Sets: | $1,060 |
| PDF File: | $1,110 |

*Pricing subject to change*

Images provided by designer/architect

## Plan #F04-051D-0737

| | |
|---|---|
| Dimensions: | 45' W x 77'4" D |
| Heated sq. ft.: | 1,680 |
| Bedrooms: 2 | Bathrooms: 2 |
| Foundation: | Basement |
| Exterior Walls: | 2" x 6" |
| 5-Sets: | $823 |
| 8-Sets: | $865 |
| PDF File: | $1,032 |
| CAD File: | $1,630 |
| Material List: | $75 |

*Pricing subject to change*

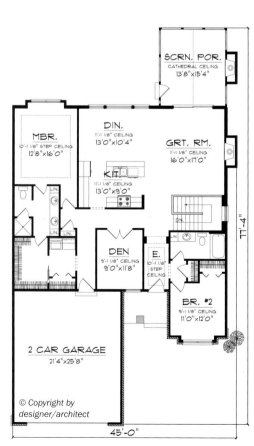

SCRN. POR.
CATHEDRAL CEILING
13'8"x15'4"

MBR.
10'-1 1/8" STEP CEILING
12'8"x16'0"

DIN.
11'-1 1/8" CEILING
13'0"x10'4"

GRT. RM.
11'-1 1/8" CEILING
16'0"x17'0"

KIT.
11'-1 1/8" CEILING
13'0"x9'0"

DEN
9'-1 1/8" CEILING
9'0"x11'8"

BR. #2
9'-1 1/8" CEILING
11'0"x12'0"

2 CAR GARAGE
21'4"x25'8"

© Copyright by designer/architect

45'-0"

77'-4"

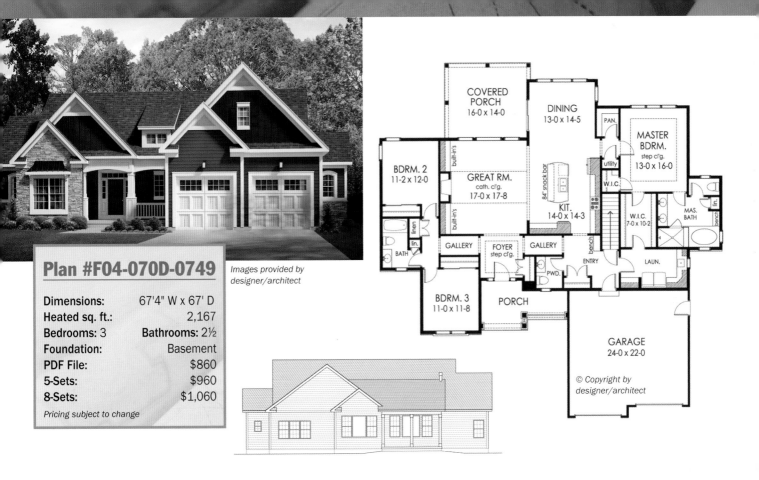

## Plan #F04-070D-0749

| | |
|---|---|
| Dimensions: | 67'4" W x 67' D |
| Heated sq. ft.: | 2,167 |
| Bedrooms: 3 | Bathrooms: 2½ |
| Foundation: | Basement |
| PDF File: | $860 |
| 5-Sets: | $960 |
| 8-Sets: | $1,060 |

*Pricing subject to change*

*Images provided by designer/architect*

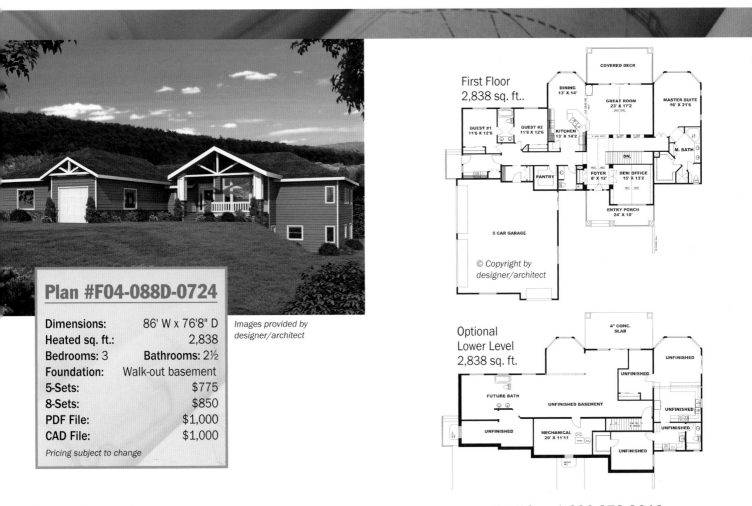

## Plan #F04-088D-0724

| | |
|---|---|
| Dimensions: | 86' W x 76'8" D |
| Heated sq. ft.: | 2,838 |
| Bedrooms: 3 | Bathrooms: 2½ |
| Foundation: | Walk-out basement |
| 5-Sets: | $775 |
| 8-Sets: | $850 |
| PDF File: | $1,000 |
| CAD File: | $1,000 |

*Pricing subject to change*

*Images provided by designer/architect*

## Plan #F04-076D-0230

**Dimensions:** 66'10" W x 67'7" D
**Heated sq. ft.:** 2,298
**Bedrooms:** 3  **Bathrooms:** 1½
**Foundation:** Crawl space or slab, please specify when ordering

| | |
|---|---|
| 5-Sets: | $875 |
| 8-Sets: | $1,125 |
| PDF File: | $1,325 |
| CAD File: | $1,650 |

*Pricing subject to change*

*Images provided by designer/architect*

## Features

- 11' ceiling heights top the family and breakfast rooms creating the most open and inviting feeling
- The kitchen is combined with both the family and breakfast rooms and includes a huge island with dining space, a double basin sink and a dishwasher
- The private master suite has an amazing amount of closetspace in addition to a luxurious bath with an oversized whirlpool tub and separate walk-in shower
- The vaulted covered patio is ideal for relaxing outdoors in any kind of weather
- 2-car side entry garage

Optional
Second Floor
240 sq. ft.

© Copyright by designer/architect

First Floor
2,298 sq. ft.

First Floor
2,397 sq. ft.

DECK
(308 SQ. FT.)

VAULTED
GREAT RM.
17/0 X 20/10

MASTER
15/2 X 20/0
(10'-6" CLG.)

DINING
12/4 X 15/0

SPA

TILE
SHWR.

FOYER
(11' CLG.)

OFFICE
10/0 X 10/8
(11' CLG.)

FURNITURE
RECESS

PANTRY

REF.

MUD

BENCH

GARAGE
35/0 X 23/0 +/-

© Copyright by
designer/architect

MEDIA
17/0 X 15/10
(9' CLG.)

REC. RM.
15/0 X 25/4
(9' CLG.)

BR. 2
12/0 X 10/8
(9' CLG.)

BR. 3
10/0 X 16/0
(9' CLG.)

STORAGE

SHELVES

UP

LINEN/STOR

TILE
SHWR.

UNFINISHED
MECH./
STORAGE

Optional
Lower Level
1,409 sq. ft.

## Plan #F04-011S-0107

| | |
|---|---|
| Dimensions: | 101'11" W x 73'6" D |
| Heated sq. ft.: | 3,806 |
| Bedrooms: 3 | Bathrooms: 2½ |
| Foundation: | Walk-out basement |
| Exterior Walls: | 2" x 6" |
| PDF File: | $1,400 |
| 5-Sets: | $1,450 |
| CAD File: | $2,700 |

*Pricing subject to change*

*Images provided by
designer/architect*

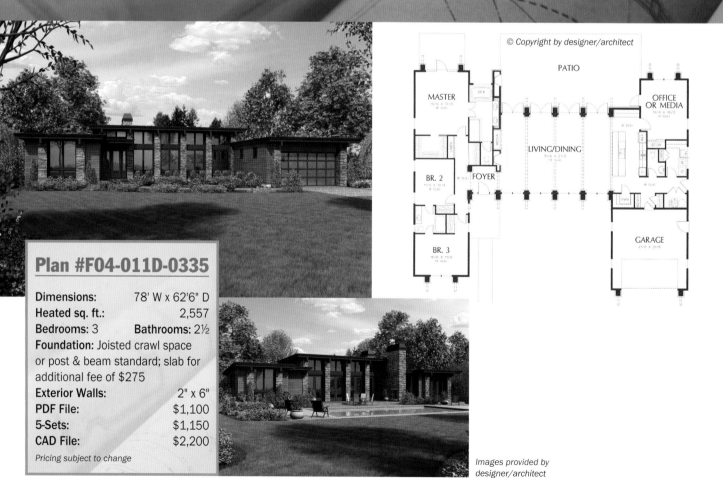

© Copyright by designer/architect

PATIO

MASTER
15/0 X 17/0
(9' CLG.)

SPA

OFFICE
OR MEDIA
13/0 X 16/0
(9' CLG.)

LIVING/DINING
31/0 X 21/0
(11' CLG.)

BR. 2
11/0 X 12/4
(9' CLG.)

FOYER

BR. 3
15/0 X 11/0
(9' CLG.)

PAN

GARAGE
21/0 X 21/6

## Plan #F04-011D-0335

| | |
|---|---|
| Dimensions: | 78' W x 62'6" D |
| Heated sq. ft.: | 2,557 |
| Bedrooms: 3 | Bathrooms: 2½ |

Foundation: Joisted crawl space
or post & beam standard; slab for
additional fee of $275

| | |
|---|---|
| Exterior Walls: | 2" x 6" |
| PDF File: | $1,100 |
| 5-Sets: | $1,150 |
| CAD File: | $2,200 |

*Pricing subject to change*

*Images provided by
designer/architect*

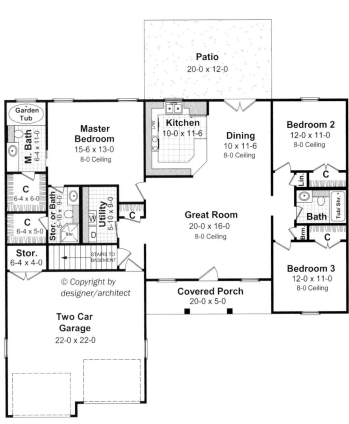

## Plan #F04-077D-0024

| | |
|---|---|
| Dimensions: | 54' W x 48' D |
| Heated sq. ft.: | 1,488 |
| Bedrooms: 3 | Bathrooms: 2 |
| Foundation: | Basement |
| 5-Sets: | $915 |
| PDF File: | $1,050 |
| Reproducible Master: | $1,130 |
| CAD File: | $1,615 |
| Material List | $130 |

*Pricing subject to change*

*Images provided by designer/architect*

Garden Tub

M. Bath 6-4 x 11-0

Master Bedroom 15-6 x 13-0
8-0 Ceiling

C 6-4 x 6-0

Stor. or Bath 5-10 x 9-0

C 6-4 x 5-0

Stor. 6-4 x 4-0

Two Car Garage 22-0 x 22-0

Utility 5-10 x 9-0

STAIRS TO BASEMENT

Patio 20-0 x 12-0

Kitchen 10-0 x 11-6

Dining 10 x 11-6
8-0 Ceiling

Great Room 20-0 x 16-0
8-0 Ceiling

Covered Porch 20-0 x 5-0

Bedroom 2 12-0 x 11-0
8-0 Ceiling

Lin.

C

Bath

C

Bedroom 3 12-0 x 11-0
8-0 Ceiling

© Copyright by designer/architect

---

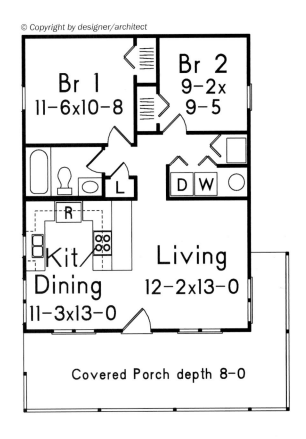

## Plan #F04-001D-0085

| | |
|---|---|
| Dimensions: | 28' W x 38' D |
| Heated sq. ft.: | 720 |
| Bedrooms: 2 | Bathrooms: 1 |
| Foundation: | Slab or crawl space, please specify when ordering |
| PDF File: | $600 |
| 5-Sets: | $650 |
| 8-Sets: | $725 |
| CAD File: | $1,110 |
| Material List: | $125 |

*Pricing subject to change*

*Images provided by designer/architect*

© Copyright by designer/architect

Br 1 11-6x10-8

Br 2 9-2x 9-5

L

D W

Kit Dining 11-3x13-0

R

Living 12-2x13-0

Covered Porch depth 8-0

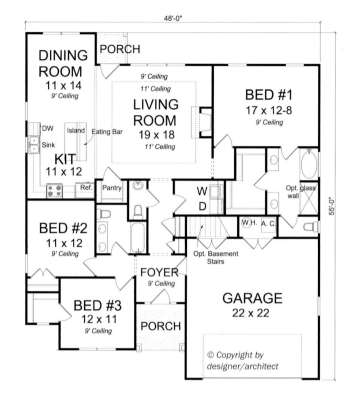

Dimensions label: 48'-0" (width), 55'-0" (depth)

DINING ROOM 11 x 14 — 9' Ceiling
PORCH
LIVING ROOM 19 x 18 — 11' Ceiling
BED #1 17 x 12-8 — 9' Ceiling
KIT 11 x 12
DW · Island · Eating Bar · Sink
Ref. · Pantry
Opt. glass wall
W D · W.H. · A.C.
BED #2 11 x 12 — 9' Ceiling
Opt. Basement Stairs
FOYER 9' Ceiling
BED #3 12 x 11 — 9' Ceiling
PORCH
GARAGE 22 x 22

© Copyright by designer/architect

## Plan #F04-130D-0336

*Images provided by designer/architect*

| | |
|---|---|
| Dimensions: | 48'W x 55'D |
| Heated sq. ft.: | 1,709 |
| Bedrooms: 3 | Bathrooms: 2½ |

Foundation: Slab standard; crawl space or basement for a fee of $150

| | |
|---|---|
| PDF File: | $885 |
| 5-Sets: | $1,110 |
| 8-Sets: | $1,185 |
| CAD File: | $1,135 |
| Upgrade to 2" x 6" Walls: | $150 |

*Pricing subject to change*

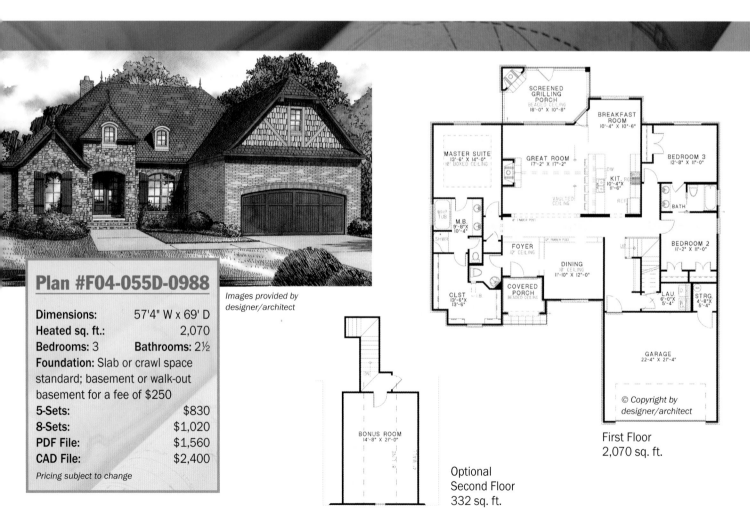

SCREENED GRILLING PORCH — BEADED CEILING 18'-0" X 10'-8"
BREAKFAST ROOM 10'-4" X 10'-6"
MASTER SUITE 13'-6" X 14'-0" — 10' BOXED CEILING
GREAT ROOM 17'-2" X 17'-2" — VAULTED CEILING
BEDROOM 3 12'-8" X 11'-0"
KIT. 10'-4" X 11'-6"
BATH
W.P. TUB · M.B. 9'-8" X 10'-4" · SHWR
FOYER 12' CEILING
BEDROOM 2 11'-2" X 11'-0"
DINING 11'-10" X 12'-0" — 10' CEILING
CLST. 13'-6" X 13'-6"
COVERED PORCH — BEADED CEILING
LAU. 6'-0" X 5'-4"
STRG. 4'-8" X 5'-4"
GARAGE 22'-4" X 21'-4"

© Copyright by designer/architect

First Floor 2,070 sq. ft.

BONUS ROOM 14'-8" X 21'-0"

Optional Second Floor 332 sq. ft.

## Plan #F04-055D-0988

*Images provided by designer/architect*

| | |
|---|---|
| Dimensions: | 57'4" W x 69' D |
| Heated sq. ft.: | 2,070 |
| Bedrooms: 3 | Bathrooms: 2½ |

Foundation: Slab or crawl space standard; basement or walk-out basement for a fee of $250

| | |
|---|---|
| 5-Sets: | $830 |
| 8-Sets: | $1,020 |
| PDF File: | $1,560 |
| CAD File: | $2,400 |

*Pricing subject to change*

## Plan #F04-020D-0365

*Images provided by designer/architect*

| | |
|---|---|
| Dimensions: | 57' W x 88'6" D |
| Heated sq. ft.: | 1,976 |
| Bedrooms: 3 | Bathrooms: 2 |
| Foundation: | Crawl space |
| Exterior Walls: | 2" x 6" |
| PDF File: | $850 |
| 5-Sets: | $875 |
| 8-Sets: | $920 |
| CAD File: | $1,638 |

*Pricing subject to change*

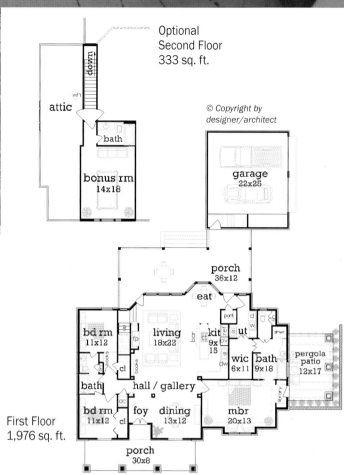

Optional
Second Floor
333 sq. ft.

© Copyright by designer/architect

First Floor
1,976 sq. ft.

## Plan #F04-051D-0678

*Images provided by designer/architect*

| | |
|---|---|
| Dimensions: | 52' W x 59' D |
| Heated sq. ft.: | 1,867 |
| Bedrooms: 3 | Bathrooms: 2 |
| Foundation: | Basement |
| Exterior Walls: | 2" x 6" |
| 5-Sets: | $853 |
| 8-Sets: | $895 |
| PDF File: | $1,070 |
| CAD File: | $1,695 |

*Pricing subject to change*

© Copyright by designer/architect

## Plan #F04-013D-0027

| | |
|---|---|
| Dimensions: | 71'2"W x 58'1"D |
| Heated sq. ft.: | 2,184 |
| Bedrooms: 3 | Bathrooms: 3 |
| Foundation: Slab standard; crawl or basement for a fee of $250 | |
| PDF File: | $995 |
| 5-Sets: | $1,045 |
| 8-Sets: | $1,095 |
| CAD File: | $1,495 |
| Material List: | $125 |
| Upgrade to 2" x 6" Walls: | $250 |

*Pricing subject to change*

*Images provided by designer/architect*

## Features

- The delightful family room has access to the screened porch for enjoyable outdoor living
- The secluded master suite is complete with a sitting area, two walk-in closets, and a luxurious bath
- The formal living room has a double-door entry easily converting it to a study or home office
- Two secondary bedrooms have their own baths and walk-in closets
- The bonus room above the garage has an additional 379 square feet of living space
- 2-car side entry garage

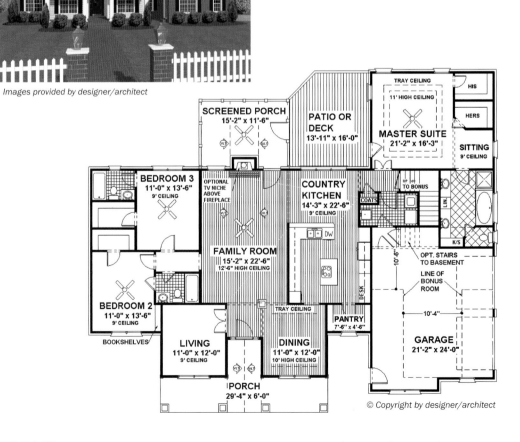

© Copyright by designer/architect

## Plan #F04-101D-0048

| | |
|---|---|
| Dimensions: | 126'6" W x 96' D |
| Heated sq. ft.: | 4,660 |
| Bedrooms: 4 | Bathrooms: 3½ |
| Foundation: | Slab |
| Exterior Walls: | 2" x 6" |
| 5-Sets: | $2,100 |
| PDF File: | $2,950 |
| CAD File: | $3,550 |

*Pricing subject to change*

## Features

- This massive home offers everything from formal to casual spaces for entertaining or everyday living
- The spacious kitchen enjoys a center island that is surrounded with additional counterspace that includes dining space, all while overlooking the great room
- The stunning master suite promises privacy and features a fireplace, two sets of double doors leading to the covered veranda, a sitting area, a plush bath with a huge walk-in closet that could also be a dressing room
- Other handy features include a garden shed, an enormous walk-in pantry in the kitchen, and a large laundry room
- 3-car front entry garage

*Images provided by designer/architect*

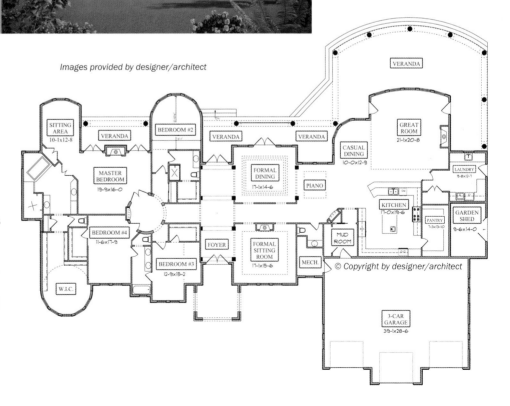

© Copyright by designer/architect

## Plan #F04-011D-0311

**Dimensions:** 64' W x 54' D
**Heated sq. ft.:** 1,988
**Bedrooms:** 3    **Bathrooms:** 3
**Foundation:** Crawl space or post & beam standard; slab for fee of $225
**Exterior Walls:** 2" x 6"
**PDF File:** $900
**5-Sets:** $950
**CAD File:** $1,800

*Pricing subject to change*

*Images provided by designer/architect*

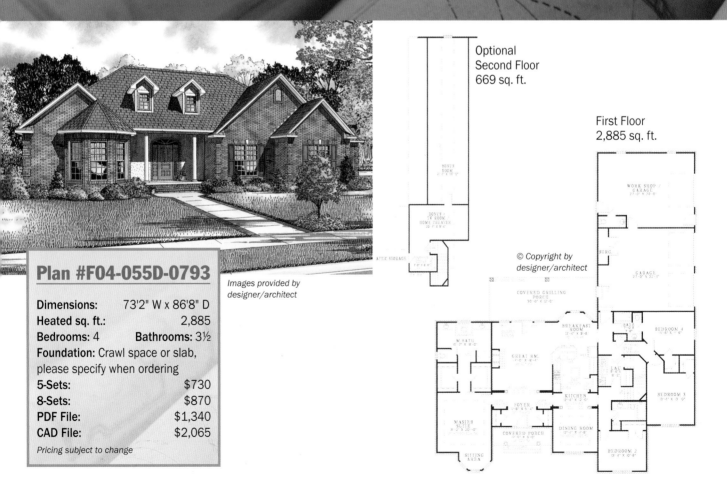

Optional Second Floor 669 sq. ft.

First Floor 2,885 sq. ft.

© Copyright by designer/architect

*Images provided by designer/architect*

## Plan #F04-055D-0793

**Dimensions:** 73'2" W x 86'8" D
**Heated sq. ft.:** 2,885
**Bedrooms:** 4    **Bathrooms:** 3½
**Foundation:** Crawl space or slab, please specify when ordering
**5-Sets:** $730
**8-Sets:** $870
**PDF File:** $1,340
**CAD File:** $2,065

*Pricing subject to change*

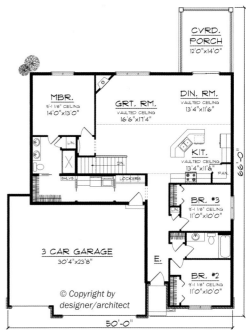

Images provided by designer/architect

## Plan #F04-051D-0714

| | |
|---|---|
| Dimensions: | 50' W x 66' D |
| Heated sq. ft.: | 1660 |
| Bedrooms: 3 | Bathrooms: 2 |
| Foundation: | Basement |
| Exterior Walls: | 2" x 6" |
| 5-Sets: | $823 |
| 8-Sets: | $865 |
| PDF File: | $1,032 |
| CAD File: | $1,630 |

*Pricing subject to change*

## Plan #F04-084D-0016

| | |
|---|---|
| Dimensions: | 56' W x 45'8" D |
| Heated sq. ft.: | 1,492 |
| Bedrooms: 3 | Bathrooms: 2 |

Foundation: Basement, slab or crawl space foundation, please specify when ordering

| | |
|---|---|
| 5-Sets: | $800 |
| 8-Sets: | $860 |
| PDF File: | $1,000 |
| CAD File: | $1,800 |
| Material List: | $65 |

*Pricing subject to change*

Images provided by designer/architect

## Plan #F04-121D-0047

| | |
|---|---|
| Dimensions: | 60' W x 70' D |
| Heated sq. ft.: | 1,983 |
| Bedrooms: 3 | Bathrooms: 2 |
| Foundation: | Basement |
| PDF File: | $750 |
| 5-Sets: | $800 |
| 8-Sets: | $875 |
| CAD File: | $1,550 |

*Pricing subject to change*

*Images provided by designer/architect*

### Features

- The kitchen overlooks the breakfast area and great room, providing an open atmosphere in the main gathering areas
- The vaulted breakfast area includes direct access to the outdoor patio, while the vaulted great room appreciates patio views
- The master bedroom becomes a private oasis for the homeowners and features a tranquil bath with a soothing corner whirlpool tub and a large walk-in closet
- 2-car side entry garage with workshop area

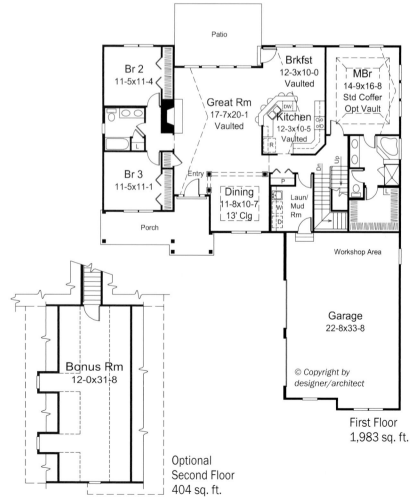

Bonus Rm
12-0x31-8

Optional
Second Floor
404 sq. ft.

First Floor
1,983 sq. ft.

## Plan #F04-011S-0108

| | |
|---|---|
| **Dimensions:** | 138' W x 91'4" D |
| **Heated sq. ft.:** | 3,557 |
| **Bedrooms:** 3 | **Bathrooms:** 2½ |
| **Foundation:** | Joisted crawl space |
| **Exterior Walls:** | 2" x 6" |
| **PDF File:** | $1,400 |
| **5-Sets:** | $1,450 |
| **CAD File:** | $2,700 |

*Pricing subject to change*

*Images provided by designer/architect*

## Features

- This sprawling one-story home allows one-level living to remain private for the bedrooms by being designed with several different wings

- The vaulted open foyer flows right into the vaulted living area with a huge dining area nearby

- The open kitchen promises ease when mealtimes occur and has plenty of prep space with a huge center island

- The vaulted kitchen/family room offers casual living that is an extension of the kitchen and enjoys views of the vaulted covered porch with fireplace

- 3-car rear entry garage

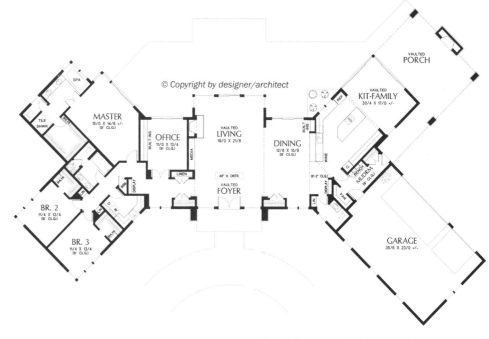

© Copyright by designer/architect

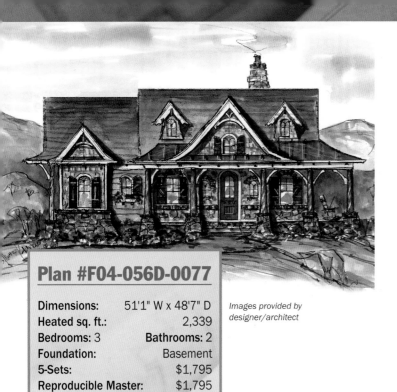

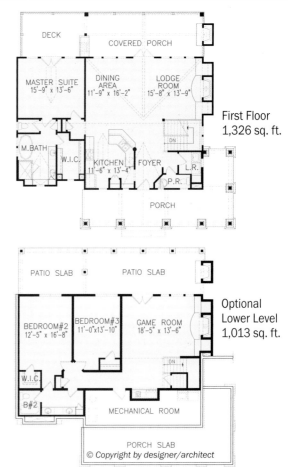

**First Floor
1,326 sq. ft.**

**Optional
Lower Level
1,013 sq. ft.**

© Copyright by designer/architect

## Plan #F04-056D-0077

| | |
|---|---|
| Dimensions: | 51'1" W x 48'7" D |
| Heated sq. ft.: | 2,339 |
| Bedrooms: 3 | Bathrooms: 2 |
| Foundation: | Basement |
| 5-Sets: | $1,795 |
| Reproducible Master: | $1,795 |
| PDF File: | $1,795 |

*Pricing subject to change*

*Images provided by
designer/architect*

## Plan #F04-121D-0052

| | |
|---|---|
| Dimensions: | 40' W x 55'4" D |
| Heated sq. ft.: | 1,366 |
| Bedrooms: 2 | Bathrooms: 2 |
| Foundation: | Basement |
| PDF File: | $675 |
| 5-Sets: | $725 |
| 8-Sets: | $800 |
| CAD File: | $1,475 |

*Pricing subject to change*

*Images provided by
designer/architect*

© Copyright by
designer/architect

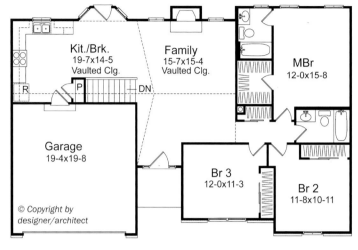

## Plan #F04-058D-0064

*Images provided by designer/architect*

| | |
|---|---|
| Dimensions: | 54' W x 35' D |
| Heated sq. ft.: | 1,323 |
| Bedrooms: 3 | Bathrooms: 2 |
| Foundation: | Basement |
| 5-Sets: | $505 |
| 8-Sets: | $575 |
| PDF File: | $575 |
| CAD File: | $675 |
| Material List: | $80 |

*Pricing subject to change*

## Plan #F04-070D-0745

*Images provided by designer/architect*

| | |
|---|---|
| Dimensions: | 54' W x 53' D |
| Heated sq. ft.: | 1,844 |
| Bedrooms: 3 | Bathrooms: 2 |
| Foundation: | Basement |
| PDF File: | $800 |
| 5-Sets: | $900 |
| 8-Sets: | $1,000 |

*Pricing subject to change*

# Plan #F04-065D-0041

| | |
|---|---|
| Dimensions: | 86'2" W x 63'8" D |
| Heated sq. ft.: | 3,171 |
| Bedrooms: 3 | Bathrooms: 2½ |

**Foundation:** Walk-out basement or basement, please specify when ordering

| | |
|---|---|
| 5-Sets: | $695 |
| 8-Sets: | $880 |
| PDF File: | $1,075 |
| Reproducible Master: | $1,075 |
| Material List: | $85 |

*Pricing subject to change*

## Features

- A double door entrance into the master bedroom leads to an amazing retreat with a stepped ceiling and a bath with a large corner shower, an oversized corner tub and an enormous walk-in closet

- The great room, breakfast area and kitchen combine with 12' ceilings to create an open feel

- The optional lower level is designed for entertaining featuring a wet bar with seating, a billiards room, a large media room, two bedrooms, and a full bath

- 3-car side entry garage

*Images provided by designer/architect*

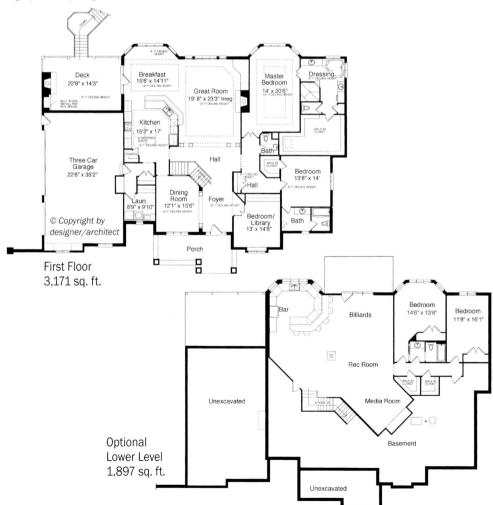

First Floor
3,171 sq. ft.

Optional
Lower Level
1,897 sq. ft.

## Plan #F04-051D-0652

| | |
|---|---|
| Dimensions: | 60' W x 56'4" D |
| Heated sq. ft.: | 1,884 |
| Bedrooms: 3 | Bathrooms: 2 |
| Foundation: | Basement |
| Exterior Walls: | 2" x 6" |
| 5-Sets: | $853 |
| 8-Sets: | $895 |
| PDF File: | $1,070 |
| CAD File: | $1,695 |
| Material List: | $75 |

*Pricing subject to change*

*Images provided by designer/architect*

Floor plan labels: DECK 12'8"x12'0", NOOK 9'-1 1/8" ceiling 11'8"x11'6", COMPUTER NOOK, BR. #2 9'-1 1/8" ceiling 11'8"x11'0", GRT. RM. 11'-1 1/8" ceiling 17'0"x19'4", KIT. 9'-1 1/8" ceiling 11'8"x11'0", MBR. 10'-1 1/8" step ceiling 13'6"x15'6", LINEN, BR. #3 9'-1 1/8" ceiling 11'8"x11'0", E. 11'-1 1/8" ceiling, DIN. 11'-1 1/8" ceiling 11'8"x13'0", PAN., BENCH, 3 CAR GARAGE 29'4"x23'8"

© Copyright by designer/architect

---

## Plan #F04-121D-0041

| | |
|---|---|
| Dimensions: | 39' W x 82' D |
| Heated sq. ft.: | 2,035 |
| Bedrooms: 3 | Bathrooms: 2½ |
| Foundation: | Basement |
| PDF File: | $825 |
| 5-Sets: | $875 |
| 8-Sets: | $950 |
| CAD File: | $1,725 |

*Pricing subject to change*

*Images provided by designer/architect*

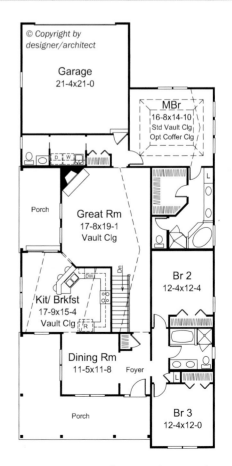

© Copyright by designer/architect

Floor plan labels: Garage 21-4x21-0, MBr 16-8x14-10 Std Vault Clg Opt Coffer Clg, Porch, Great Rm 17-8x19-1 Vault Clg, Br 2 12-4x12-4, Kit/Brkfst 17-9x15-4 Vault Clg, Dining Rm 11-5x11-8, Foyer, Porch, Br 3 12-4x12-0

## Plan #F04-011S-0115

**Dimensions:** 73' W x 56' D
**Heated Sq. Ft.:** 4,126
**Bedrooms:** 4     **Bathrooms:** 3½
**Foundation:** Partial crawl space/
walk-out basement standard; slab
for fee of $350
**Exterior Walls:** 2" x 6"
**PDF File:** $1,550
**5-Sets:** $1,600
**CAD File:** $3,200
*Pricing subject to change*

First Floor
2,698 sq. ft.

*Images provided by
designer/architect*

Lower Level
1,428 sq. ft.

## Plan #F04-055D-0543

**Dimensions:** 55'10" W x 52' D
**Heated sq. ft.:** 1,763
**Bedrooms:** 3     **Bathrooms:** 2
**Foundation:** Crawl space or slab,
please specify when ordering
**5-Sets:** $730
**8-Sets:** $870
**PDF File:** $1,340
**CAD File:** $2,065
*Pricing subject to change*

*Images provided by
designer/architect*

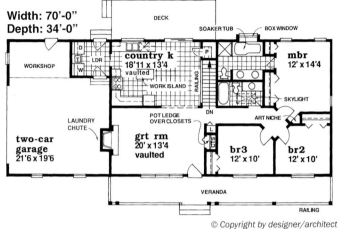

Width: 70'-0"
Depth: 34'-0"

© Copyright by designer/architect

## Plan #F04-062D-0050

| | |
|---|---|
| Dimensions: | 70' W x 34' D |
| Heated sq. ft.: | 1,408 |
| Bedrooms: 3 | Bathrooms: 2 |
| Foundation: Basement or crawl space, please specify when ordering | |
| Exterior Walls: | 2" x 6" |
| PDF File: | $750 |
| 5-Sets: | $800 |
| 8-Sets: | $875 |
| CAD File: | $1,550 |
| Material List: | $125 |
| *Pricing subject to change* | |

*Images provided by designer/architect*

---

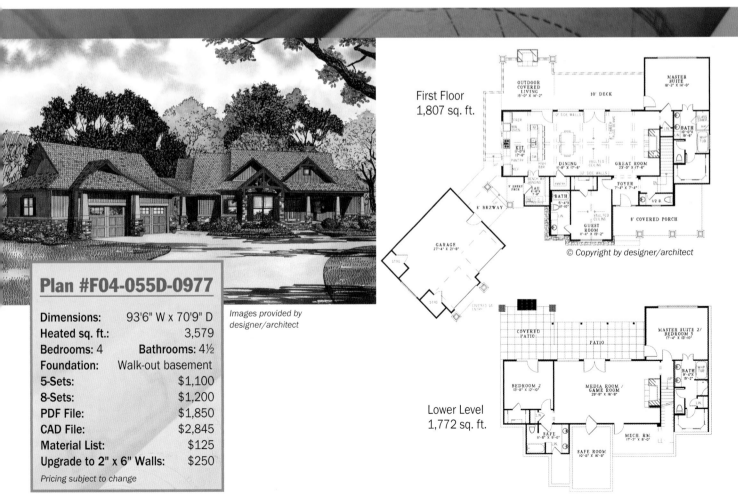

First Floor
1,807 sq. ft.

© Copyright by designer/architect

Lower Level
1,772 sq. ft.

## Plan #F04-055D-0977

| | |
|---|---|
| Dimensions: | 93'6" W x 70'9" D |
| Heated sq. ft.: | 3,579 |
| Bedrooms: 4 | Bathrooms: 4½ |
| Foundation: | Walk-out basement |
| 5-Sets: | $1,100 |
| 8-Sets: | $1,200 |
| PDF File: | $1,850 |
| CAD File: | $2,845 |
| Material List: | $125 |
| Upgrade to 2" x 6" Walls: | $250 |
| *Pricing subject to change* | |

*Images provided by designer/architect*

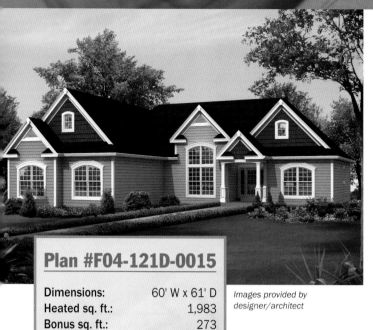

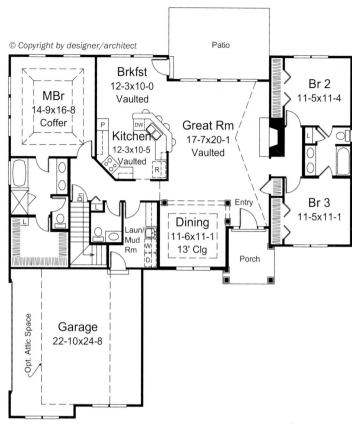

## Plan #F04-121D-0015

| | |
|---|---|
| Dimensions: | 60' W x 61' D |
| Heated sq. ft.: | 1,983 |
| Bonus sq. ft.: | 273 |
| Bedrooms: 3 | Bathrooms: 2½ |
| Foundation: | Basement |
| PDF File: | $750 |
| 5-Sets: | $800 |
| 8-Sets: | $875 |
| CAD File: | $1,550 |
| Material List: | $125 |

*Pricing subject to change*

*Images provided by designer/architect*

---

## Plan #F04-077D-0039

| | |
|---|---|
| Dimensions: | 64' W x 39' D |
| Heated sq. ft.: | 1,654 |
| Bedrooms: 3 | Bathrooms: 2 |

Foundation: Basement, slab or crawl space, please specify when ordering

| | |
|---|---|
| 5-Sets: | $1,015 |
| PDF File: | $1,125 |
| Reproducible Master: | $1,200 |
| CAD File: | $1,680 |
| Material List: | $130 |

*Pricing subject to change*

*Images provided by designer/architect*

## Plan #F04-007D-0085

| | |
|---|---|
| Dimensions: | 59'8" W x 40' D |
| Heated sq. ft.: | 1,787 |
| Bedrooms: 3 | Bathrooms: 2 |
| Foundation: | Walk-out basement |
| PDF File: | $750 |
| 5-Sets: | $800 |
| Reproducible Master: | $800 |
| 8-Sets: | $875 |
| Material List: | $125 |

*Pricing subject to change*

## Features

- The large great room with fireplace and vaulted ceiling features three large skylights and windows galore
- Cooking is sure to be a pleasure in this L-shaped well-appointed kitchen that includes a bayed breakfast area with access to the rear deck
- Every bedroom offers a spacious walk-in closet with the convenient laundry room just steps away
- Living will be simple and comfortable in this beautiful ranch home
- 2-car drive under rear entry garage

*Images provided by designer/architect*

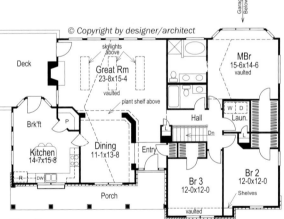

First Floor
1,787 sq. ft.

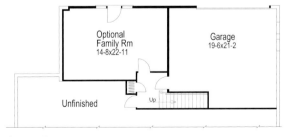

Optional
Lower Level
415 sq. ft.

## Plan #F04-055D-0211

| | |
|---|---|
| **Dimensions:** | 66'4" W x 67'2" D |
| **Heated sq. ft.:** | 2,405 |
| **Bedrooms:** 4 | **Bathrooms:** 3 |

**Foundation:** Slab or crawl space, standard; basement or walk-out basement for a fee of $250

| | |
|---|---|
| **5-Sets:** | $780 |
| **8-Sets:** | $945 |
| **PDF File:** | $1,450 |
| **CAD File:** | $2,235 |

*Pricing subject to change*

*Images provided by designer/architect*

## Features

- The grilling and covered porches combine for a relaxing outdoor living area
- The master suite enjoys a bayed sitting area and a luxurious bath with a large walk-in closet
- The kitchen, breakfast and hearth rooms combine for a cozy family living area
- 3-car side entry garage

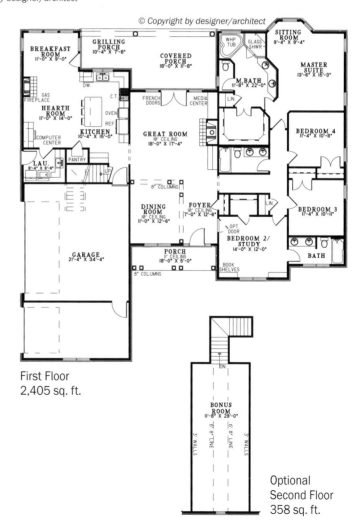

© Copyright by designer/architect

**First Floor**
2,405 sq. ft.

**Optional
Second Floor**
358 sq. ft.

## Plan #F04-034D-0105

| | |
|---|---|
| Dimensions: | 52' W x 55'2" D |
| Heated sq. ft.: | 1,598 |
| Bedrooms: 3 | Bathrooms: 2 |
| Foundation: | Concrete block |
| Exterior Walls: | 2" x 6" |
| PDF File: | $750 |
| 5-Sets: | $800 |
| Reproducible Master: | $800 |
| 8-Sets: | $875 |

*Pricing subject to change*

*Images provided by designer/architect*

## Plan #F04-116D-0030

| | |
|---|---|
| Dimensions: | 40' W x 64' D |
| Heated sq. ft.: | 1659 |
| Bedrooms: 4 | Bathrooms: 2 |
| Foundation: | Slab |
| Exterior Walls: | Concrete block |
| PDF File: | $1,050 |
| 5-Sets: | $1,100 |
| 8-Sets: | $1,175 |
| CAD File: | $1,950 |

*Pricing subject to change*

*Images provided by designer/architect*

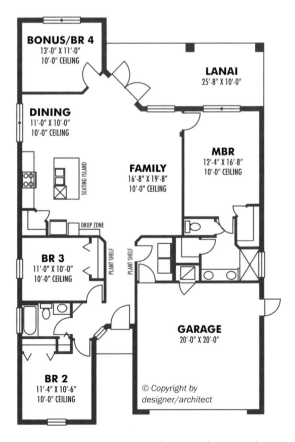

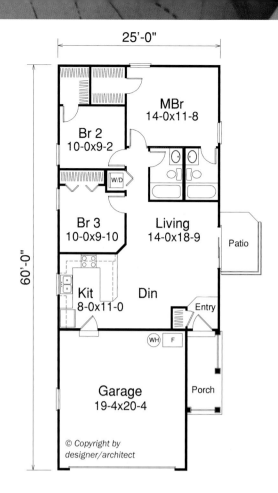

## Plan #F04-007D-0108

**Dimensions:** 25' W x 60' D
**Heated sq. ft.:** 983
**Bedrooms:** 3    **Bathrooms:** 2
**Foundation:** Crawl space or slab, please specify when ordering

| | |
|---|---|
| **PDF File:** | $675 |
| **5-Sets:** | $725 |
| **Reproducible Master:** | $725 |
| **8-Sets:** | $800 |
| **Material List:** | $125 |

*Pricing subject to change*

*Images provided by designer/architect*

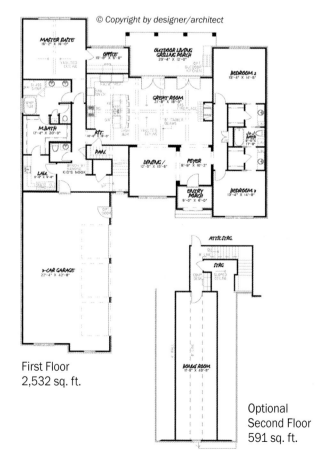

## Plan #F04-155D-0013

**Dimensions:** 63'2" W x 90' D
**Heated sq. ft.:** 2,532
**Bedrooms:** 3    **Bathrooms:** 2½
**Foundation:** Crawl space or slab standard; basement or walk-out basement for fee of $250

| | |
|---|---|
| **5-Sets:** | $1,100 |
| **8-Sets:** | $1,200 |
| **PDF File:** | $1,850 |
| **CAD File:** | $2,845 |

*Pricing subject to change*

*Images provided by designer/architect*

First Floor
2,532 sq. ft.

Optional
Second Floor
591 sq. ft.

## Plan #F04-047D-0057

| | |
|---|---|
| Dimensions: | 79'6" W x 91' D |
| Heated sq. ft.: | 3,064 |
| Bedrooms: 3 | Bathrooms: 3½ |
| Foundation: | Slab |
| Exterior Walls: | Concrete block |
| PDF File: | $1,050 |
| 5-Sets: | $1,100 |
| Reproducible Master: | $1,100 |
| CAD File: | $1,950 |

*Pricing subject to change*

## Features

- The eye-catching den with an enchanting balcony has a coffered ceiling
- The master suite has views of a private garden, shares a see-through fireplace with the outdoor spa, and accesses the patio
- The living room has a wet bar and a cozy corner fireplace
- The summer kitchen allows for outdoor grilling and cooking in warmer months
- The optional second floor has an additional 366 square feet of living area
- Framing - only concrete block available
- 3-car side entry garage

*Images provided by designer/architect*

© Copyright by designer/architect

First Floor
3,064 sq. ft.

Optional
Second Floor
366 sq. ft.

## Plan #F04-028D-0054

| | |
|---|---|
| **Dimensions:** | 60' W x 76' D |
| **Heated sq. ft.:** | 2,123 |
| **Bedrooms:** 3 | **Bathrooms:** 3½ |

**Foundation:** Slab or crawl space, please specify when ordering

| | |
|---|---|
| **5-Sets:** | $860 |
| **8-Sets:** | $960 |
| **PDF File:** | $1,010 |

*Pricing subject to change*

*Images provided by designer/architect*

### Features

- Bedroom #2 enjoys its own private sitting area
- The large rear covered porch is perfect for providing a great outdoor retreat
- Accessing the home is easy with two separate entries off of the large wrap-around porch
- Bedroom 2 is a second master suite with its own sitting area

© Copyright by designer/architect

Images provided by
designer/architect

## Plan #F04-011D-0349

| | |
|---|---|
| Dimensions: | 103' W x 67'8" D |
| Heated sq. ft.: | 2,122 |
| Bedrooms: 3 | Bathrooms: 2½ |
| Foundation: | Joisted crawl space |
| Exterior Walls: | 2" x 6" |
| PDF File: | $1,000 |
| 5-Sets: | $1,050 |
| CAD File: | $2,000 |

*Pricing subject to change*

## Plan #F04-007D-0161

| | |
|---|---|
| Dimensions: | 70' W x 36' D |
| Heated sq. ft.: | 1,480 |
| Bedrooms: 2 | Bathrooms: 2 |
| Foundation: | Slab |
| Exterior Walls: | 2" x 6" |
| PDF File: | $750 |
| 5-Sets: | $800 |
| 8-Sets: | $875 |
| CAD File: | $1,550 |
| Material List: | $125 |

*Pricing subject to change*

Images provided by
designer/architect

© Copyright by
designer/architect

## Plan #F04-121D-0043

| | |
|---|---|
| Dimensions: | 69'8" W x 42'4" D |
| Heated sq. ft.: | 2,033 |
| Bedrooms: 3 | Bathrooms: 2½ |
| Foundation: | Basement |
| PDF File: | $825 |
| 5-Sets: | $875 |
| 8-Sets: | $950 |
| CAD File: | $1,725 |
| *Pricing subject to change* | |

*Images provided by designer/architect*

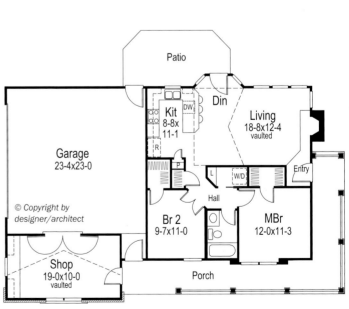

## Plan #F04-007D-0135

| | |
|---|---|
| Dimensions: | 23' W x 23'4" D |
| Heated sq. ft.: | 801 |
| Bedrooms: 2 | Bathrooms: 1 |
| Foundation: | Slab |
| PDF File: | $675 |
| 5-Sets: | $725 |
| Reproducible Master: | $725 |
| 8-Sets: | $800 |
| Material List: | $125 |
| *Pricing subject to change* | |

*Images provided by designer/architect*

## Plan #F04-076D-0252

**Dimensions:** 103'5" W x 93'10" D
**Heated sq. ft.:** 2,971
**Bedrooms:** 4 **Bathrooms:** 3½
**Foundation:** Basement, crawl space or slab, please specify when ordering

| | |
|---|---|
| **5-Sets:** | $1,000 |
| **8-Sets:** | $1,325 |
| **PDF File:** | $1,825 |
| **CAD File:** | $2,150 |

*Pricing subject to change*

*Images provided by designer/architect*

## Features

- Charming Craftsman and country style collide creating a fantastic looking one-story home with angled garage bays
- Upon entering, you'll be greeted by a study/bedroom on the left and a formal dining room on the right
- A ultra private master suite is tucked away on the right side of the home and offers the homeowners a huge walk-in closet and a plush bath
- Two other bedrooms reside on the left side of the home each with direct bath access
- 3-car angled front entry garage

Optional Bonus Room 755 sq. ft.

First Floor 2,971 sq. ft.

© Copyright by designer/architect

## Plan #F04-077D-0001

| | |
|---|---|
| **Dimensions:** | 72'10" W x 41' D |
| **Heated sq. ft.:** | 1,638 |
| **Bedrooms:** 3 | **Bathrooms:** 2 |

**Foundation:** Basement, crawl space or slab, please specify when ordering

| | |
|---|---|
| **5-Sets:** | $1,015 |
| **PDF File:** | $1,125 |
| **Reproducible Master:** | $1,200 |
| **CAD File:** | $1,680 |
| **Material List:** | $130 |

*Pricing subject to change*

*Images provided by designer/architect*

### Features

- The great room features a fireplace with flanking double doors that access the covered porch
- The centrally located kitchen serves the breakfast and dining areas with ease and has a raised breakfast bar
- Two secondary bedrooms skillfully share the full bath between them
- There is plenty of storage space located in the garage
- 2-car side entry garage

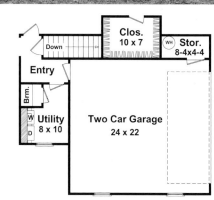

Optional Basement
Stair Location

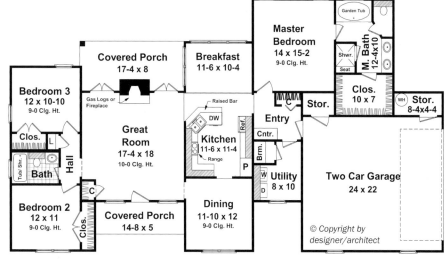

First Floor
1,638 sq. ft.

# Take Living OUTDOORS

You wake to a perfectly sunny day. After a long stretch to awaken your senses you head to the French doors and swing them open to reveal an amazing oasis with stunning gardens, patios, and a waterfall. No, you are not on vacation – you are experiencing and living the luxury of your very own outdoor living area!

It seems homeowners have taken the idea of a "staycation" to a whole new level. Instead of jetting off to pricey tropical vacation destinations all the time, now more homeowners than ever are looking to invest their income into something more gratifying, their home. Why not invest in something you can truly enjoy every single day? Homeowners are enjoying staying at home more, and that includes entertaining on a more regular basis. With many home designs being designed smaller, more compact, and efficient, it seems only natural that entertaining and everyday living is now heading outdoors. The line between the interior spaces and the exterior ones has been blurred now more than ever before.

Both home and landscape designers have seen a huge desire for homeowners to bring an indoor entertainment experience to the outdoors. Through adding things like fireplaces, fire pits, outdoor kitchens, televisions, sound systems, etc., the party has moved to the outdoors.

Think of your outdoor space as another room in your home. Gone are the days of rickety old rusted patio furniture and a wilted plant in one corner of the concrete slab patio. The best outdoor living areas rival the interior ones by creating an open flow that encourages easy entertaining, dining and relaxing.

*Page 234, top: Plan #F04-047D-0083 on page 127; bottom: Plan #F04-055D-0748 on page 8; Page 235 top: 2006 ASLA Award Winner, Marmol Radziner and Associates, Los Angeles, California, photo by John Ellis; middle: water and fire elements collide, Copyright © 2010 Doug Bennett, www.dougbennett. net; Bottom, left: Plan #055D-0215, houseplansandmore.com; Bottom, right: Green Guys, greenguysstl.com.*

## Get Started!

List some features you want to incorporate into your outdoor area so you can determine what the focal point should be.

Do you love the idea of an outdoor kitchen? Then, make that one of the focal points. If your budget or area is small, maybe a deluxe grill is all you need to get the area ready for entertaining. Or, if you plan to spare no expense, then there are countless amenities available including: built-in grills, stovetops, refrigerators, and even a pizza oven can be a family fun spot that no doubt will be a conversation starter when friends are over for memorable get-togethers.

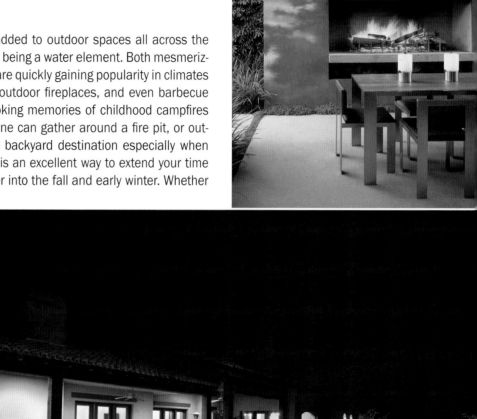

There are two other popular features being added to outdoor spaces all across the country - one being a fire source, and the other being a water element. Both mesmerizing as well as relaxing, fire and water features are quickly gaining popularity in climates of all types. When it comes to fire - fire pits, outdoor fireplaces, and even barbecue grills fall into this popular category. Often evoking memories of childhood campfires and family time, adding a place where everyone can gather around a fire pit, or outdoor fireplace is bound to become a favorite backyard destination especially when the weather starts to cool down. This feature is an excellent way to extend your time in the outdoors earlier into the spring and later into the fall and early winter. Whether it's an intimate gathering with couples enjoying some wine on a fall evening, or a lively night with the entire family roasting marshmallows, one thing is for sure; a backyard fireplace or fire pit is bound to create countless memories.

Another focal point cropping up in outdoor spaces everywhere are water features. From waterfalls and fountains, to hot tubs and swimming pools, a water feature is a welcomed amenity that appeals to the senses. Nothing says refreshing like the cool, crystal blue waters of a swimming pool. And, the bubbling sound of a fountain or waterfall instantly refreshes and relaxes the soul. So, whatever your budget, there is a water solution for your outdoor space.

## HOW TO CREATE A SEAMLESS FEEL FROM YOUR OUTDOOR ROOM TO THE INDOOR SPACES OF YOUR HOME:

 for your patio that mimics your interior flooring and instantly expand your living space visually. Homeowners are taking a lot of time and putting a lot of thought into treating and decorating outdoor patios like indoor rooms – again, sort of bringing the look and feel of the home's interior to its outdoor spaces creating a cohesive experience between the indoors and the outdoors. While many homeowners may stick with traditional concrete or stamped concrete that comes in a variety of colors, what some designers believe is more aesthetically pleasing are pavers and flagstone products. These have also proven to be a wiser investment in terms of long term value and durability. So, start with the floor and select a beautiful foundation that mirrors your interior spaces. It will create a solid design anchor that will merge your indoor and outdoor rooms seamlessly. If your outdoor space is covered like many are today, you may even wish to use ceramic tile, or other stone tile surfaces that can be used both indoors and outdoors for the ultimate seamless look.

# select furniture

that resembles the interior style when it comes to colors and textures. This will further enhance the open feel of these merging spaces naturally and will keep the areas from looking disjointed. When investing in outdoor furniture, it is sometimes best to stick to natural neutral colors such as brown, beige, white, and other earth tones. These are timeless colors that make the perfect backdrop for highlighting outdoor artwork, textiles such as pillows, and other exciting colorful accessories. However, although neutral furniture is a wise investment, current trends in outdoor spaces show wildly bright and neon colored furniture gaining popularity. Regardless of its color, group furniture pieces creating several types of spaces for dining, intimate conversation spots, and seating areas for larger parties. If you have a special focal point in nature, don't forget to arrange a seating area so this can be enjoyed to its fullest. If you're lucky enough to have panoramic ocean or lake views, arrange one seating area so it completely enjoys this scenic vista with little or no visual distractions.

*Page 236, top: Plan #071S-0051, houseplansandmore.com; middle: Plan #F04-011S-0001 on page 36, Bob Greenspan, photographer; bottom Plan #F04-101D-0056 on page 270, Warren Diggles Photography; Page 237 top: Outdoor Kitchen/Grill; Pergola and Pizza Oven, Green Guys, greenguysstl.com; middle: Plan #F04-065D-0041 on page 218; Bottom: istock-photos.com.*

## Fire or Rain?

What would you choose for
your outdoor living area?
Fire, water, or both? Why?

Last, don't forget to incorporate lighting that highlights all of the amazing features and design ideas you have added to your own outdoor paradise. Not only will "lightscaping" call attention to a focal point like a water feature, it can designate a space. For example, a chandelier or statement light fixture can spotlight a special dining spot, or a unique side table lamp will make an intimate outdoor space even more cozy and comfortable.

Don't let another season go by without finding a way to smoothly transition your indoor and outdoor spaces into something truly spectacular. Use some or all of these great outdoor design trends to provide a year-round outdoor oasis that creates a sanctuary for your senses just steps from your home's interior.

## select color

including vibrant colors that have really made a comeback recently and add a tremendous amount of personality to any space both indoors and out. So, choose three to four colors for your scheme and have fun! Rich reds, bold oranges, vivid blues or garden-inspired greens all offer personality. Then, pair up some plants and flowers native to your area for easy maintenance. Select matching or contrasting colors and you'll have an outdoor area that exudes your own personal style.

# eat, play & live: using your outdoor space

Outdoor living is a trend that is here to stay. For many homeowners the opportunity to have a backyard paradise is too good to be true. However, as thoughts of swimming pools, gardens, outdoor televisions, fireplaces, gorgeous stonework, kitchens, fabrics and furniture swirl through the mind, it can create a sense of overwhelming confusion causing you to see major dollar signs. Sure, outdoor living space is great, but beyond the grill, where do you even start? How extensive is this outdoor project going to be?

## BELOW ARE SOME TIPS FOR PLANNING YOUR OUTDOOR LIVING EXPANSION:

*1* Remember, outdoor living can be made as simple or as grand as you desire.

*2* Set a budget. This will also help determine what outdoor living components can become a reality and are must-haves.

*3* Evaluate the space. A small patio for hosting dinner parties with friends and family may be closer to reality than a huge swimming pool and spa. Will it be better to have one multi-purpose area or designated zones for dining, resting, and play? Take note of the space available and determine which amenities are most important to your lifestyle.

## TODAY'S MOST POPULAR OPTIONS INCLUDE:

### outdoor kitchens are the most popular feature in outdoor living spaces right now. People naturally tend to gather in the kitchen anyway, so combining hosting and cooking with the pleasure of visiting with guests in an outdoor setting is truly a winning combination. To ensure function, look at how the outdoor kitchen will be used with your lifestyle. The basic outdoor kitchen is an extension of the home and typically contains a small prep sink, grill, and limited counter space for small tasks. Close proximity to the indoor kitchen allows easy transport of ingredients, dishes, and drinks not stored outdoors. On the other end of the spectrum, an outdoor kitchen can be fully independent from the one inside the home and can include a dishwasher, refrigerator, cooktop, and storage. These elaborate kitchens are typically L- or U-shaped with an island, creating a work atmosphere with similar distinct zones for food preparation and cooking like an indoor kitchen utilizes. These outdoor kitchens are ideal for hosting large groups. Outdoor kitchens of any size can be fully built-in with massive grills and impressive hardware, or comprised of rolling carts that move when necessary. Permanent versus flexible kitchen options are often determined by budget and local climate.

## outdoor social spaces

outdoor social spaces fill the need for a place to retreat to. The options are endless when it comes to creating a space that is perfect for private or social use. Again, determined by budget and need, outdoor living rooms can be sprawling extensions of the indoors, full of cozy couches and chairs, fireplaces, and even outdoor media centers. There can be separate dining and resting spaces, or these can be combined into one multi-purpose space with a few well-chosen pieces of furniture. The choice is up to you, but either option can be a haven of comfort. Part of keeping outdoor living spaces functional is keeping them comfortable. Outdoor fans and fireplaces add decorative touches with practical purposes. Outdoor fans are the same as indoor fans since they circulate the air, provide a light breeze, and help shoo away disruptive bugs. Whether placed over dining or sitting areas, outdoor fans are rated for damp or wet use, meaning they can be placed in partially uncovered situations.

Outdoor fireplaces come in numerous shapes and sizes, and are the perfect accessory for any outdoor space. Two-sided fireplaces can be placed in the home's exterior wall and enjoyed both inside and out. Chimineas are freestanding pot-bellied fireplaces, perfect for smaller patios and situations that may require mobility. Fire pits can be permanent or portable and radiate warmth from all sides. These are the most popular choices in today's homes. Lastly, is the built-in outdoor fireplace. These are permanent masterpieces of masonry, fully constructed like indoor fireplaces with surrounds and mantles. Stunning and functional, built-in fireplaces can be prohibitively expensive and do require regular maintenance, but they are a stunning addition to any backyard landscape.

# outdoor play

reminds us that the outdoors is a place for fun and maintaining an active, healthy lifestyle, too. While outdoor living areas are typically ideal for creating a relaxing paradise close to home; they usually only designate space for dining and resting. Keep in mind, the need for play space is equally important. Many families are choosing to include outdoor sport courts into their landscape. Whether tennis is your game, or a quick game of hoops with your rising star basketball player, sport courts can handle active families and their need for a variety of the active options they crave. And, not just for looks, a backyard swimming pool is beautiful, but it also provides a healthy active option for people of all ages even during the hottest months of the year. To attractively separate play from relaxation areas, try using hedges and landscaping to create play areas in the yard. Not only are these dividers decorative, they keep errant balls and other toys from interrupting the flow of conversation on the patio. In addition to sport courts, outdoor play areas allow for outdoor meditation areas or yoga nooks. Playing outside is not just for the young, but for the young at heart as well.

Whether dividing the outdoors into "rooms," or openly sharing the space for activities, it is important to be aware of how the outdoor living space will be used. Specialty landscaping and outdoor storage can be used to keep various activities from interrupting one another. However you choose to use your space, remember to take advantage of every corner, so your relaxing retreat not so far from home has everything you could possible want right in your own backyard.

*Page 238, top: Outdoor kitchen/grill with pergola, Green Guys, greenguysstl.com; middle: Plan #026D-0252, houseplansandmore.com; bottom: Outdoor fireplace, Green Guys, greenguysstl.com; Page 239 top: Plan #106S-0046, houseplansandmore.com; bottom: Outdoor pool house with kitchen and living area, Green Guys, greenguysstl.com; Page 240, top: Plan #011S-0001, houseplansandmore.com; middle: Plan #055D-0817, houseplansandmore.com; bottom: Plan #065S-0033, houseplansandmore.com; Page 241, top to bottom: Plan #091D-0476, houseplansandmore.com; Backyard tennis/basketball sport court, sportcourtstlouis.com; Plan #F04-011S-0003 on page 108; Plan #071S-0002, houseplansandmore.com.*

## Plan #F04-011D-0526

| | |
|---|---|
| Dimensions: | 72' W x 65'6" D |
| Heated Sq. Ft.: | 2,735 |
| Bedrooms: 3 | Bathrooms: 2½ |

**Foundation:** Crawl space or post & beam standard; slab or basement for a fee of $295

| | |
|---|---|
| Exterior Walls: | 2" x 6" |
| PDF File: | $1,250 |
| 5-Sets: | $1,300 |
| CAD File: | $2,400 |

*Pricing subject to change*

*Images provided by designer/architect*

## Features

- The vaulted great room with fireplace and covered porch views commands full attention when you enter this home
- A quiet home office is tucked away near the foyer
- The kitchen has an efficient angled island and breakfast bar that overlooks the great room and breakfast nook
- Two secondary bedrooms find themselves located behind the kitchen and share a full bath
- 3-car front entry garage

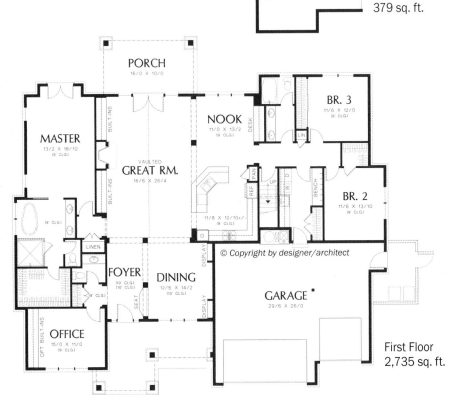

Optional Second Floor 379 sq. ft.

First Floor 2,735 sq. ft.

© Copyright by designer/architect

## Plan #F04-011D-0340

| | |
|---|---|
| Dimensions: | 50' W x 56'6" D |
| Heated sq. ft.: | 2,795 |
| Bedrooms: 3 | Bathrooms: 2½ |
| Foundation: | Slab |
| Exterior Walls: | 2" x 6" |
| PDF File: | $1,100 |
| 5-Sets: | $1,150 |
| CAD File: | $2,200 |

*Pricing subject to change*

First Floor 1,655 sq. ft.

Optional Lower Level 1,140 sq. ft.

*Images provided by designer/architect*

© Copyright by designer/architect

## Plan #F04-020D-0362

| | |
|---|---|
| Dimensions: | 64' W x 77' D |
| Heated Sq. Ft.: | 1,837 |
| Bedrooms: 4 | Bathrooms: 2½ |
| Foundation: | Basement |
| Exterior Walls: | 2" x 6" |
| 5-Sets: | $1,015 |
| PDF File: | $1,125 |
| CAD File: | $1,680 |

*Pricing subject to change*

*Images provided by designer/architect*

© Copyright by designer/architect

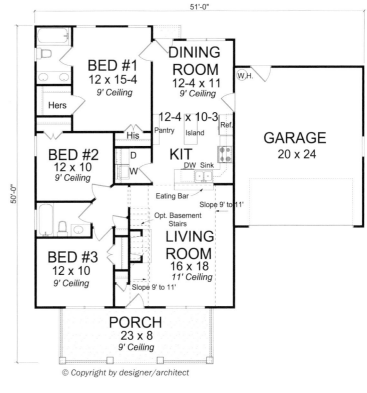

51'-0"

50'-0"

BED #1
12 x 15-4
*9' Ceiling*

DINING ROOM
12-4 x 11
*9' Ceiling*

W.H.

Hers

His

12-4 x 10-3

Pantry

Island

Ref.

KIT

GARAGE
20 x 24

BED #2
12 x 10
*9' Ceiling*

D

W

DW

Sink

Eating Bar

Slope 9' to 11'

Opt. Basement
Stairs

LIVING ROOM
16 x 18
*11' Ceiling*

BED #3
12 x 10
*9' Ceiling*

Slope 9' to 11'

PORCH
23 x 8
*9' Ceiling*

© Copyright by designer/architect

## Plan #F04-130D-0367

*Images provided by designer/architect*

| | |
|---|---|
| **Dimensions:** | 51' W x 50' D |
| **Heated Sq. Ft.:** | 1,277 |
| **Bedrooms:** 3 | **Bathrooms:** 2 |

**Foundation:** Slab standard; crawl space or basement for a fee of $150

| | |
|---|---|
| **PDF File:** | $845 |
| **5-Sets:** | $970 |
| **8-Sets:** | $1,045 |
| **CAD File:** | $1,095 |
| **Upgrade to 2" x 6" Walls:** | $150 |

*Pricing subject to change*

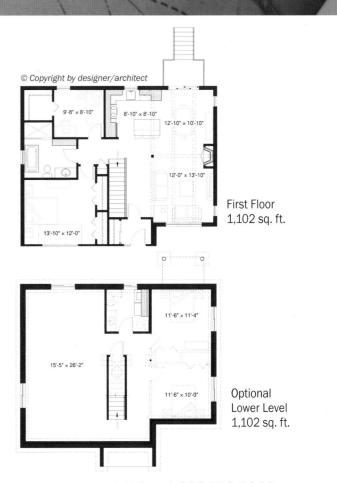

© Copyright by designer/architect

9'-8" × 8'-10"

8'-10" × 8'-10"

12'-10" × 10'-10"

12'-0" × 13'-10"

13'-10" × 12'-0"

First Floor
1,102 sq. ft.

11'-6" × 11'-4"

15'-5" × 28'-2"

11'-6" × 10'-0"

Optional Lower Level
1,102 sq. ft.

## Plan #F04-032D-0932

*Images provided by designer/architect*

| | |
|---|---|
| **Dimensions:** | 38' W x 30' D |
| **Heated Sq. Ft.:** | 1,102 |
| **Bedrooms:** 4 | **Bathrooms:** 2 |
| **Foundation:** | Basement |
| **Exterior Walls:** | 2" x 6" |
| **5-Sets:** | $725 |
| **8-Sets:** | $755 |
| **PDF File:** | $870 |
| **CAD File:** | $1,440 |
| **Material List:** | $110 |

*Pricing subject to change*

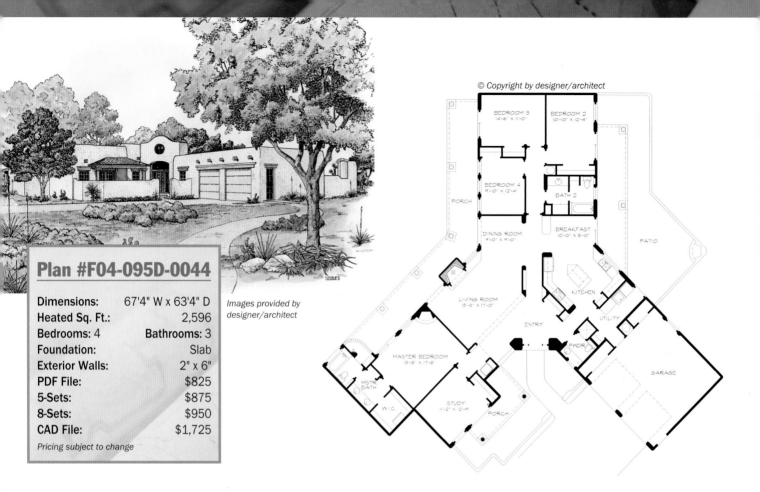

## Plan #F04-095D-0044

| Dimensions: | 67'4" W x 63'4" D |
|---|---|
| Heated Sq. Ft.: | 2,596 |
| Bedrooms: 4 | Bathrooms: 3 |
| Foundation: | Slab |
| Exterior Walls: | 2" x 6" |
| PDF File: | $825 |
| 5-Sets: | $875 |
| 8-Sets: | $950 |
| CAD File: | $1,725 |

*Pricing subject to change*

*Images provided by designer/architect*

## Plan #F04-155D-0021

| Dimensions: | 72'2" W x 64'10" D |
|---|---|
| Heated Sq. Ft.: | 2,272 |
| Bedrooms: 3 | Bathrooms: 2½ |

Foundation: Crawl space or slab, please specify when ordering

| 5-Sets: | $1,100 |
|---|---|
| 8-Sets: | $1,200 |
| PDF File: | $1,850 |
| CAD File: | $2,845 |

*Pricing subject to change*

*Images provided by designer/architect*

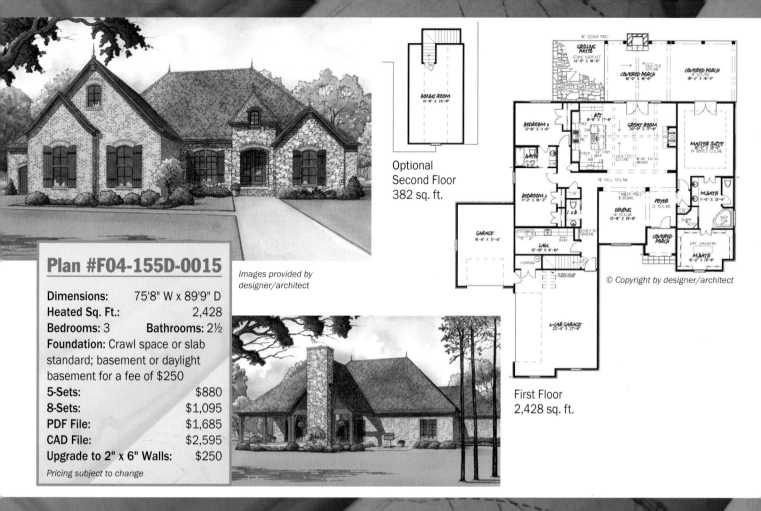

Images provided by designer/architect

Optional
Second Floor
382 sq. ft.

© Copyright by designer/architect

First Floor
2,428 sq. ft.

## Plan #F04-155D-0015

| | |
|---|---|
| Dimensions: | 75'8" W x 89'9" D |
| Heated Sq. Ft.: | 2,428 |
| Bedrooms: 3 | Bathrooms: 2½ |

Foundation: Crawl space or slab standard; basement or daylight basement for a fee of $250

| | |
|---|---|
| 5-Sets: | $880 |
| 8-Sets: | $1,095 |
| PDF File: | $1,685 |
| CAD File: | $2,595 |
| Upgrade to 2" x 6" Walls: | $250 |

*Pricing subject to change*

Images provided by designer/architect

© Copyright by designer/architect

## Plan #F04-034D-0104

| | |
|---|---|
| Dimensions: | 52' W x 55'2" D |
| Heated Sq. Ft.: | 1,598 |
| Bedrooms: 3 | Bathrooms: 2 |
| Foundation: | Concrete block |
| PDF File: | $750 |
| 5-Sets: | $800 |
| Reproducible Master: | $800 |
| 8-Sets: | $875 |
| 2" x 6" Wall Upgrade: | $150 |

*Pricing subject to change*

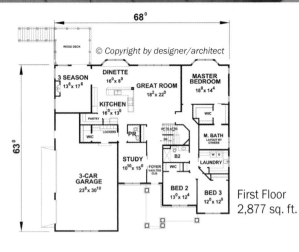

© Copyright by designer/architect

**First Floor**
2,877 sq. ft.

**Optional Lower Level**
2,111 sq. ft.

## Plan #F04-026D-1924

*Images provided by designer/architect*

| | |
|---|---|
| Dimensions: | 68' W x 63' D |
| Heated Sq. Ft.: | 2,877 |
| Bedrooms: 3 | Bathrooms: 3 |
| Foundation: | Basement |
| Exterior Walls: | 2" x 6" |
| PDF File: | $915 |
| 5-Sets: | $1,025 |
| 8-Sets: | $1,205 |
| CAD File: | $1,415 |

*Pricing subject to change*

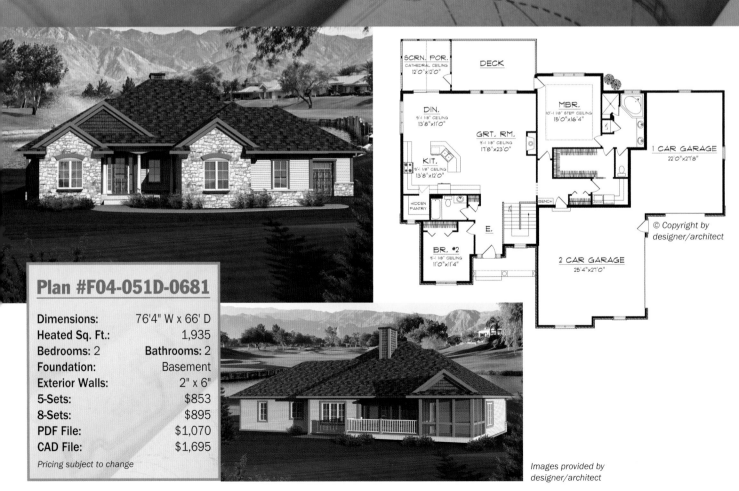

© Copyright by designer/architect

## Plan #F04-051D-0681

| | |
|---|---|
| Dimensions: | 76'4" W x 66' D |
| Heated Sq. Ft.: | 1,935 |
| Bedrooms: 2 | Bathrooms: 2 |
| Foundation: | Basement |
| Exterior Walls: | 2" x 6" |
| 5-Sets: | $853 |
| 8-Sets: | $895 |
| PDF File: | $1,070 |
| CAD File: | $1,695 |

*Pricing subject to change*

*Images provided by designer/architect*

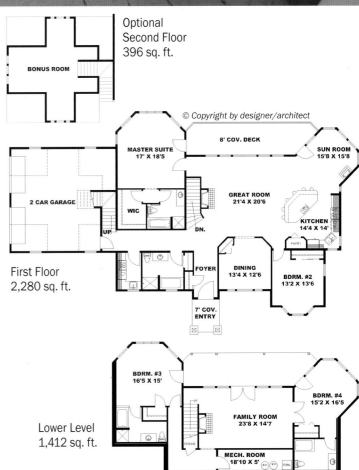

**Optional Second Floor 396 sq. ft.**

BONUS ROOM

MASTER SUITE 17' X 18'5

8' COV. DECK

SUN ROOM 15'8 X 15'8

2 CAR GARAGE

WIC

UP

DN.

GREAT ROOM 21'4 X 20'6

KITCHEN 14'4 X 14'

FOYER

DINING 13'4 X 12'6

BDRM. #2 13'2 X 13'6

7' COV. ENTRY

**First Floor 2,280 sq. ft.**

BDRM. #3 16'5 X 15'

BDRM. #4 15'2 X 16'5

FAMILY ROOM 23'8 X 14'7

**Lower Level 1,412 sq. ft.**

MECH. ROOM 18'10 X 5'

## Plan #F04-088D-0733

| | |
|---|---|
| Dimensions: | 89'5" W x 50'4" D |
| Heated Sq. Ft.: | 3,692 |
| Bedrooms: 5 | Bathrooms: 4 |
| Foundation: | Walk-out basement |
| 5-Sets: | $875 |
| 8-Sets: | $950 |
| PDF File: | $1,250 |
| CAD File: | $1,250 |

*Pricing subject to change*

*Images provided by designer/architect*

---

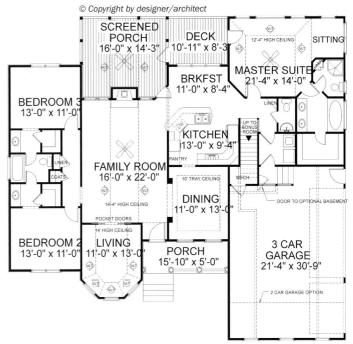

SCREENED PORCH 16'-0" x 14'-3"

DECK 10'-11" x 8'-3"

12'-4" HIGH CEILING

SITTING

BRKFST 11'-0" x 8'-4"

MASTER SUITE 21'-4" x 14'-0"

BEDROOM 3 13'-0" x 11'-0"

KITCHEN 13'-0" x 9'-4"

LINEN

UP TO BONUS ROOM

PANTRY

MECH

FAMILY ROOM 16'-0" x 22'-0"

14'-4" HIGH CEILING

LINEN

COATS

10' TRAY CEILING

DOOR TO OPTIONAL BASEMENT

DINING 11'-0" x 13'-0"

3 CAR GARAGE 21'-4" x 30'-9"

POCKET DOORS

14' HIGH CEILING

BEDROOM 2 13'-0" x 11'-0"

LIVING 11'-0" x 13'-0"

PORCH 15'-10" x 5'-0"

2 CAR GARAGE OPTION

## Plan #F04-013D-0021

| | |
|---|---|
| Dimensions: | 63' W x 58' D |
| Heated Sq. Ft.: | 1,982 |
| Bonus Sq. Ft.: | 386 |
| Bedrooms: 3 | Bathrooms: 2½ |
| Foundation: | Basement standard; crawl space or slab for a fee of $250 |
| PDF File: | $895 |
| 5-Sets: | $945 |
| 8-Sets: | $995 |
| CAD File: | $1,395 |
| Material List: | $125 |
| Upgrade to 2" x 6" Walls: | $250 |

*Pricing subject to change*

*Images provided by designer/architect*

© Copyright by designer/architect

*Images provided by designer/architect*

## Plan #F04-055D-0974

| | |
|---|---|
| Dimensions: | 72' W x 73' D |
| Heated Sq. Ft.: | 2,988 |
| Bedrooms: 3 | Bathrooms: 3½ |
| Foundation: Slab or crawl space standard; basement or walk-out basement for a fee of $250 | |
| 5-Sets: | $830 |
| 8-Sets: | $1,020 |
| PDF File: | $1,560 |
| CAD File: | $2,400 |
| Upgrade to 2" x 6" Walls: | $250 |

*Pricing subject to change*

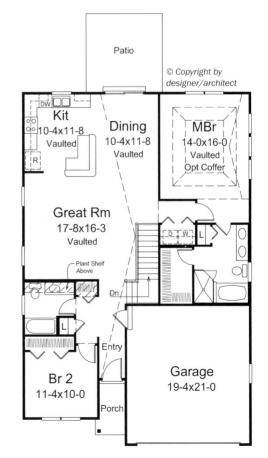

© Copyright by designer/architect

*Images provided by designer/architect*

## Plan #F04-121D-0028

| | |
|---|---|
| Dimensions: | 36' W x 54' D |
| Heated Sq. Ft.: | 1,433 |
| Bedrooms: 2 | Bathrooms: 2 |
| Foundation: | Basement |
| PDF File: | $675 |
| 5-Sets: | $725 |
| 8-Sets: | $800 |
| CAD File: | $1,475 |
| Material List: | $125 |

*Pricing subject to change*

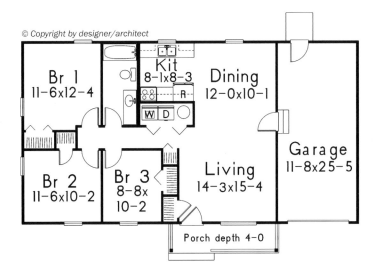

© Copyright by designer/architect

Br 1
11-6x12-4

Kit
8-1x8-3

Dining
12-0x10-1

Garage
11-8x25-5

Br 2
11-6x10-2

Br 3
8-8x
10-2

Living
14-3x15-4

Porch depth 4-0

## Plan #F04-001D-0018

*Images provided by designer/architect*

| | |
|---|---|
| Dimensions: | 50' W x 30' D |
| Heated Sq. Ft.: | 988 |
| Bedrooms: 3 | Bathrooms: 1 |
| Foundation: Basement or crawl space, please specify when ordering | |
| PDF File: | $600 |
| 5-Sets: | $650 |
| Reproducible Master: | $650 |
| 8-Sets: | $725 |
| Material List: | $125 |

*Pricing subject to change*

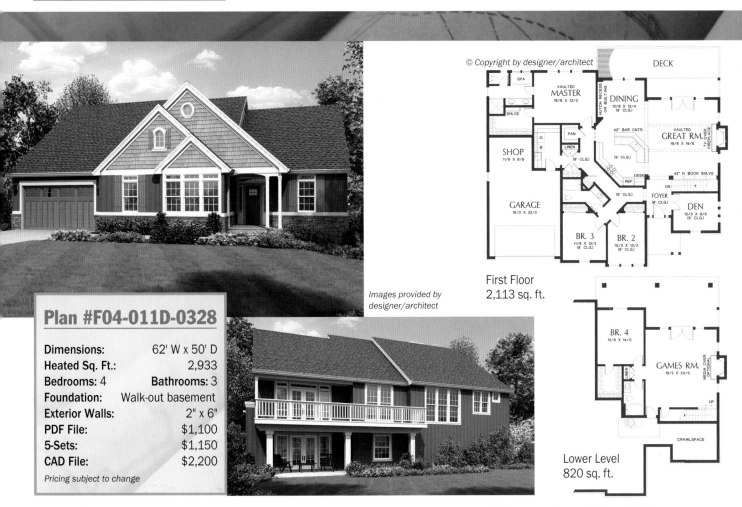

© Copyright by designer/architect

DECK

SPA

VAULTED
MASTER
16/6 X 13/0

DINING
12/8 X 13/4
(9' CLG.)

SHLVS

42" BAR CNTR.

VAULTED
GREAT RM.
19/6 X 19/6
TV OVER FIREPLACE

SHOP
11/6 X 8/8

PAN

LINEN

(9' CLG.)

42" H. BOOK SHLVS

DESK

REF

FOYER
(9' CLG.)

DEN
12/0 X 9/8
(9' CLG.)

GARAGE
19/0 X 22/0

BR. 3
11/6 X 12/2
(9' CLG.)

BR. 2
10/0 X 13/2
(9' CLG.)

First Floor
2,113 sq. ft.

BR. 4
12/8 X 14/0

GAMES RM.
19/2 X 20/0

LINEN

CRAWLSPACE

Lower Level
820 sq. ft.

## Plan #F04-011D-0328

| | |
|---|---|
| Dimensions: | 62' W x 50' D |
| Heated Sq. Ft.: | 2,933 |
| Bedrooms: 4 | Bathrooms: 3 |
| Foundation: | Walk-out basement |
| Exterior Walls: | 2" x 6" |
| PDF File: | $1,100 |
| 5-Sets: | $1,150 |
| CAD File: | $2,200 |

*Pricing subject to change*

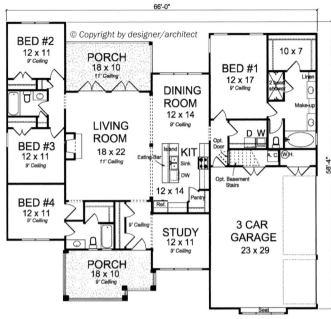

## Plan #F04-130D-0323

| | |
|---|---|
| Dimensions: | 66' W x 58'4" D |
| Heated Sq. Ft.: | 2,193 |
| Bedrooms: 4 | Bathrooms: 3 |
| Foundation: Slab standard; crawl space or basement for a fee of $150 | |
| PDF File: | $925 |
| 5-Sets: | $1,150 |
| CAD File: | $1,175 |
| 8-Sets: | $1,225 |
| Upgrade to 2" x 6" Walls: | $150 |
| *Pricing subject to change* | |

*Images provided by designer/architect*

## Plan #F04-065D-0381

| | |
|---|---|
| Dimensions: | 60' W x 69'9" D |
| Heated Sq. Ft.: | 2,335 |
| Bedrooms: 3 | Bathrooms: 2 |
| Foundation: | Basement |
| 5-Sets: | $795 |
| 8-Sets: | $880 |
| PDF File: | $1,075 |
| CAD File: | $1,620 |
| Material List: | $85 |
| *Pricing subject to change* | |

*Images provided by designer/architect*

## Plan #F04-055D-0196

| | |
|---|---|
| Dimensions: | 60'6" W x 91'4" D |
| Heated Sq. Ft.: | 2,039 |
| Bedrooms: 4 | Bathrooms: 3 |

Foundation: Slab or crawl space, please specify when ordering

| | |
|---|---|
| 5-Sets: | $730 |
| 8-Sets: | $870 |
| PDF File: | $1,340 |
| CAD File: | $2,065 |

*Pricing subject to change*

*Images provided by designer/architect*

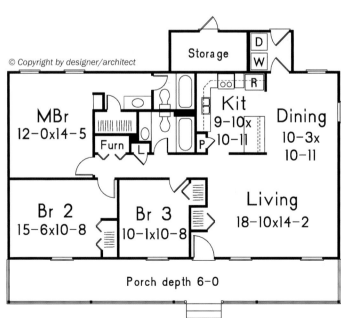

Optional
Second Floor
1,155 sq. ft.

First Floor
2,039 sq. ft.

## Plan #F04-001D-0068

| | |
|---|---|
| Dimensions: | 48' W x 37'8" D |
| Heated Sq. Ft.: | 1,285 |
| Bedrooms: 3 | Bathrooms: 2 |

Foundation: Basement, slab or crawl space, please specify when ordering

| | |
|---|---|
| PDF File: | $750 |
| 5-Sets: | $800 |
| Reproducible Master: | $800 |
| 8-Sets: | $875 |
| Material List: | $125 |
| Upgrade to 2" x 6" Walls: | $150 |

*Pricing subject to change*

*Images provided by designer/architect*

Images provided by designer/architect

## Plan #F04-051D-0680

| | |
|---|---|
| Dimensions: | 69'8" W x 46' D |
| Heated Sq. Ft.: | 1,928 |
| Bedrooms: 3 | Bathrooms: 2½ |
| Foundation: | Basement |
| Exterior Walls: | 2" x 6" |
| 5-Sets: | $853 |
| 8-Sets: | $895 |
| PDF File: | $1,070 |
| CAD File: | $1,695 |

*Pricing subject to change*

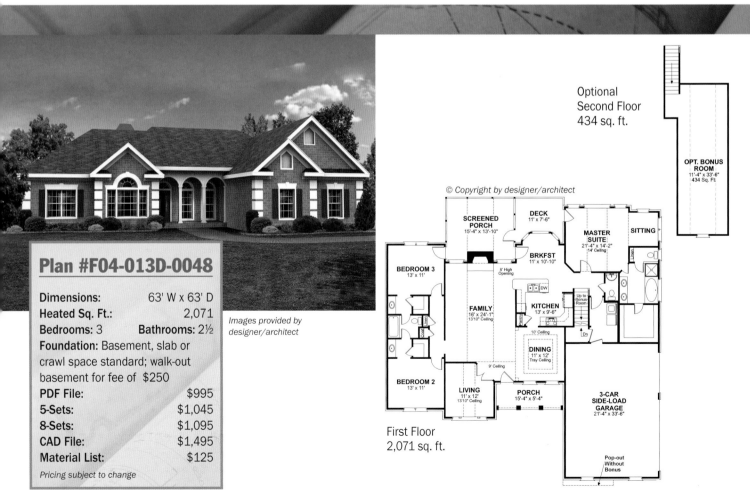

## Plan #F04-013D-0048

| | |
|---|---|
| Dimensions: | 63' W x 63' D |
| Heated Sq. Ft.: | 2,071 |
| Bedrooms: 3 | Bathrooms: 2½ |
| Foundation: Basement, slab or crawl space standard; walk-out basement for fee of $250 | |
| PDF File: | $995 |
| 5-Sets: | $1,045 |
| 8-Sets: | $1,095 |
| CAD File: | $1,495 |
| Material List: | $125 |

*Pricing subject to change*

Images provided by designer/architect

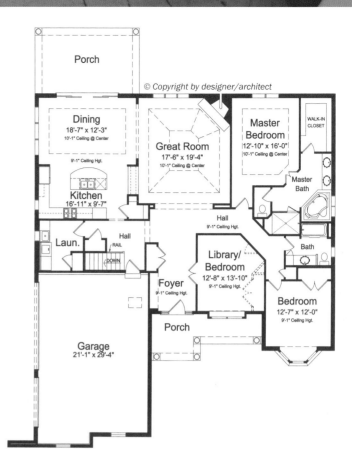

## Plan #F04-065D-0363

| | |
|---|---|
| **Dimensions:** | 67'6" W x 76'8" D |
| **Heated Sq. Ft.:** | 2,252 |
| **Bedrooms:** 3 | **Bathrooms:** 2 |
| **Foundation:** | Basement |
| **5-Sets:** | $695 |
| **8-Sets:** | $880 |
| **PDF File:** | $1,075 |
| **CAD File:** | $1,620 |
| **Material List:** | $85 |

*Pricing subject to change*

*Images provided by designer/architect*

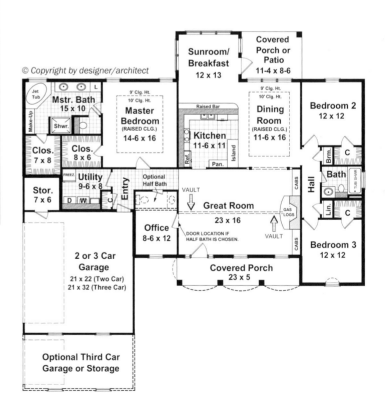

## Plan #F04-077D-0057

| | |
|---|---|
| **Dimensions:** | 64' W x 54'4" D |
| **Heated Sq. Ft.:** | 2,001 |
| **Bedrooms:** 3 | **Bathrooms:** 2 |

**Foundation:** Slab, crawl space or basement, please specify when ordering

| | |
|---|---|
| **Exterior Walls:** | 2" x 6" |
| **5-Sets:** | $1,060 |
| **PDF File:** | $1,200 |
| **Reproducible Master:** | $1,270 |
| **CAD File:** | $1,820 |
| **Material List:** | $130 |

*Pricing subject to change*

*Images provided by designer/architect*

## Plan #F04-055D-0932

**Dimensions:** 144'3" W x 104'11" D
**Heated Sq. Ft.:** 4,183
**Bedrooms:** 3      **Bathrooms:** 3½
**Foundation:** Crawl space or slab, please specify when ordering

| | |
|---|---|
| 5-Sets: | $1,325 |
| 8-Sets: | $1,500 |
| PDF File: | $2,300 |
| CAD File: | $3,540 |
| Upgrade to 2" x 6" Walls: | $250 |

*Pricing subject to change*

*Images provided by designer/architect*

### Features

- Mediterranean style split bedroom home has vaulted ceilings
- From the impressive porte cochere entrance, you're welcomed by a huge vaulted great room with a sky window above for natural light and a fireplace flanked by built-ins
- The large kitchen makes entertaining easy with an island bar, a prep island and nearby dining
- The large pool room has a kitchen with an eating bar, a full bath, and dressing room
- 3-car garage with storm room and storage space

© Copyright by designer/architect

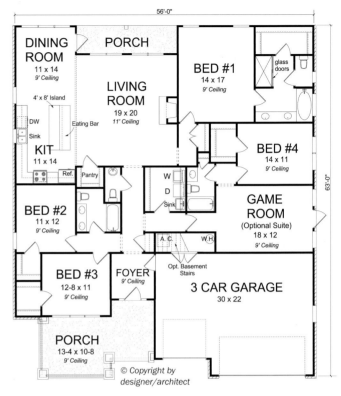

## Plan #F04-130D-0338

*Images provided by designer/architect*

| | |
|---|---|
| **Dimensions:** | 56' W x 63' D |
| **Heated Sq. Ft.:** | 2,425 |
| **Bedrooms:** 4 | **Bathrooms:** 3½ |

**Foundation:** Slab standard; basement or crawl space for a fee of $150

| | |
|---|---|
| **PDF File:** | $955 |
| **5-Sets:** | $1,180 |
| **8-Sets:** | $1,255 |
| **CAD File:** | $1,205 |
| **Upgrade to 2" x 6" Walls:** | $150 |

*Pricing subject to change*

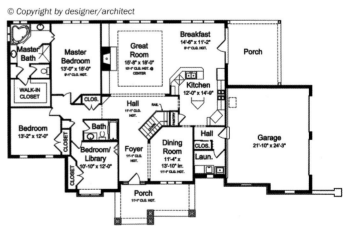

## Plan #F04-065D-0307

*Images provided by designer/architect*

| | |
|---|---|
| **Dimensions:** | 80'2" W x 44'6" D |
| **Heated Sq. Ft.:** | 2,246 |
| **Bedrooms:** 3 | **Bathrooms:** 2 |
| **Foundation:** | Basement |
| **5-Sets:** | $695 |
| **8-Sets:** | $880 |
| **PDF File:** | $1,075 |
| **CAD File:** | $1,620 |
| **Material List:** | $85 |

*Pricing subject to change*

## Plan #F04-055D-0790

| | |
|---|---|
| Dimensions: | 66' W x 52' D |
| Heated Sq. Ft.: | 2,075 |
| Bedrooms: 4 | Bathrooms: 3 |

Foundation: Crawl space or slab, please specify when ordering

| | |
|---|---|
| 5-Sets: | $780 |
| 8-Sets: | $945 |
| PDF File: | $1,450 |
| CAD File: | $2,235 |

*Pricing subject to change*

*Images provided by designer/architect*

© Copyright by designer/architect

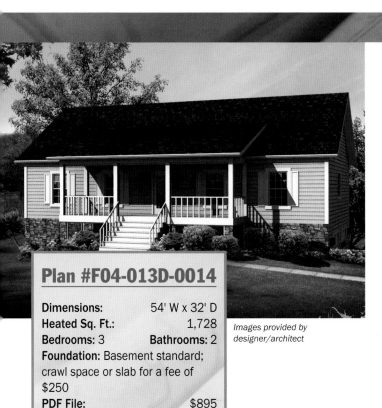

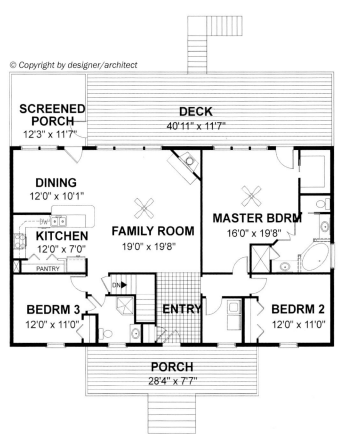

## Plan #F04-013D-0014

| | |
|---|---|
| Dimensions: | 54' W x 32' D |
| Heated Sq. Ft.: | 1,728 |
| Bedrooms: 3 | Bathrooms: 2 |

Foundation: Basement standard; crawl space or slab for a fee of $250

| | |
|---|---|
| PDF File: | $895 |
| 5-Sets: | $945 |
| 8-Sets: | $995 |
| Reproducible Master: | $1,045 |
| Material List: | $125 |

*Pricing subject to change*

*Images provided by designer/architect*

## Plan #F04-020D-0364

*Images provided by designer/architect*

| | |
|---|---|
| Dimensions: | 71' W x 50' D |
| Heated Sq. Ft.: | 1,806 |
| Bedrooms: 3 | Bathrooms: 2½ |
| Foundation: | Slab |
| Exterior Walls: | 2" x 6" |
| PDF File: | $850 |
| 5-Sets: | $875 |
| 8-Sets: | $920 |
| CAD File: | $1,638 |

*Pricing subject to change*

© Copyright by designer/architect

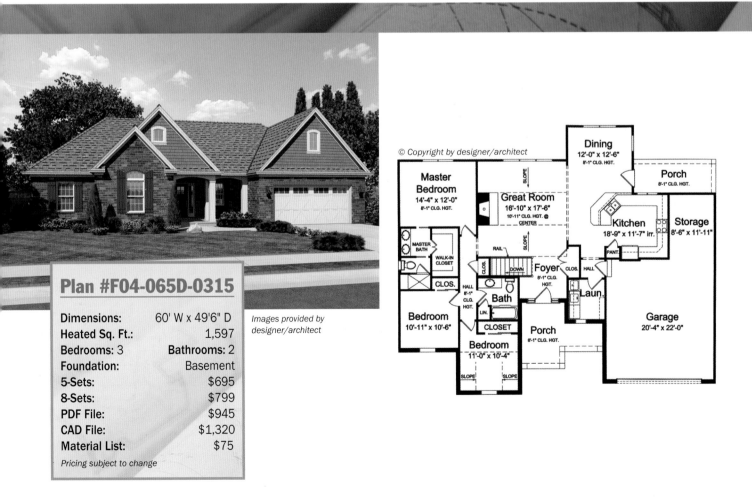

## Plan #F04-065D-0315

*Images provided by designer/architect*

| | |
|---|---|
| Dimensions: | 60' W x 49'6" D |
| Heated Sq. Ft.: | 1,597 |
| Bedrooms: 3 | Bathrooms: 2 |
| Foundation: | Basement |
| 5-Sets: | $695 |
| 8-Sets: | $799 |
| PDF File: | $945 |
| CAD File: | $1,320 |
| Material List: | $75 |

*Pricing subject to change*

© Copyright by designer/architect

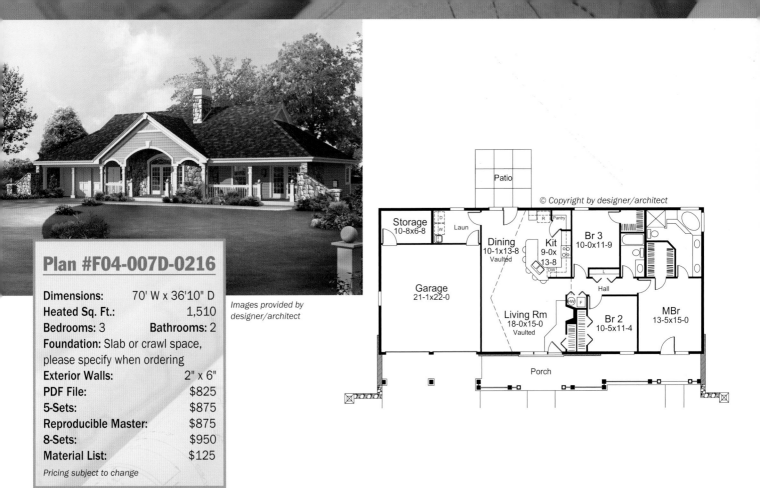

## Plan #F04-007D-0216

| | |
|---|---|
| Dimensions: | 70' W x 36'10" D |
| Heated Sq. Ft.: | 1,510 |
| Bedrooms: 3 | Bathrooms: 2 |
| Foundation: Slab or crawl space, please specify when ordering | |
| Exterior Walls: | 2" x 6" |
| PDF File: | $825 |
| 5-Sets: | $875 |
| Reproducible Master: | $875 |
| 8-Sets: | $950 |
| Material List: | $125 |

*Pricing subject to change*

*Images provided by designer/architect*

## Plan #F04-070D-0738

| | |
|---|---|
| Dimensions: | 56'4" W x 42' D |
| Heated Sq. Ft.: | 1,351 |
| Bedrooms: 3 | Bathrooms: 2 |
| Foundation: | Basement |
| PDF File: | $700 |
| 5-Sets: | $800 |
| 8-Sets: | $900 |

*Pricing subject to change*

*Images provided by designer/architect*

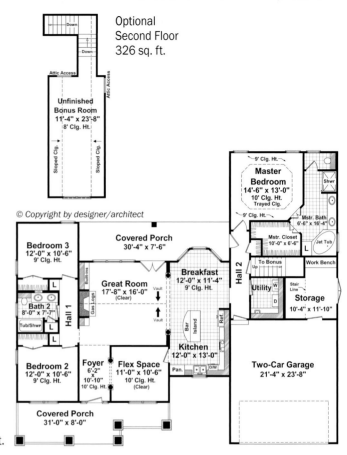

**Optional Second Floor**
326 sq. ft.

Unfinished Bonus Room
11'-4" x 23'-8"
8' Clg. Ht.

Attic Access

Sloped Clg.

Master Bedroom
14'-6" x 13'-0"
10' Clg. Ht.
Trayed Clg.

Mstr. Bath
6'-6" x 16'-4"

Mstr. Closet
10'-0" x 6'-6"

Shwr

Jet Tub

Work Bench

9' Clg. Ht.

Bedroom 3
12'-0" x 10'-6"
9' Clg. Ht.

Covered Porch
30'-4" x 7'-6"

Breakfast
12'-0" x 11'-4"
9' Clg. Ht.

Hall 2

To Bonus

Utility

Stair Line

Storage
10'-4" x 11'-10"

Great Room
17'-8" x 16'-0"
(Clear)

Hall 1

Gas Logs

Bath 2
8'-0" x 7'-7"

Tub/Shwr

Vault

Vault

Kitchen
12'-0" x 13'-0"

Bar Island

Ref

Two-Car Garage
21'-4" x 23'-8"

Bedroom 2
12'-0" x 10'-6"
9' Clg. Ht.

Foyer
6'-2" x
10'-10"

Flex Space
11'-0" x 10'-6"
10' Clg. Ht.
(Clear)

Pan.

D/W

Covered Porch
31'-0" x 8'-0"

**First Floor**
1,800 sq. ft.

## Plan #F04-077D-0140

*Images provided by designer/architect*

| | |
|---|---|
| Dimensions: | 65' W x 56'8" D |
| Heated Sq. Ft.: | 1,800 |
| Bedrooms: 3 | Bathrooms: 2 |
| Foundation: Slab or crawl space, please specify when ordering | |
| 5-Sets: | $1,015 |
| PDF File: | $1,125 |
| CAD File: | $1,680 |
| Material List: | $130 |

*Pricing subject to change*

## Plan #F04-121D-0017

*Images provided by designer/architect*

| | |
|---|---|
| Dimensions: | 40' W x 52' D |
| Heated Sq. Ft.: | 1,379 |
| Bedrooms: 2 | Bathrooms: 1 |
| Foundation: | Basement |
| PDF File: | $750 |
| 5-Sets: | $800 |
| 8-Sets: | $875 |
| CAD File: | $1,550 |
| Material List: | $125 |

*Pricing subject to change*

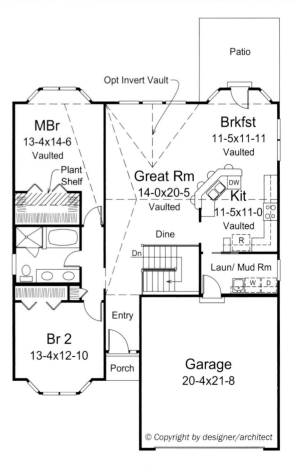

Patio

Opt Invert Vault

MBr
13-4x14-6
Vaulted

Plant Shelf

Brkfst
11-5x11-11
Vaulted

Great Rm
14-0x20-5
Vaulted

DW

Kit
11-5x11-0
Vaulted

R

Dine

Dn

Laun/ Mud Rm

W D

Entry

Br 2
13-4x12-10

Porch

Garage
20-4x21-8

© Copyright by designer/architect

*Images provided by designer/architect*

## Plan #F04-007D-0008

| | |
|---|---|
| Dimensions: | 70'8" W x 70'4" D |
| Heated Sq. Ft.: | 2,452 |
| Bedrooms: 3 | Bathrooms: 2½ |
| Foundation: | Basement |
| PDF File: | $900 |
| 5-Sets: | $950 |
| 8-Sets: | $1,025 |
| CAD File: | $1,800 |
| Material List: | $125 |
| Upgrade to 2" x 6" Walls: | $150 |

*Pricing subject to change*

*Images provided by designer/architect*

© Copyright by designer/architect

## Plan #F04-007D-0212

| | |
|---|---|
| Dimensions: | 72'8" W x 37'4" D |
| Heated Sq. Ft.: | 1,568 |
| Bedrooms: 3 | Bathrooms: 2 |
| Foundation: | Crawl space or slab, please specify when ordering |
| PDF File: | $825 |
| 5-Sets: | $875 |
| 8-Sets: | $950 |
| CAD File: | $1,725 |
| Material List: | $125 |
| Upgrade to 2" x 6" Walls: | $150 |

*Pricing subject to change*

## Plan #F04-101D-0049

| | |
|---|---|
| Dimensions: | 87'9" W x 68'6" D |
| Heated Sq. Ft.: | 2,008 |
| Bedrooms: 2 | Bathrooms: 2½ |
| Foundation: | Basement |
| Exterior Walls: | 2" x 6" |
| 5-Sets: | $850 |
| PDF File: | $1,150 |
| CAD File: | $1,650 |

*Pricing subject to change*

*Images provided by designer/architect*

### Features

- Modern and rustic collide to create this stunning luxury home with tons of personality
- The kitchen overlooks the living room featuring a fireplace for added coziness
- The master bedroom offers many amenities including a private bath with large walk-in closet, and direct access through sliding glass doors to the covered deck with an outdoor fireplace
- Vaulted ceilings throughout contribute to the overall spacious feeling
- The lower level recreation room is large enough for a pool table and media room space
- 2-car side entry garage, and a 1-car front entry garage

© Copyright by designer/architect

First Floor
2,008 sq. ft.

Optional
Lower Level
2,008 sq. ft.

## Plan #F04-076D-0210

| | |
|---|---|
| **Dimensions:** | 91'9" W x 76'4" D |
| **Heated Sq. Ft.:** | 2,650 |
| **Bedrooms:** 3 | **Bathrooms:** 2½ |

**Foundation:** Basement, crawl space or slab, please specify when ordering

| | |
|---|---|
| **5-Sets:** | $875 |
| **8-Sets:** | $1,125 |
| **PDF File:** | $1,325 |
| **CAD File:** | $1,650 |

*Pricing subject to change*

*Images provided by designer/architect*

## Features

- Stylish ranch home with rustic Craftsman details give the exterior plenty of curb appeal
- Open family room is topped with beamed ceilings
- A grilling terrace can be found on the back of the home near the kitchen, perfect when the weather is warm enough to grill
- Split bedroom floor plan is ideal for every family member and ensures privacy
- 2-car side entry garage

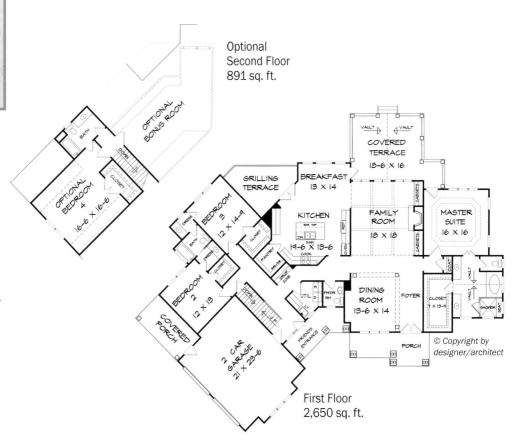

Optional Second Floor 891 sq. ft.

First Floor 2,650 sq. ft.

© Copyright by designer/architect

*Images provided by designer/architect*

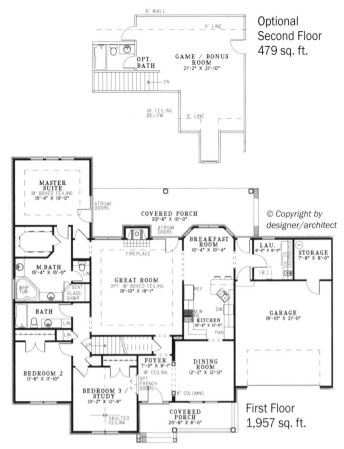

Optional Second Floor 479 sq. ft.

GAME / BONUS ROOM 21'-2" X 21'-10"

OPT. BATH

10' CEILING BELOW

© Copyright by designer/architect

First Floor 1,957 sq. ft.

MASTER SUITE 10' BOXED CEILING 15'-4" X 13'-0"

COVERED PORCH 33'-8" X 10'-0"

BREAKFAST ROOM 10'-4" X 10'-4"

LAU. 8'-0" X 8'-0"

STORAGE 7'-8" X 8'-0"

M.BATH 15'-4" X 15'-0"

GREAT ROOM OPT. 10' BOXED CEILING 18'-10" X 19'-1"

GARAGE 19'-10" X 21'-0"

BATH

KITCHEN 10'-4" X 12'-0"

BEDROOM 2 11'-6" X 11'-10"

FOYER 7'-0" X 9'-1" 10' CEILING

DINING ROOM 12'-2" X 12'-0"

BEDROOM 3 / STUDY 13'-2" X 12'-9"

COVERED PORCH 20'-8" X 6'-0"

## Plan #F04-055D-0053

| | |
|---|---|
| Dimensions: | 66' W x 55' D |
| Heated Sq. Ft.: | 1,957 |
| Bedrooms: 3 | Bathrooms: 2 |

Foundation: Basement, crawl space or slab standard; walk-out basement for a fee of $250

| | |
|---|---|
| 5-Sets: | $680 |
| 8-Sets: | $795 |
| PDF File: | $1,225 |
| CAD File: | $1,885 |

*Pricing subject to change*

---

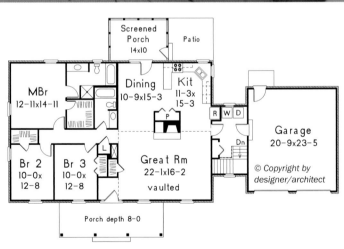

Screened Porch 14x10

Patio

MBr 12-11x14-11

Dining 10-9x15-3

Kit 11-3x 15-3

Garage 20-9x23-5

Br 2 10-0x 12-8

Br 3 10-0x 12-8

Great Rm 22-1x16-2 vaulted

© Copyright by designer/architect

Porch depth 8-0

*Images provided by designer/architect*

## Plan #F04-006D-0003

| | |
|---|---|
| Dimensions: | 78'4" W x 50' D |
| Heated Sq. Ft.: | 1,674 |
| Bedrooms: 3 | Bathrooms: 2 |

Foundation: Basement, crawl space or slab, please specify when ordering

| | |
|---|---|
| PDF File: | $825 |
| 5-Sets: | $875 |
| Reproducible Master: | $875 |
| 8-Sets: | $950 |
| Material List: | $125 |

*Pricing subject to change*

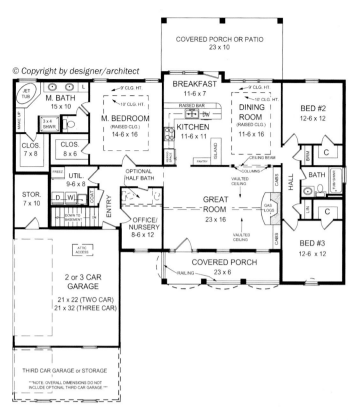

© Copyright by designer/architect

*Images provided by designer/architect*

## Plan #F04-077D-0058

| | |
|---|---|
| Dimensions: | 64'6" W x 61'4" D |
| Heated Sq. Ft.: | 2,002 |
| Bedrooms: 3 | Bathrooms: 2 |
| Foundation: | Slab, crawl space or basement, please specify when ordering |
| Exterior Walls: | 2" x 6" |
| 5-Sets: | $1,060 |
| PDF File: | $1,200 |
| 8-Sets: | $1,270 |
| CAD File: | $1,820 |
| Material List: | $130 |

*Pricing subject to change*

© Copyright by designer/architect

*Images provided by designer/architect*

## Plan #F04-076D-0256

| | |
|---|---|
| Dimensions: | 39' W x 77'10" D |
| Heated Sq. Ft.: | 1,771 |
| Bedrooms: 3 | Bathrooms: 2 |
| Foundation: | Slab |
| 5-Sets: | $655 |
| 8-Sets: | $800 |
| PDF File: | $975 |
| CAD File: | $1,250 |

*Pricing subject to change*

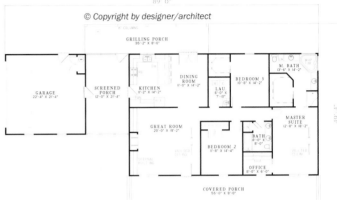

© Copyright by designer/architect

*Images provided by designer/architect*

## Plan #F04-055D-0651

| | |
|---|---|
| **Dimensions:** | 89' W x 49'4" D |
| **Heated Sq. Ft.:** | 1,800 |
| **Bedrooms:** 3 | **Bathrooms:** 2 |

**Foundation:** Crawl space or slab, please specify when ordering

| | |
|---|---|
| **5-Sets:** | $630 |
| **8-Sets:** | $720 |
| **PDF File:** | $1,105 |
| **CAD File:** | $1,700 |

*Pricing subject to change*

## Plan #F04-021D-0006

*Images provided by designer/architect*

| | |
|---|---|
| **Dimensions:** | 75' W x 37' D |
| **Heated Sq. Ft.:** | 1,600 |
| **Bedrooms:** 3 | **Bathrooms:** 2 |

**Foundation:** Slab standard; crawl space or basement for a fee of $100

| | |
|---|---|
| **Exterior Walls:** | 2" x 6" |
| **PDF File:** | $850 |
| **5-Sets:** | $875 |
| **8-Sets:** | $920 |
| **CAD File:** | $1,638 |
| **Material List:** | $90 |

*Pricing subject to change*

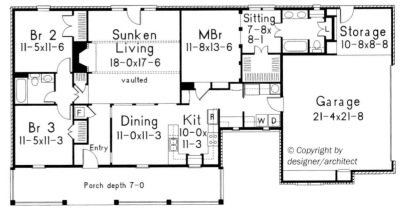

© Copyright by designer/architect

## Plan #F04-051D-0784

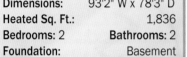

| | |
|---|---|
| Dimensions: | 93'2" W x 78'3" D |
| Heated Sq. Ft.: | 1,836 |
| Bedrooms: 2 | Bathrooms: 2 |
| Foundation: | Basement |
| Exterior Walls: | 2" x 6" |
| 5-Sets: | $853 |
| 8-Sets: | $895 |
| PDF File: | $1,070 |
| CAD File: | $1,695 |

*Pricing subject to change*

*Images provided by designer/architect*

## Plan #F04-076D-0213

| | |
|---|---|
| Dimensions: | 71'8" W x 79'7" D |
| Heated Sq. Ft.: | 2,896 |
| Bedrooms: 3 | Bathrooms: 2½ |
| Foundation: | Crawl space |
| 5-Sets: | $875 |
| 8-Sets: | $1,125 |
| PDF File: | $1,325 |
| CAD File: | $1,650 |

*Pricing subject to change*

*Images provided by designer/architect*

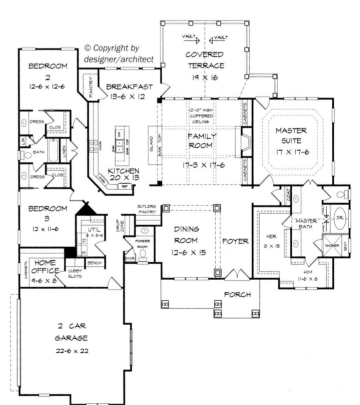

## Plan #F04-101D-0056

| | |
|---|---|
| **Dimensions:** | 72' W x 77' D |
| **Heated Sq. Ft.:** | 2,593 |
| **Bedrooms:** | 4 |
| **Bathrooms:** | 4 full, 2 half |
| **Foundation:** Basement or daylight basement, please specify when ordering | |
| **Exterior Walls:** | 2" x 6" |
| **5-Sets:** | $950 |
| **PDF File:** | $1,250 |
| **CAD File:** | $1,800 |

*Pricing subject to change*

### Features

- This stunning home has the look and feel homeowners love with its sleek interior and open floor plan
- The great room, kitchen and dining combine maximizing the square footage and making these spaces functional and comfortable
- The master bedroom enjoys a first floor location adding convenience to the homeowners
- The lower level adds extra amenities like a media area, billiards space, recreation and exercise rooms
- 3-car front entry garage

*Images provided by designer/architect*

© © Copyright by designer/architect

First Floor
2,593 sq. ft.

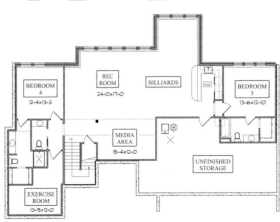

Optional
Lower Level
1,892 sq. ft.

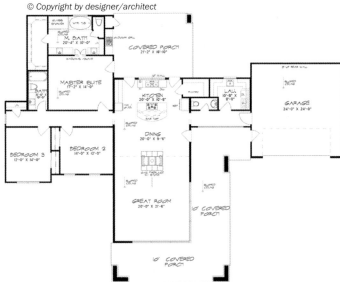

© Copyright by designer/architect

Images provided by designer/architect

## Plan #F04-155D-0019

| | |
|---|---|
| Dimensions: | 90'8" W x 69'4" D |
| Heated Sq. Ft.: | 2,154 |
| Bedrooms: 3 | Bathrooms: 2½ |

Foundation: Crawl space or slab, please specify when ordering

| | |
|---|---|
| 5-Sets: | $880 |
| 8-Sets: | $1,095 |
| PDF File: | $1,685 |
| CAD File: | $2,595 |

*Pricing subject to change*

---

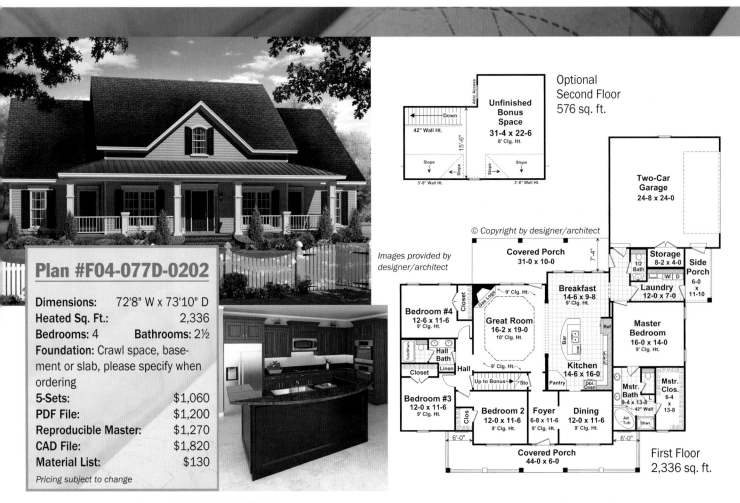

Optional Second Floor 576 sq. ft.

Attic Access

**Unfinished Bonus Space** 31-4 x 22-6 8' Clg. Ht.

42" Wall Ht.
15'-6"
Down
Slope    Slope
3'-8" Wall Ht.    3'-8" Wall Ht.

**Two-Car Garage** 24-8 x 24-0

© Copyright by designer/architect

Images provided by designer/architect

**Covered Porch** 31-0 x 10-0     7'-4"

Storage 8-2 x 4-0

Side Porch 6-0 x 11-10

**Breakfast** 14-6 x 9-8 9' Clg. Ht.

1/2 Bath

Laundry 12-0 x 7-0

W D

Bedroom #4 12-6 x 11-6 9' Clg. Ht.

Closet
Gas Logs   9' Clg. Ht.

**Great Room** 16-2 x 19-0 10' Clg. Ht.

Ref

**Master Bedroom** 16-0 x 14-0 9' Clg. Ht.

Tub/Shwr
Hall Bath
Closet   Linen

9' Clg. Ht.
Bar
Dw

**Kitchen** 14-6 x 16-0

Hall
Up to Bonus   Sto
Pantry
Dbl. Oven

Mstr. Bath 9-4 x 13-8
42" Wall

Mstr. Clos. 6-4 x 13-8

**Bedroom #3** 12-0 x 11-6 9' Clg. Ht.

Clos

**Bedroom 2** 12-0 x 11-6 9' Clg. Ht.

**Foyer** 6-8 x 11-6 9' Clg. Ht.

**Dining** 12-0 x 11-6 9' Clg. Ht.

Jet Tub   Shwr

6'-0"    6'-0"

**Covered Porch** 44-0 x 6-0

**First Floor** 2,336 sq. ft.

## Plan #F04-077D-0202

| | |
|---|---|
| Dimensions: | 72'8" W x 73'10" D |
| Heated Sq. Ft.: | 2,336 |
| Bedrooms: 4 | Bathrooms: 2½ |

Foundation: Crawl space, basement or slab, please specify when ordering

| | |
|---|---|
| 5-Sets: | $1,060 |
| PDF File: | $1,200 |
| Reproducible Master: | $1,270 |
| CAD File: | $1,820 |
| Material List: | $130 |

*Pricing subject to change*

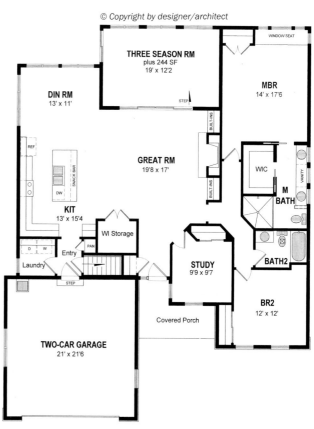

## Plan #F04-034D-0108

| | |
|---|---|
| Dimensions: | 50' W x 61'8" D |
| Heated Sq. Ft.: | 1,771 |
| Bedrooms: 2 | Bathrooms: 2 |
| Foundation: | Concrete block |
| Exterior Walls: | 2" x 6" |
| PDF File: | $675 |
| 5-Sets: | $725 |
| Reproducible Master: | $725 |
| 8-Sets: | $800 |

*Pricing subject to change*

*Images provided by designer/architect*

First Floor 1,285 sq. ft.

Lower Level 789 sq. ft.

## Plan #F04-065D-0261

| | |
|---|---|
| Dimensions: | 53'4" W x 45'6" D |
| Heated Sq. Ft.: | 1,285 |
| Bedrooms: 3 | Bathrooms: 2 |
| Foundation: | Basement |
| 5-Sets: | $695 |
| 8-Sets: | $799 |
| PDF File: | $945 |
| CAD File: | $1,320 |
| Material List: | $75 |

*Pricing subject to change*

*Images provided by designer/architect*

Images provided by designer/architect

## Plan #F04-051D-0674

| | |
|---|---|
| Dimensions: | 60'4" W x 46' D |
| Heated Sq. Ft.: | 1,520 |
| Bedrooms: 3 | Bathrooms: 2 |
| Foundation: | Basement |
| Exterior Walls: | 2" x 6" |
| 5-Sets: | $823 |
| 8-Sets: | $865 |
| PDF File: | $1,032 |
| CAD File: | $1,630 |

*Pricing subject to change*

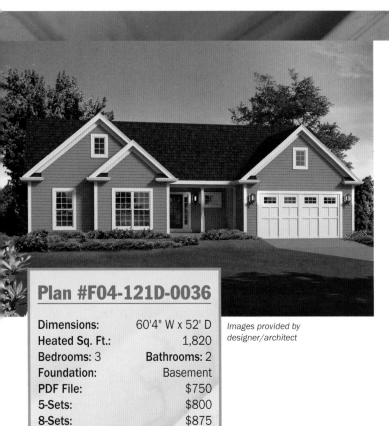

## Plan #F04-121D-0036

| | |
|---|---|
| Dimensions: | 60'4" W x 52' D |
| Heated Sq. Ft.: | 1,820 |
| Bedrooms: 3 | Bathrooms: 2 |
| Foundation: | Basement |
| PDF File: | $750 |
| 5-Sets: | $800 |
| 8-Sets: | $875 |
| CAD File: | $1,550 |
| Material List: | $125 |

*Pricing subject to change*

Images provided by designer/architect

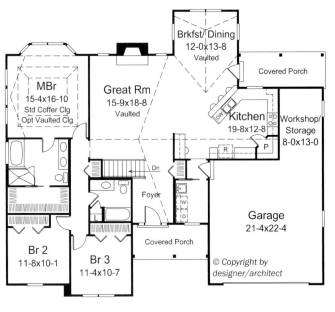

## Plan #F04-116D-0031

| | |
|---|---|
| Dimensions: | 40' W x 64' D |
| Heated Sq. Ft.: | 1,721 |
| Bedrooms: 4 | Bathrooms: 2 |
| Foundation: | Slab |
| Exterior Walls: | Concrete block |
| PDF File: | $1,050 |
| 5-Sets: | $1,100 |
| 8-Sets: | $1,175 |
| CAD File: | $1,950 |

*Pricing subject to change*

*Images provided by designer/architect*

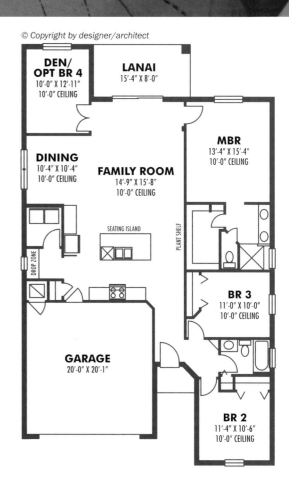

**DEN/ OPT BR 4**
10'-0" X 12'-11"
10'-0" CEILING

**LANAI**
15'-4" X 8'-0"

**MBR**
13'-4" X 15'-4"
10'-0" CEILING

**DINING**
10'-4" X 10'-4"
10'-0" CEILING

**FAMILY ROOM**
14'-9" X 15'-8"
10'-0" CEILING

SEATING ISLAND

PLANT SHELF

DROP ZONE

**GARAGE**
20'-0" X 20'-1"

**BR 3**
11'-0" X 10'-0"
10'-0" CEILING

**BR 2**
11'-4" X 10'-6"
10'-0" CEILING

## Plan #F04-007D-0196

| | |
|---|---|
| Dimensions: | 27' W x 27' D |
| Heated Sq. Ft.: | 421 |
| Bedrooms: 1 | Bathrooms: 1 |
| Foundation: | Slab |
| PDF File: | $600 |
| 5-Sets: | $650 |
| 8-Sets: | $725 |
| CAD File: | $1,110 |
| Material List: | $125 |
| Upgrade to 2" x 6" Walls: | $150 |

*Pricing subject to change*

*Images provided by designer/architect*

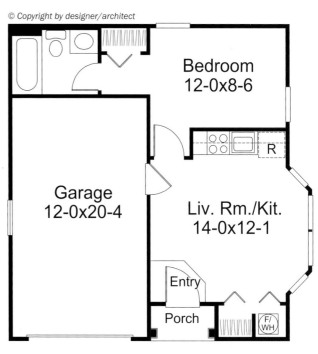

**Bedroom**
12-0x8-6

**Garage**
12-0x20-4

**Liv. Rm./Kit.**
14-0x12-1

Entry

Porch

R

F/ WH

## Plan #F04-032D-0887

| | |
|---|---|
| Dimensions: | 42' W x 40' D |
| Heated Sq. Ft.: | 1,212 |
| Bedrooms: 2 | Bathrooms: 1 |
| Foundation: | Basement |
| Exterior Walls: | 2" x 6" |
| 5-Sets: | $785 |
| 8-Sets: | $815 |
| PDF File: | $930 |
| CAD File: | $1,500 |
| Material List: | $120 |

*Pricing subject to change*

### Features

- This highly efficient home offers an open floor plan with beamed ceilings above adding a tremendous amount of architectural interest to the interior
- A fireplace acts like a partition between the bedrooms and the gathering spaces
- The large covered porch is a wonderful extension of the interior living spaces
- The island in the kitchen includes casual dining space and a double basin sink and dishwasher

*Images provided by designer/architect*

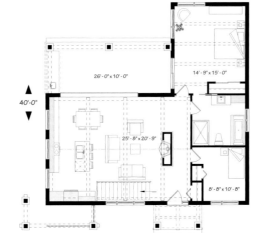

First Floor
1,212 sq. ft.

◀ 42'-0" ▶

© Copyright by designer/architect

Basement
1,212 sq. ft.

## Plan #F04-076D-0222

| | |
|---|---|
| Dimensions: | 93'2" W x 77'9" D |
| Heated Sq. Ft.: | 2,767 |
| Bedrooms: 3 | Bathrooms: 2½ |

Foundation: Basement, crawl space or slab, please specify when ordering

| | |
|---|---|
| 5-Sets: | $1,000 |
| 8-Sets: | $1,325 |
| PDF File: | $1,825 |
| CAD File: | $2,150 |

Pricing subject to change

### Features

- A vaulted beamed ceiling tops the spacious and open family room
- The kitchen is efficient thanks to the center island, walk-in pantry and plenty of counterspace
- The covered terrace offers a lovely outdoor living area, perfect all year long
- 2-car side entry garage

Images provided by designer/architect

© Copyright by designer/architect

First Floor
2,767 sq. ft.

Optional
Second Floor
898 sq. ft.

Optional
Lower Level
2,671 sq. ft.

# Home Plans Index

# Home Plans Index

# why buy
# stock plans?

*Building a home yourself presents many opportunities to showcase a homeowner's creativity, individuality, and dreams turned into reality. Within these opportunities, many challenges and questions crop up. Location, size, and budget are all important to consider, as well as special features and amenities. When one really examines everything that must be determined, it can become overwhelming to search for your dream home. But, before you get too anxious, start the search process an easier way and consider choosing a home design that's a stock home plan.*

Custom home plans as well as stock home plans offer positives and negatives; what is "best" can only be determined by your lifestyle, budget, and time. A customized home plan is one that a homeowner and designer or architect work together to develop from scratch, taking ideas and putting them down on paper. These plans require extra patience, as it may be months before the architect has them ready. A stock plan is a pre-developed plan that fits the needs and desires of a group of people or the general population. These are often available within days of purchasing and typically cost up to one-tenth the price of customized home plans, yet they still have all of the amenities you were looking for and usually at a much more affordable price than having custom plans drawn for you.

When compared to a customized plan, some homeowners fear that a stock home will be carbon copy home, taking away the opportunity for individualism and creating a unique design. This is a common misconception that can waste a lot of money and time!

As you can see from the home designs throughout this book, the variety of stock plans available is truly impressive, encompassing the most up-to-date features including square footage, room dimensions, layout, and amenities. With a little patience and determination, carefully look at the numerous available stock plans throughout this book, which can be easily purchased and ready to go almost immediately.

Plus, stock plans can be customized. For example, perhaps you see a stock plan that is just about perfect, but you wish the mud room was a tad larger. Rather than go through the cost and time of having a custom home design drawn, you could have our customizing service modify the stock home plan and have your new dream plans ready to go in no time. Also, stock home plans often have a material list available, helping to eliminate unknown costs from developing during construction.

It's often a good idea to speak with someone who has recently built. Did they use stock or custom plans? What would they recommend you do, or do not undertake? Can they recommend professionals that will help you narrow down your options? As you take a look at plans throughout this publication, don't hesitate to take notes, or write down questions. Also, take advantage of our website, houseplansandmore.com. This website is very user-friendly, allowing you to search for the perfect house design by style, size, budget, and a home's features. With all of these tools readily available to you, you'll have the home design of your dreams in no time at all and with so much more ease thanks to the innovative stock plans available today that take into account your wishes in a floor plan as well as your wallet.

# how can I find out if I can afford to build a home?

The most important question for someone wanting to build a new home is, "How much is it going to cost?" Obviously, you must have an accurate budget set prior to ordering house plans and beginning construction, or your dream home will quickly turn into a nightmare. Our goal is to make building your dream home a much simpler reality that's within reach thanks to the estimated cost-to-build report available for all of the home plans in this book and on our website, houseplansandmore.com.

Price is always the number one factor when selecting a new home. Price dictates the size and the quality of materials you will choose. So, it comes as no surprise that having an accurate building estimate prior to making your final decision on a home plan is quite possibly the most important step in the entire process.

If you feel you've found "the" home, then before taking the step of purchasing plans, order an estimated cost-to-build report for the zip code where you want to build. When you order this report created specifically for you, it will educate you on all costs associated with building your new home. Simply order the cost-to-build report on houseplansandmore.com for the home you want to build and gain knowledge of the material and labor cost associated with the home. Not only does the report allow you to choose the quality of the materials, you can also select options in every aspect of the project from lot condition to contractor fees. This report will allow you to successfully manage your construction budget in all areas, clearly see where the majority of the costs lie, and save you money from start to finish.

Listed to the right are the categories included in every cost-to-build report. Each category breaks down labor cost, material cost, funds needed, and the report offers the ability to manipulate over/under adjustments if necessary.

282

**BASIC INFORMATION** includes your contact information, the state and zip code where you intend to build. First, select material class. It will include details of the home such as square footage, number of windows, fireplaces, balconies, and bathrooms. Deck, basement, or bonus room square footage is included. Garage location and number of bays, and your lot size are also included.

**GENERAL SOFT COSTS** include cost for plans, customizing (if applicable), building permits, pre-construction services, and planning expenses.

**SITE WORK & UTILITIES** include water, sewer, electric, and gas. Choose the type of site work you will need prior to building and if you'll need a driveway.

**FOUNDATION** is selected from a menu that lists the most common types.

**FRAMING ROUGH SHELL** calculates your rough framing costs including framing for fireplaces, balconies, decks, porches, basements and bonus rooms.

**ROOFING** includes several options so you can see how it will affect your overall price.

**DRY OUT SHELL** allows you to select doors, windows, siding and garage doors.

**ELECTRICAL** includes wiring and the quality of the light fixtures.

**PLUMBING** includes plumbing materials, plumbing fixtures, and fire proofing materials. It includes labor costs, and the ability to change fixture quality.

**HVAC** includes costs for both labor and materials.

**INSULATION** includes costs for both labor and materials.

**FINISH SHELL** includes drywall, interior doors and trim, stairs, shower doors, mirrors, and bath accessories - costs for both labor and materials.

**CABINETS & VANITIES** select the grade of your cabinets, vanities, kitchen countertops, and bathroom vanity materials, as well as appliances.

**PAINTING** includes all painting materials, their quality, and labor.

**FLOORING** includes over a dozen flooring material options.

**SPECIAL EQUIPMENT NEEDS** calculate cost for unforeseen expenses.

**CONTRACTOR FEE / PROJECT MANAGER** includes the cost of your cost-to-build report, project manager and/or general contractor fees. If you're doing the managing yourself, your costs will be tremendously lower in this portion.

**LAND PAYOFF** includes the cost of your land.

**RESERVES / CLOSING COSTS** includes interest, contingency reserves, and closing costs.

We've taken the guesswork out of what your new home will cost. Take control of your homebuilding project, determine the major expenses and save money. Easily supervise all costs, from labor to materials. Manage your home building with confidence and avoid costly mistakes and unforeseen expenses. If you want to order a Cost-To-Build Report for a home plan, visit houseplansandmore.com and search for the plan. Then, look for the orange button that says, "Request Your Report" and get started.

# what kind of plan package do I need?

## SELECT AND ORDER THE TYPES OF BLUEPRINTS THAT BEST FIT YOUR SITUATION

**PLEASE NOTE:** *Not all plan packages listed below are available for every plan. Please refer to the specific plan page in this book for a plan's options and pricing. There may be additional plan options available, please visit houseplansandmore.com, or call 1-800-373-2646 for all current options. The plan pricing shown in this book is subject to change without notice.*

**5-SET PLAN PACKAGE** includes five complete sets of construction drawings. Besides one set for yourself, additional sets of blueprints will be required for your lender, your local building department, your contractor, and any other tradespeople working on your project. Please note: These 5 sets of plans are copyrighted, so they can't be altered or copied.

**8-SET PLAN PACKAGE** includes eight complete sets of construction drawings. Besides one set for yourself, additional sets of blueprints will be required for your lender, your local building department, your contractor, and any other tradespeople working on your project. Please note: These 8 sets of plans are copyrighted, so they can't be altered or copied.

**REPRODUCIBLE MASTERS** is one complete paper set of construction drawings that can be modified. They include a one-time build copyright release that allows you to draw changes on the plans. This allows you, your builder, or local design professional to make the necessary drawing changes without the major expense of entirely redrawing the plans. Easily make minor drawing changes by using correction fluid to cover up small areas of the existing drawing, then draw in your modifications. Once the plan has been altered to fit your needs, you have the right to copy, or reproduce the modified plans as needed for building your home. Please note: The right of building only one home from these plans is licensed exclusively to the buyer. You may not use this design to build a second or multiple dwelling(s) without purchasing a multi-build license.

**PDF FILE FORMAT** is our most popular plan option because of how fast you can receive them (usually within 24 to 48 hours Monday through Friday), and their ability to be easily shared via email with your contractor, subcontractors, and local building officials. The PDF file format is a complete set of construction drawings in an electronic file format. It includes a one-time build copyright release that allows you to make changes and copies of the plans. Typically you will receive a PDF file via email within 24-48 hours (Mon-Fri, 7:30am-4:30pm CST) allowing you to save money on shipping. Upon receiving, visit a local copy or print shop and print the number of plans you need to build your home, or print one and alter the plan by using correction fluid and drawing in your modifications. Please note: These are flat image files and cannot be altered electronically. PDF files are non-refundable and not returnable.

**CAD FILE FORMAT** is the actual computer files for a plan directly from AutoCAD, or another computer aided design program. CAD files are the best option if you have a significant amount of changes to make to the plan, or if you need to make the plan fit your local codes. If you purchase a CAD File, it allows you, or a local design professional the ability to modify the plans electronically in a CAD program, so making changes to the plan is easier and less expensive than using a paper set of plans when modifying. A CAD package also includes a one-time build copyright release that allows you to legally make your changes, and print multiple copies of the plan. See the specific plan page for availability and pricing. Please note: CAD files are non-refundable and not returnable.

**MIRROR REVERSE SETS** Sometimes a home fits a site better if it is flipped left to right. A mirror reverse set of plans is simply a mirror image of the original drawings causing the lettering and dimensions to read backwards. Therefore, when ordering a mirror reverse set of plans, you must purchase at least one set of the original plans to read from, and use the mirror reverse set for construction. Some plans offer right reading reverse for an additional fee. This means the plan has been redrawn by the designer as the mirrored version and can easily be read.

**ADDITIONAL SETS** You can order additional sets of a plan for an additional fee. A 5-set, 8-set, or reproducible master must have been previously purchased. Please note: Only available within 90 days after purchase of a plan package.

**2" X 6" EXTERIOR WALLS** 2" x 6" exterior walls can be purchased for some plans for an additional fee (see specific plan for availability and pricing).

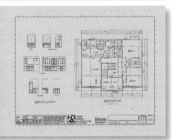

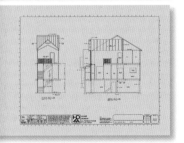

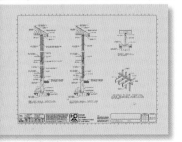

# our
# **plan packages** include...

*Quality plans for building your future, with extras that provide unsurpassed value, ensure good construction and long-term enjoyment. A quality home - one that looks good, functions well, and provides years of enjoyment - is a product of many things - design, materials, and craftsmanship. But it's also the result of outstanding blueprints - the actual plans and specifications that tell the builder exactly how to build your home.*

And with our BLUEPRINT PACKAGES you get the absolute best. A complete set of blueprints is available for every design in this book. These "working drawings" are highly detailed, resulting in two key benefits:

- **BETTER UNDERSTANDING BY THE CONTRACTOR OF HOW TO BUILD YOUR HOME AND...**

- **MORE ACCURATE CONSTRUCTION ESTIMATES THAT WILL SAVE YOU TIME AND MONEY.**

Below is a sample of the plan information included for most of the designs in this book. Specific details may vary with each designer's plan. While this information is typical of most plans, we cannot assure the inclusion of all the following referenced items. Please contact us at 1-800-373-2646 for a plan's specific information, including which of the following items are included.

*1* cover sheet is included with many of the plans, the cover sheet is the artist's rendering of the exterior of the home. It will give you an idea of how your home will look when completed and landscaped.

*2* foundation plan shows the layout of the basement, walk-out basement, crawl space, slab or pier foundation. All necessary notations and dimensions are included. See plan page for the foundation types included. If the home plan you choose does not have your desired foundation type, our Customer Service Representatives can advise you on how to customize your foundation to suit your specific needs or site conditions.

*3* floor plans show the placement of walls, doors, closets, plumbing fixtures, electrical outlets, columns, and beams for each level of the home.

*4* interior elevations provide views of special interior elements such as fireplaces, kitchen cabinets, built-in units and other features of the home.

*5* exterior elevations illustrate the front, rear and both sides of the house, with all details of exterior materials and the required dimensions.

*6* sections show detail views of the home or portions of the home as if it were sliced from the roof to the foundation. This sheet shows important areas such as load-bearing walls, stairs, joists, trusses and other structural elements, which are critical for proper construction.

*7* details show how to construct certain components of your home, such as the roof system, stairs, deck, etc.

# do you want to make **changes** to your plan?

*We understand that sometimes it is difficult to find blueprints that meet all of your specific needs.*
*That is why we offer home plan modification services so you can build a home exactly the way you want it!*

## ARE YOU THINKING ABOUT CUSTOMIZING A PLAN?

If you're like many customers, you may want to make changes to your home plan to make it the dream home you've always wanted. That's where our expert design and modification partners come in. You won't find a more efficient and economic way to get your changes done than by using our home plan customizing services.

Whether it's enlarging a kitchen, adding a porch, or converting a crawl space to a basement, we can customize any plan and make it perfect for your needs. Simply create your wish list and let us go to work. Soon you'll have the blueprints for your new home and at a fraction of the cost of hiring a local architect!

## IT'S EASY!

- We can customize any of plans in this book.
- We provide a FREE cost estimate for your home plan modifications within 24-48 hours (Monday-Friday, 7:30am-4:30pm CST).
- Average turn-around time to complete the modifications is typically 2-3 weeks.
- You will receive one-on-one design consultations.

## CUSTOMIZING FACTS

- The average cost to have a house plan customized is typically less than 1 percent of the building costs — compare that to the national average of 7 percent of building costs.
- The average modification cost for a home is typically $800 to $1,500. This does not include the cost of purchasing the PDF file format of the blueprints, which is required to legally make plan changes.

## OTHER HELPFUL INFORMATION

- Sketch, or make a specific list of changes you'd like to make on the Home Plan Modification Request Form.
- One of our home plan modification specialists will contact you within 24-48 hours with your free estimate.
- Upon accepting the estimate, you will need to purchase the PDF file format.
- A contract, which includes a specific list of changes and fees will be sent to you prior for your approval.
- Upon approving the contract, our design partners will keep you up to date by emailing sketches throughout the project.
- Plans can be converted to metric, or to a Barrier-free layout (also referred to as a universal home design, which allows easy mobility for an individual with limitations of any kind).

## 2 Easy Steps

### 1 visit

houseplansandmore.com and click on the Resources tab at the top of the home page, or scan the QR code here to download the Home Plan Modification Request Form.

### 2 email

your completed form to: customize@designamerica.com, or fax it to: 651-602-5050.

If you are not able to access the Internet, please call 1-800-373-2646 (Monday-Friday, 7:30am - 4:30pm CST)

# helpful **building aids**

*Your Blueprint Package will contain all of the necessary construction information you need to build your home. But, we also offer the following products and services to save you time and money in the building process.*

**MATERIAL LIST** Many of the home plans in this book have a material list available for purchase that gives you the quantity, dimensions, and description of the building materials needed to construct the home (see the specific plan page for availability and pricing). Keep in mind, due to variations in local building code requirements, exact material quantities cannot be guaranteed. Note: Material lists are created with the standard foundation type only. Please review the material list and the construction drawings with your material supplier to verify measurements and quantities of the materials listed before ordering supplies.

**THE LEGAL KIT** Avoid many legal pitfalls and build your home with confidence using the forms and contracts featured in this kit. Included are request for proposal documents, various fixed price and cost plus contracts, instructions on how and when to use each form, warranty statements and more. Save time and money before you break ground on your new home or start a remodeling project. All forms are reproducible. This kit is ideal for homebuilders and contractors. Cost: $35.00

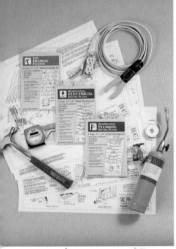

**DETAIL PLAN PACKAGES - ELECTRICAL, FRAMING & PLUMBING** Three separate packages offer homebuilders details for constructing various foundations; numerous floor, wall and roof framing techniques; simple to complex residential wiring; sump and water softener hookups; plumbing connection methods; installation of septic systems, and more. Each package includes three dimensional illustrations and a glossary of terms. Purchase one or all three. Cost: $20.00 each or all three for $40.00 Please note: These drawings do not pertain to a specific home plan, but they include general guidelines and tips for construction in all 3 of these trades.

**EXPRESS DELIVERY** Most orders are processed within 24 hours of receipt. Please allow 7-10 business days for standard delivery. If you need to place a rush order, please call us by 11:00 am Monday through Friday CST and ask for express service (allow 1-2 business days). Please see page 287 for specific pricing information for shipping and handling.

**TECHNICAL ASSISTANCE** If you have questions about your blueprints, we offer technical assistance by calling 1-314-770-2228 between 7:30 am and 4:30 pm Monday through Friday CST. Whether it involves design modifications or field assistance, our home plans team is extremely familiar with all of our designs and will be happy to help you. We want your home to be everything you expect it to be.

# before you **order**

*Please note: Plan pricing is subject to change without notice.*
*For current pricing, visit houseplansandmore.com, or call us at 1-800-373-2646.*

**BUILDING CODE REQUIREMENTS** At the time the construction drawings were prepared, every effort was made to ensure that these plans and specifications met nationally recognized codes. These plans conform to most national building codes. Because building codes vary from area to area, some drawing modifications and/or the assistance of a professional designer or architect may be necessary to comply with your local codes, or to accommodate your specific building site conditions. We advise you to consult with your local building official, or a local builder for information regarding codes governing your area prior to ordering blueprints.

**COPYRIGHT** Plans are protected under Copyright Law. Reproduction by any means is strictly prohibited. The right of building only one structure from all plan packages is licensed exclusively to the buyer and the plans may not be resold unless by express written authorization from the home designer, or architect. You may not use this design to build a second or multiple structure(s) without purchasing a multi-build license. Each violation of the Copyright Law is punishable in a fine.

**LICENSE TO BUILD** When you purchase a "full set of construction drawings" from Design America, Inc., you are purchasing an exclusive one-time "License to Build," not the rights to the design. Design America, Inc. is granting you permission on behalf of the plan's designer or architect to use the construction drawings one-time for the building of the home. The construction drawings (also referred to as blueprints/plans and any derivative of that plan whether extensive or minor) are still owned and protected under copyright laws by the original designer. The blueprints/plans cannot be resold, transferred, rented, loaned or used by anyone other than the original purchaser of the "License to Build" without written consent from Design America, Inc. or the plan designer. If you are interested in building the plan more than once, please call 1-800-373-2646 and inquire about purchasing a Multi-Build License that will allow you to build a home design more than one time. Please note: A "full set of construction drawings" consists of either CAD files or PDF files.

## SHIPPING & HANDLING CHARGES

**U.S. SHIPPING -**
(AK and HI express only)

| | |
|---|---|
| Regular (allow 7-10 business days) | $27.00 |
| Priority (allow 3-5 business days) | $47.00 |
| Express* (allow 1-2 business days) | $67.00 |

**CANADA SHIPPING\*\***

| | |
|---|---|
| Regular (allow 8-12 business days) | $50.00 |
| Express* (allow 3-5 business days) | $100.00 |

**OVERSEAS SHIPPING/INTERNATIONAL**
Call, fax, or e-mail
(customerservice@designamerica.com) for shipping costs.

\*  For express delivery please call us by 11:00 am Monday-Friday CST

\*\*  Orders may be subject to custom's fees and or duties/taxes.

*Note: Shipping and handling does not apply on PDF files and CAD Package orders. PDF and CAD orders will be emailed within 24-48 hours (Monday - Friday, 7:30 am - 4:30 pm CST) of purchase.*

**EXCHANGE POLICY** Since blueprints are printed in response to your order, we cannot honor requests for refunds.

# Order Form

**Please note: Plan pricing is subject to change without notice.
For current pricing, visit houseplansandmore.com, or call us at 1-800-373-2646**

## Please send me the following:

Plan Number: F04-_____

Select Foundation Type: (Select ONE- see plan page for available options).

❑ Slab ❑ Crawl space ❑ Basement

❑ Walk-out basement ❑ Pier

❑ Optional Foundation for an additional fee

Enter foundation cost here $ _____

## Plan Package     Cost

❑ CAD File $ _____

❑ PDF File Format (recommended) $ _____

❑ Reproducible Masters $ _____

❑ 8-Set Plan Package $ _____

❑ 5-Set Plan Package $ _____

See the plan page for the most commonly ordered plan packages, or visit houseplansandmore.com to see current pricing and all plan package options available.

## Important Extras

For pricing and availability of Material Lists, see the plan page.
For the other plan options listed below, visit houseplansandmore.com, or call 1-800-373-2646.

❑ Additional plan sets*:

_____ set(s) at $_____ per set $ _____

❑ Print in mirror reverse:

_____ set(s) at $_____ per set $ _____
(where right reading reverse is not available)

❑ Print in right-reading reverse:

one-time additional fee of $_____ $ _____

❑ Material list (see plan page for availability) $ _____

Shipping (see page 287) $ _____

SUBTOTAL $ _____

Sales Tax (MO residents only, add 8.425%) $ _____

**TOTAL** $ _____

*Available only within 90 days after purchase of plan.

### HELPFUL TIPS

- You can upgrade to a different plan package within 90 days of your original plan purchase.
- Additional sets cannot be ordered without the purchase of a 5-Set, 8-Set, or Reproducible Masters.

Name _____
(Please print or type)

Street _____
(Please do not use a P.O. Box)

City _____ State _____

Country _____ Zip _____

Daytime telephone ( _____ ) _____

E-Mail _____
(For invoice and tracking information)

Payment   ❑ Bank check/money order. No personal checks.
Make checks payable to Design America, Inc.

❑ MasterCard   ❑ VISA   ❑ DISCOVER   ❑ AMERICAN EXPRESS Cards

Credit card number _____

Expiration date (mm/yy) _____ CID _____

Signature _____

❑ I hereby authorize Design America, Inc. to charge this purchase to my credit card.

Please check the appropriate box:
❑ Building home for myself
❑ I'm building home for someone else

## ORDER ONLINE

houseplansandmore.com

## ORDER TOLL-FREE BY PHONE

1-800-373-2646
Fax: 314-770-2226

## EXPRESS DELIVERY

Most orders are processed within 24 hours of receipt. If you need to place a rush order, please call us by 11:00 am CST and ask for express service.

Business Hours: Monday - Friday (7:30 am-4:30 pm CST)

## MAIL YOUR ORDER

Design America, Inc.
734 West Port Plaza, Suite #208
St. Louis, MO 63146

### Best-Selling 1-Story Home Plans

**SOURCE CODE F04**